Romancing the Brand

Romancing the Brand

The Power of Advertising and How to Use It

David N. Martin

American Management Association

This book is available at a special
discount when ordered in bulk quantities.
For information, contact Special Sales Department,
AMACOM, a division of American Management Association,
135 West 50th Street, New York, NY 10020.

Library of Congress Cataloging-in-Publication Data

Martin, David N.
    Romancing the brand : the power of advertising and how to use it /
David N. Martin.
        p.   cm.
    Bibliography: p.
    Includes index.
    ISBN 0-8144-5949-8
    1. Advertising—Brand name products.   I. American Management
Association.   II. Title.
    HF5823.M268   1989
    659.1—dc 19   88-48032
                                                                    CIP

Printing number

10   9   8   7   6   5   4   3   2   1

▪ CONTENTS ▪

Contents

Contents

▪ Some Words of Thanks ▪

To:

David Ogilvy, who inspired me to write this book back in 1979, and again in 1987.

John O'Toole, the first to read it, who applauded and, like the good creative director he is, refrained from taking pencil in hand to make changes.

Marilyn Bockman and her librarians at the AAAA, who guided me through a storehouse of information and didn't nag when the books I borrowed were overdue.

The editors at AMACOM, who, like all great marketers, take risks and thus had the nerve to publish it.

Alan Donnahoe, who, after writing his first book, suggested I complete the manuscript before sending it to a publisher in order to avoid finishing it under pressure.

Maura Saucer, who read early drafts of several chapters and made helpful suggestions that prompted me to throw all those early attempts away and start over from scratch.

Carolyn Coates, who typed endless revisions of those first attempts, kept track of everything through three moves, and stayed on top of all those permissions you see in the Chapter Notes.

Barbara Corby-Martin, who pushed and encouraged me and insisted that I learn to use a word processor (without which I would never have gotten past Chapter One).

Everyone in my family, who never complained, waited on and for me, showed interest, gave helpful advice, and endured being ignored while this work was being done.

My colleagues at The Martin Agency, Scali, and Ogilvy, who, along with Jim Cargill, Bob Wilson, Ed Acree and Harry Jacobs, provided material for some of the stories told and the illustrations used.

Jerry Torchia, that creative revolutionary from the South whose creative work never lays an egg and who used several dozen of them while designing and producing the jacket for this book.

Joel Raphaelson, whose viewpoint I respect and who took the time to help tie up some loose ends.

My clients, past and present, who love great advertising as much as I do.

▪INTRODUCTION▪

Romancing the Brand

> *The use of advertising—to add a subjective value to the product—becomes increasingly important as the trends in our technology lead to competing products being more and more alike.*
>
> —James Webb Young, in
> *How to Become an Advertising Man*

Business people, and especially young MBAs who manage brands, are left-side thinkers. That means they think logically. They are goal oriented. That is the way they were taught, and that is the way they are.

You may be a left-sider, and if you are, let me put you at ease. A smart, step-by-step approach to problem solving takes you straight to the head of the class; I'm sure you learned that a long time ago.

Logic leads to results. If you manage a brand, you want results *now*. In the short term. You need to make your numbers. As you look around for available tactics to help you do this, the question of advertising often arises. Should you step it up or cut it out? That is the question, and most managers are ill equipped by training or experience to deal with it.

Whom can you trust to tell you? Who doesn't have an ax to grind? The advertising manager wants to do more, and so of course does your advertising agency. The sales manager wants to put the money into trade deals or premiums—something tangible, palpable, easy to understand and measure. To the logical left-sider, advertising is often a mysterious, unmeasurable activity of doubtful value even in the long term. Meanwhile, short-term pressures must be dealt with.

The easiest and most practical thing to do is to cut both cost and price. This will boost sales and protect margins. Advertising, of course, in this scenario, will be reduced somewhat. You think about the savings to be gained from cutting an insertion here, a radio flight there. Coupons will make up the difference. So you do it. Margins improve. Customers continue to buy. And the brand takes a share point or two from its category competitors. As far as the practical manager can see, an advertising dollar saved is a profit dollar earned.

So who needs advertising? Brands need it, that's who. Stick with me and you'll see why.

Right-Side vs. Left-Side Thinking

Advertising people are right-side thinkers. You might think of them as poets and artists—romantics caught up in the world of commerce. They deal in ideas and art. They dedicate themselves to romancing products, to giving brands a personality and some kind of value mystique. This noble and high-minded objective often prompts the practical left-sider to ask, "so what?"

This book is an attempt to bridge the differences between left-side and right-side thinking, to interpret one to the other, to meld the two sides into a single force in the interests of building successful brands and dominant category share.

The methods advertising people use are often puzzling to left-side thinkers. Managers despair of the arty and flashy men and women in advertising agencies with their "silly" right-side thinking. They want those ideas, and that art, to help them make their numbers.

"Patience," says the advertising agency.

"Sales," says the client.

"This is a long-term undertaking," says the advertising agency.

"It is nebulous and unproductive," says the client.

Yet it isn't. What these poets and artists do, if they do it right, is to reach out to customers with their ideas and art, to touch emotions and build up the desire to make a brand the brand of choice in a particular category. The practical value of all this "art" is to insulate the brand from pressures that drive down price. Category leaders have bargaining power, benefit from economies of scale, and give their owners a greater return on investment.

Note the caveat "if they do it right." Much advertising today seems poorly done and pointless, flashy and lacking a firm footing. It *is* therefore "nebulous and unproductive." The point of this book is to help make your advertising more productive.

Left-side thinkers want advertising to make sense—to them. "Say what you mean," they demand. "Lay out the facts. Tell people straight out why they should buy my brand." The problem is, customers are not always logical. They may be pragmatic, but they buy out of emotion. The intangible mystique that surrounds some brands and gives them added value is not logical. It is an alluring impression put there by poets and artists to pull the brand through from manufacturing to the kitchen shelf.

At this point, let me say that this book is *not* just about items in a pasteboard box sporting a colorful label. It's true, products like cereal, soap, or toothpaste are brands, but the material presented here takes the meaning of "brand" beyond that to include any product or service promoted to build a customer base. Crest toothpaste is a brand. And so is a bank called Crestar. The principles discussed in this book apply whether you manage popular consumer brands, sell products and services to other businesses, own a retail shop, or guide a *Fortune* 500 company.

Added Value

Each product, service, or company with a brand name that people recognize stands for something slightly different from anything else in the same category. If the difference is a desirable one, and that difference is known and understood by the universe of potential customers, the brand will be the category leader. Sometimes the difference is only imagined. But perceived or real, a desirable difference translates into *added value* to broaden the gap between the marketer's cost and the retail selling price. In a land of free choice and parity products, value characteristics set the brand apart from other products in the category. *Now, more than ever before, the perception of a quality difference is essential for survival in the marketplace.*

The category is the battlefield where the war for market share is won or lost. Every strategy or tactic must be calculated to advance the perception of quality for the brand within a particular category. To do this, a *dominant value point* must be identified and communicated. The brand must be softer, cleaner, brighter, faster, smoother, lighter, more durable, more convenient, better tasting, whatever. Of course, the value point must be believable as well as relevant. To get this message across, the advertising must be witty and wise, perhaps indirect, but sufficiently clear so that the customer himself can discover the value point of difference and thus make it his own permanent link with the brand.

The value point must be seen as desirable. Only the customer can tell us what attributes are important from both a rational and emotional perspective. Before we write a line of copy we should talk to customers and find out what really does make a difference. Finally, the unique benefit must be broadly understood by a large percentage of the category's target universe so that it is associated with the brand at the critical moment when a buying decision is made.

For many brands, value point awareness is needed only when the vagaries of life return the customer to a category classification to meet a need or satisfy a desire. Tires wear thin, the car gets old, toothpaste runs out, replacements are needed. Satisfied customers tend to reorder, providing the brand has met expectations. In this brief moment of decision, however, an upstart brand has a window of opportunity that a competitive point of difference, perceived or real, can open.

This book will show you how to open that window.

The Value of Leadership

It's not easy to do. Established brands, especially pioneers in the category, are well entrenched. This was driven home to me the other day when I was browsing through the library at the American Association of Advertising Agencies (AAAA) in New York. I came across a rare book published by Doubleday in 1923 called *The Leadership of Advertised Brands*. It lists the brands that had "mental dominance" with consumers at that time. The brands below were mentioned by more than twice as many persons as mentioned the next brand in their respective fields. As you can see, many have endured for sixty-five years. Others have not for various reasons.

Commodity	*Brand*
Soap	Ivory
Flour	Gold Medal
Soft drinks	Coca-Cola
Underwear	B.V.D.
Hats	Stetson
Breakfast food	Kellogg's Cornflakes
Dentifrice	Colgate
Tires	Goodyear
Guns	Winchester
Men's clothing	Hart Schaffner & Marx
Hair tonic	Ed Pinaud
Pianos	Steinway
Automobiles	Ford
Coffee	Arbuckle [*Yuban*]
Raincoats	Goodyear
Spaghetti	Heinz
Canned fruits	Del Monte
Rubber boots	Goodyear
Laundry soap	Fels Naptha
Face powder	Djer Kiss
Bicycles	Iver Johnson
Lamps	Mazda
Yarns	Fleischer's
Leather goods	Cross

This list demonstrates the enduring nature of established brands. To dislodge a leader takes considerable cunning by a competitor—or considerable neglect by those responsible for maintaining the brand franchise. Why are some of the brands shown here still household words today while others have faded from memory? Would you buy Fels Naptha for a quarter less than Tide? Brand loyalty is not a matter of "what did you do for me today?" but stems from a kaleidoscope of impressions and experience, from form as well as function. Advertising reinforces these impressions to solidify the customer base, convert infrequent users into frequent ones, and turn frequent users into single-brand loyalists.

This Book's for You

This book is especially for business managers who may know a great deal about such things as frequency distribution, manufacturing, weighted averages, present value analysis, pricing and distribution, personnel administration, and dealing with unions, but who haven't given much thought or study to the greatest corporate responsibility of all: *protecting and building the brand franchise*.

It is also for company advertising professionals who need ammunition that will convince management to use advertising to carve out a bigger piece of the category pie.

You will find this book easy to read. Even when complicated studies are discussed, I've taken out the "tech talk" to make them interesting and useful in the real world. If you are a client who has never worked in an agency, you'll find out how to deal with agency mentality to your brand's advantage. You will also learn how to avoid mistakes that pour so many advertising dollars down the drain.

If you're a student, I hope you'll put this book on your list to read along with *Ogilvy on Advertising,* John Philip Jones's *What's in a Name?* John O'Toole's *The Trouble With Advertising,* Claude Hopkins's *My Life in Advertising,* John Lyons's *Guts,* Stephen Fox's *The Mirror Makers,* Bob Levenson's *Bill Bernbach's Book,* and *How to Advertise* by Ken Roman and Jane Maas. There are others mentioned in the notes to each chapter. You'll come away understanding the advertising business and the people in it. You'll see why we love our work and the brands we create for.

This book is also for my friends and colleagues in the agency business—that small band of men and women, only 150,000 strong, who plan, create, and place $60 billion in advertising each year. If you're good at what you do—writing, designing, media buying, account work, whatever—chances are you concentrate on that and haven't given much thought to advertising's long-term role: building and maintaining a strong brand franchise. Because rules are unacceptable to talented creative people, you eschew them and get caught up in the job at hand: How the hell to make "this job"—the assignment before you—different! How to make it the most startling, compelling ad ever to be seen by an award show judging committee. How to get people to stop and say "wow!"

I haven't written rules here. But I do ask you: Does the ad you're doing enhance the brand in addition to enhancing your reputation as an innovative creative genius? Does it romance the brand? Does it start with the product, and the product's value point, from the customer's perspective, and then knock the viewer's (reader's) socks off?

Do the style and tone of the ad echo what the customer vaguely remembers having seen or read previously about this product? What users feel about it? As unique as you make the message this time, does it have *déja vu* quality? Advertising is more than a one-night stand.

With all the clutter and confusion today, with marketers fighting for share, with price pressures and new and improved products threatening established brands, you've got to play to consumer memory. You have to add a value point people will associate everlastingly with the brand. That perception of difference *has* to stick. It is the only way a brand can survive. It is the value-added essential I'm talking about. The brand must have it to carve out solid category share. Because, in the world of commerce, category share is everything.

Romancing the Brand

·1·

The Angry Lion

> *You are not right if in your ad you stand a man on*
> *his head just to get attention. You are right if*
> *you have him on his head to show how your prod-*
> *uct keeps things from falling out of his pockets.*
>
> Bill Bernbach, copywriter,
> from *Bill Bernbach said . . .*

After a morning creative session in May 1987 at the Hotel Cipriani in Venice, my partner Harry Jacobs, creative head of the Martin Agency, approached David Ogilvy, tape recorder in hand. He came to ask what Ogilvy thought about making each advertisement an "event"—a "happening"—somewhere out there beyond strategy, beyond technique, where the sheer uniqueness and cleverness of the work calls out to the consumer and gives it a life of its own. What did advertising's greatest living legend think about that?

Harry wanted a pithy comment on tape to use for an upcoming *Advertising Age* creative workshop. He thought Ogilvy would be a good subject, in that he had stirred the advertising industry a number of years before with "event" advertising of his own: the eyepatch ad for Hathaway shirts and the Commander Whitehead series for Schweppes. Ogilvy had plenty to say. His comments were pithy, but not something Harry could use to underscore the value of event advertising.

Sales vs. Applause

Ogilvy was agitated. The "legend" had just seen a composite reel of television commercials that Sam Scali, partner and creative director of Scali, McCabe, Sloves, had put together to illustrate what the best agencies throughout the world were doing. Sam's reel had rolled out the work of Chiat/Day, Hal Riney, Ammeriti & Puris, as well as that by agencies attending the meeting. They were Scali, McCabe, Sloves, and representatives of its offices around the world, along with some of Scali's "confederation" members such as Fallon McElligott and us. The commercials Ogilvy saw were the best being done at the time. There was plenty to see: Bartles & Jaymes, Pizza Hut, Federal Express, Nike, Perdue, California Raisins, Volvo, and a wide variety of belly-laughers from Great Britain.

Although Ogilvy was amused during the showing, the spots didn't seem to fit his idea of great advertising.

"The advertising business is going down the drain," he said, slamming his hand down for emphasis. "It is being pulled down by the people who create it, who don't know how to sell anything, who have never sold anything in their lives . . . who despise selling, whose mission in life is to be clever and show-offs, and con clients into giving them money to display their originality and genius!"

This outburst put Harry into a mild state of shock. He didn't know what to expect next. After a pause, Ogilvy mused, "Claude Hopkins lived in vain." Hopkins is the legendary copywriter who worked early in the twentieth century, the man who is widely credited with making advertising what it is today: a powerful selling force that can build brands and corporations through mass persuasion (see Chapter 4).

Ogilvy waved his hand to encompass the people leaving the room—among them, some of the best creative minds in advertising, but his gesture extended to writers and artists everywhere. "Fancy Dan amateurs intoxicated with their own genius," he said scornfully. "Amateurs playing the fool!" Ogilvy obviously agreed with Claude Hopkins, who had once said, "Ad writers forget they are salesmen and try to be performers. Instead of sales, they seek applause."

It was an interesting situation. Here was Ogilvy in Venice at a meeting of agencies in which The Ogilvy Group had a financial interest, including Scali, McCabe, Sloves. These agencies were among the best in the world, with outstanding creative reputations. But the writers and art directors in the session with Ogilvy tended to be from the colorful, witty Bernbach school of advertising. He was like an old king lion presiding over a pride that agency chairman Marvin Sloves had gathered together. It was as if Ogilvy had at age 76, and in semi-retirement, adopted the kids that his old rival, Bill Bernbach, had raised. And he disapproved of them.

Some who heard about the confrontation dismissed Ogilvy as a grand old man who had lost touch with reality. Today's situation is different, they believe. There is too much competition for attention. The 73 million baby boomers raised in front of the tube want to be entertained, charmed into buying. Who will sit still and listen to a sales pitch when, with the flick of a zapper, they can change channels from across the room?

The "Young Turks" in Venice admired Ogilvy for the breakthroughs he fathered. His ads from the 1950s were events and as such they are the shintos of modern "image" advertising. What is often overlooked by today's practitioners, however, is the fact that his famous campaigns projected brand image in the guise of soft sell. There was, in fact, a hard selling edge in each of them.

The Twig Is Bent

Ogilvy's convictions can be traced to the "claim" school of Hopkins. When he first came to America from England in 1947, Ogilvy was strongly influenced by what he later called "the wicked old Chicago philosophy as practiced by Claude Hopkins." This demanded that each ad stand on its own, pay for itself at a profit.[1] But even then his style projected brand image.

Ogilvy's enduring eye-patch campaign for Hathaway shirts had made him famous by 1952, when he sought out Raymond Rubicam, founder of Young & Rubicam, in retirement and became a disciple of that agency's friendly-persuasion, image style of advertising.[2] He felt Rubicam had missed a bet by not placing his views between the covers of a book. Observing that Claude Hopkins had written a book while Rubicam had not, he suggested, "That is why so many of the younger generation, including myself, tend to accept the rightness of Hopkins and his ilk."

Under Rubicam's influence Ogilvy followed what he termed the "great Y&R tradition—a tradition which defies stereotypes but does so with perfect manners and with no sacrifice to sell."[3] His style lent grace to the selling of Hathaway, Schweppes, Shell, British Travel, Puerto Rico, and Rolls-Royce. "At 60 miles an hour the loudest noise in this new Rolls-Royce comes from the electric clock," went one of his ads. He began to see the value of long-term effect as a brand's image was built by each succeeding advertisement over time. But, while he considered each ad part of the long-term investment in the brand's reputation, each one he created also included an extremely strong element of salesmanship. There was nothing "soft" about them.

Over the years, Ogilvy and his (then) brother-in-law, Rosser Reeves, spent many hours arguing the fine points of advertising at family gatherings. For Reeves, Hopkins had always been an extremely seminal figure, and at Ted Bates, Rosser Reeves became the father of the "unique selling proposition" and exponent of the hard-sell, repetitious, hammer-on-the-head school of advertising. Thus, although the discussions pitted the leading advocates of "claim" versus "image," both agreed the purpose of advertising is to persuade.

David Ogilvy was a "late bloomer" in advertising. His early training came from door-to-door selling and from a stint as a researcher for Dr. George Gallup in Princeton. This honed his left-side thinking and gave him a healthy respect for the opinions of customers. He was 39 before he wrote his first advertisement, a task that never came easily to him. For his

Take away the eyepatch and what do you have? An ordinary ad laden with reasons to buy.
The eyepatch and this ad created an aura of mystery and romance for the product and made
a legend of Ogilvy when it first appeared nearly forty years ago.

The man in the Hathaway shirt

AMERICAN MEN are beginning to realize that it is ridiculous to buy good suits and then spoil the effect by wearing an ordinary, mass-produced shirt. Hence the growing popularity of HATHAWAY shirts, which are in a class by themselves.

HATHAWAY shirts *wear* infinitely longer—a matter of years. They make you look younger and more distinguished, because of the subtle way HATHAWAY cut collars. The whole shirt is tailored more *generously*, and is therefore more *comfortable*. The tails are longer, and stay in your trousers. The buttons are mother-of-pearl. Even the stitching has an ante-bellum elegance about it.

Above all, HATHAWAY make their shirts of remarkable *fabrics*, collected from the four corners of the earth—Viyella, and Aertex, from England, woolen taffeta from Scotland, Sea Island cotton from the West Indies, hand-woven madras from India, broadcloth from Manchester, linen batiste from Paris, hand-blocked silks from England, exclusive cottons from the best weavers in America. You will get a great deal of quiet satisfaction out of wearing shirts which are in such impeccable taste.

HATHAWAY shirts are made by a small company of dedicated craftsmen in the little town of Waterville, Maine. They have been at it, man and boy, for one hundred and twenty years.

At better stores everywhere, or write C. F. HATHAWAY, Waterville, Maine, for the name of your nearest store. In New York, telephone OX 7-5566. Prices from $5.95 to $20.00.

famous Rolls-Royce ad, for example, he wrote twenty-six different headlines and had other writers in his agency pick the best one. He wrote 3,500
words of copy, then got other writers to "cut out the dull and obscure
parts and reduce it down."[4]

Going for the Jugular

Although Ogilvy's outburst in Venice was a surprise to most of us, the
view he expressed is consistent. Back in the mid-1960s in the midst of
advertising's creative revolution, a *Newsweek* writer caught up with him
long enough to report this observation on the prevailing crop of copywriters:

> The new breed has no regard for how well an ad sells the
> product. These pseudo-intellectuals who are now flocking to advertis-
> ing, these callow, half baked, overpaid young men and women haven't
> the slightest interest in how the consuming public reacts. They are
> departing from tested formulae and going to things that are very
> doubtful.[5]

Yet, at that time, he didn't apply this criticism to the ground-breaking
campaign for Volkswagen created by his rival, Doyle Dane Bernbach. "I
couldn't write the Volkswagen campaign if I live to be 100," he said then,
"but I admire it very much and it seems to me that it opens new doors."[6]
Bernbach shared Ogilvy's belief that advertising exists to persuade people
to buy. "Our job is to sell our clients' merchandise—not ourselves,"
Bernbach once said. "Our job is to kill the cleverness that makes us shine
instead of the product."[7]

So, it seems Reeves, Ogilvy, and Bernbach—champions of hard sell,
image, and wit—used different methods to achieve the same purpose. As
Ogilvy sees it, today's ad creators have strayed far away from the job of
selling. He admires work that goes for the jugular and finds it in the field
of direct response. "The people who know what they're doing are the
direct [marketing] people," he told Harry. "They know exactly what
they've sold. And you don't. You haven't the faintest idea whether the
advertising sells anything or not. And you don't really care. You want to
win an award at the Cannes Festival, or some Clio, or one of those
rackets."

Most general advertising today is concerned with the first two stages
in the dynamics of selling, *getting attention* and *arousing interest*. By
contrast, direct marketers move straight to the final two phases, *creating
desire* and *producing action*. The best creators want to be sure that the
advertising they do is noticed in the maze of media clutter. The first goal,
they are convinced, is to break through and touch the viewer or reader, to
be seen and remembered for their dozen or so television exposures out of

Ogilvy drew on the heritage of mail order advertising to drive home nineteen persuasive reasons why a customer should buy the Silver Cloud, then selling for $13,550. Despite its hard selling edge, this classic ad is imagery at its best.

The Rolls-Royce Silver Cloud—$13,550.

"At 60 miles an hour the loudest noise in this new Rolls-Royce comes from the electric clock"

*What makes Rolls-Royce the best car in the world? "There is really no magic about it—
it is merely patient attention to detail," says an eminent Rolls-Royce engineer.*

1. "At 60 miles an hour the loudest noise comes from the electric clock," reports the Technical Editor of THE MOTOR. The silence of the engine is uncanny. Three mufflers tune out sound frequencies—acoustically.

2. Every Rolls-Royce engine is run for seven hours at full throttle before installation, and each car is test-driven for hundreds of miles over varying road surfaces.

3. The Rolls-Royce is designed as an owner-driven car. It is eighteen inches shorter than the largest domestic cars.

4. The car has power steering, power brakes and automatic gear-shift. It is very easy to drive and to park. No chauffeur required.

5. There is no metal-to-metal contact between the body of the car and the chassis frame—except for the speedometer drive. The entire body is insulated and under-sealed.

6. The finished car spends a week in the final test-shop, being fine-tuned. Here it is subjected to ninety-eight separate ordeals. For example, the engineers use a stethoscope to listen for axle-whine.

7. The Rolls-Royce is guaranteed for three years. With a new network of dealers and parts-depots from

Coast to Coast, service is no longer any problem.

8. The famous Rolls-Royce radiator has never been changed, except that when Sir Henry Royce died in 1933 the monogram RR was changed from red to black.

9. The coachwork is given five coats of primer paint, and hand rubbed between each coat, before fourteen coats of finishing paint go on.

10. By moving a switch on the steering column, you can adjust the shock-absorbers to suit road conditions. (The lack of fatigue in driving this car is remarkable.)

11. Another switch defrosts the rear window, by heating a network of 1360 invisible wires in the glass. There are two separate ventilating systems, so that you can ride in comfort with all the windows closed. Air conditioning is optional.

12. The seats are upholstered with eight hides of English leather—enough to make 128 pairs of soft shoes.

13. A picnic table, veneered in French walnut, slides out from under the dash. Two more swing out behind the front seats.

14. You can get such optional extras as an Espresso coffee-making machine, a dictating machine, a bed, hot and cold water for washing, an electric razor

15. You can lubricate the entire chassis by simply pushing a pedal from the driver's seat. A gauge on the dash shows the level of oil in the crankcase.

16. Gasoline consumption is remarkably low and there is no need to use premium gas; a happy economy.

17. There are two separate systems of power brakes, hydraulic and mechanical. The Rolls-Royce is a very safe car—and also a very lively car. It cruises serenely at eighty-five. Top speed is in excess of 100 m.p.h.

18. Rolls-Royce engineers make periodic visits to inspect owners' motor cars and advise on service.

ROLLS-ROYCE AND BENTLEY

19. The Bentley is made by Rolls-Royce. Except for the radiators, they are identical motor cars, manufactured by the same engineers in the same works. The Bentley costs $300 less, because its radiator is simpler to make. People who feel diffident about driving a Rolls-Royce can buy a Bentley.

PRICE. The car illustrated in this advertisement—f.o.b. principal port of entry—costs $13,550.
If you would like the rewarding experience of driving a Rolls-Royce or Bentley, get in touch with our dealer. His name is on the bottom of this page. Rolls-Royce Inc., 10 Rockefeller Plaza, New York, N.Y.

JET ENGINES AND THE FUTURE

Certain airlines have chosen Rolls-Royce turbo-jets for their Boeing 707's and Douglas DC8's. Rolls-Royce prop-jets are in the Vickers Viscount, the Fairchild F-27 and the Grumman Gulfstream.

Rolls-Royce engines power more than half the turbo-jet and prop-jet airliners supplied to or in order for world airlines.

Rolls-Royce now employ 42,000 people and the company's engineering experience does not stop at motor cars and jet engines. There are Rolls-Royce diesel and gasoline engines for many other applications.

The huge research and development resources of the company are now at work on many projects for the future, including nuclear and rocket propulsion.

Reprinted by permission of Rolls-Royce Motor Cars Inc.

the 50,000 some aired by the networks each year. This takes emotion, drama, or humor as persuasion is crafted into a cloak of entertainment. I suspect Ogilvy understands this as he observes the advertising scene from Touffou, his twelfth-century chateau 150 miles southwest of Paris. But he obviously feels that much of today's advertising is too flashy and pointless in its attempts to scale the wall of distraction, indifference, and confusion. Each year, the wall gets higher and wider as media options multiply and commercial minutes are split like amoebas from 60 seconds and 30s into 15s. And the commercials *are* getting flashier.

True, some of the commercials we most admire do a terrific job of scaling the wall to make contact and shake hands with the consumer. However, when the consumer smiles back and is receptive, the spots often stop short of a clear sales pitch. The point is sometimes lost. There has been no attempt to romance product benefits. That's what Ogilvy is concerned about when he rages against "self-conscious, brilliant, original crap." "It hasn't got to be an event," he argues, "it's got to persuade people to do things. Persuade them to do things!"

Hall of Giants

That evening we took a motor launch across the lagoon to the Palazzo Pisani Moretta, where Ogilvy was scheduled to speak before dinner. The men were decked out in tuxedos, the ladies in formal concoctions. Ogilvy was dressed in a black Nehru jacket buttoned up to his Adam's apple. Above the collar his face was reddish brown. He appeared to be playing the part of a fashionable Englishman stopping over in Venice on his return from a holiday in India.

At 7:25, we settled into the stiff-backed sixteenth-century chairs in the second floor grand ballroom. A large table, draped with a crimson cloth, was positioned high on a platform at one end of the hall in front of a giant window overlooking the canal. On the table was a single microphone, no lectern. Behind the table was a chair. At precisely 7:30, Ogilvy mounted the platform and sat down. He reached under the table and brought out the famous Russian doll with a series of progressively smaller dolls inside. This he placed to one side to use at the close of his talk.

"I've been to India," he said. I presumed this was a reference to his jacket. "It was a wonderful experience." (Long pause.) "Show-biz advertising hasn't reached India yet. In India they still believe the purpose of advertising is to sell the product."

This was as far as he went in admonishing the audience. He went on to deliver an eloquent talk on his principles of advertising and managing an advertising agency. Most of us had read what he had to say in his various books, but in this setting the words took on special significance when spoken in the deep, James Mason voice by the old lion himself.

With the Grand Canal outside the window, the Grand Master, David Ogilvy, addresses assembled managers and creative supervisors of the worldwide Scali, McCabe, Sloves confederation. The Russian Doll awaits his final point.

He concluded with the Russian doll he gave to every new manager of an Ogilvy office. He opened it up and took out a smaller one. Then again, until he had reached the smallest doll, inside of which was a slip of paper bearing these words of advice: "If you always hire people who are smaller than you are, we shall become a company of dwarfs. If, on the other hand, you always hire people who are bigger than you are, we shall become a company of giants."

There were many giants in the room, but they didn't necessarily see eye to eye with him on the best way to sell today's consumers.

The Product Is the Star

The next morning at breakfast by the lagoon on the white terrace at the Cipriani, I asked Sam Scali about Ogilvy's reaction to the commercials.

"You have to understand that's his way, to overreact to make a point," Sam said. "He doesn't object to entertainment or funny advertising. He liked a lot of it. He objects if the product is tacked on the end as an afterthought."

When I asked for an example, he described this one:

There was a cigar commercial from Europe. I forget the product name. A bald man in a photo booth was fiddling with the buttons on the machine. He wanted to have his photo taken without showing he was bald. He couldn't make the machine work. The scene was hilarious. It ended with him hunching down to push the buttons and the photo came out with nothing but the top of the head with three strands of hair showing. The spot had nothing to do with cigars.

I've since seen the spot on the *Tonight Show*. Johnny Carson showed it along with other crowd-pleasing spots from Europe. It was funny. But I too forget the product name. Maybe Ogilvy would have approved if the product had been film, or photo equipment, or toupees, anything that registered the brand on your memory string and made you want to buy it. On the other hand, perhaps the cigar is so well known in Europe that it simply needs a funny little "tweak" now and then to remind people it is still around.

You will be hard pressed to find a client who disagrees with David Ogilvy that today's advertising is long on entertainment and short on persuasion. Marketers want advertising to sell the product. To do that, they think, you need to spell out the advantages, say what you mean—straight out—and not beat around the bush.

You will also have a hard time finding a truly gifted creative person who thinks that straightforward, rational persuasion will be noticed in today's media clutter. Even when consumers do notice it, they are so streetwise about advertising that you have to do more than simply show them. You have to romance and entertain them to get around defenses, which, like layers of scar tissue, have formed around most viewers' minds.

I agree with Ogilvy that much of today's advertising has strayed too far in the direction of "show biz" and too far away from dramatizing a product's unique advantage. Each message must indelibly lodge the brand in the viewer's memory and seed the mind with reasons to buy, in addition to providing entertainment. The brand deserves to be more than simply a member of the supporting cast. This can be, and is, being done. A good example is Batten Barton, Durstine, and Osborn's (BBDO) Diet Pepsi commercial featuring Michael J. Fox dashing out in a rainstorm. The casting is superb, and even an attractive neighbor and Fox's considerable talent can't steal the limelight. The product is the true star of the show.

Great advertising is a storyteller, a romantic voice, an emotional persuader. It must have style and intrigue as it shines a bright light on the product, its advantages and value point. The brand and its uniqueness must be remembered when the TV set goes dark, or the page is turned. To do this, advertising must combine the thinking of a Claude Hopkins with the staging of a George Lucas. It must persuade in a way that romances and lures the customer unsuspecting into the brand's sticky web.

Sum & Substance

Many corporate managers agree that the creators of today's television commercials and print advertising seem to be more interested in enhancing their own reputations by winning awards than they are in selling the product.

This ad for Lee jeans is a superb example of today's indirect sell. It tells a story by implication to a sophisticated target audience. Consumers draw their own conclusions and form their own link with the brand and what it offers. Fallon McElligott, Minneapolis, also used this scenario in television.

Separate loads. Mutual interests. Lee jeans.

It is true, writers and art directors want the fame and peer admiration that comes from winning award shows like Communications Arts (CA), New York Art Directors, Cannes, Clios, The One Show, and MPA/Stephen Kelly. But to win the most coveted awards, the work must have both style and substance. It must convey a persuasive point through an unexpected idea. Judges admire smart and inventive graphics and copy and reward them when they are used to present product advantages in new and unusual ways.

Talented young people are attracted to advertising by the glamour of a business that trades in art and ideas. They want to try their hand at creating images and ideas even more exciting than those they grew up with. Without training, the fact that advertising is supposed to sell something is often a secondary consideration. Some never grasp that this is what advertising is all about.

The other day our agency (The Martin Agency) hosted eighteen students from a dozen colleges for two weeks of intensive study. One of the projects in the program involved planning a marketing communications strategy—and advertising—for our client Reynolds Aluminum Recycling. The group broke into three teams, and on the final day my colleagues and I, along with the client, judged the results. We were amazed at the insight of these neophytes. The ideas were innovative and sound. They had been given direction and instructed that advertising must deliver a selling proposition. If their ideas were executed by skilled art directors and producers, I'm convinced the campaigns could run, be effective salesmen, and win awards as well.

How about television spots directed to children featuring Oscar the Grouch? Not a bad idea, eh? The copy they turned out for Oscar made him a very persuasive spokesman for recycling. Even after eight days of training, the students had learned that the purpose of an advertisement is to sell.

It is a mistake to sell young people short. They are quick studies. What is needed is the guidance of wise creative directors and a solid agency philosophy demanding that advertising sell as well as entertain.

▪2▪

Something of Value

*It seems to be taken for granted that productivity
is simply a synonym for cost reduction or manufacturing efficiency. The* value *of the product,
particularly in terms of its consumer meaning,
seems never to be taken into account.*

—Peter Georgescu, president,
Young & Rubicam

We had just settled comfortably into a well-worn wooden booth in Akron's Diamond Grill.

"This place is a good example of value added." My dinner companion, Jim DeVoe, was introducing me to one of his favorite restaurants. He was right. The place didn't look like much. It was circa 1930, straight out of an Edward Hopper painting, outfitted with wood and chrome. The outside walls needed some tile work, the interior was sparse, but the soft lighting brought everything together in a diffused haze, and the product that counted was reasonably priced and served with sizzling flair. I cut my filet with a fork.

Our subject was advertising. Our discussion covered a number of concerns facing manufacturers today. It set the stage for issues developed more fully in the following pages.

DeVoe's Iceberg

"I see advertising as the tip of the iceberg, the visible peak above the surface," DeVoe said. Goodyear's advertising vice-president, and a custodian of one of America's most enduring brands, was launching into his favorite subject along with his steak. He reached for a cocktail napkin and drew a triangle. "The base below the surface makes advertising possible," he said. "The foundation is distribution, everything rests on that. Next is a quality product. Then the sales force. Up here, near the water line, is product publicity." He had drawn four layers below the surface.

"Advertising agencies, especially big ones, tend to concentrate up

12

here.'' Jim tapped his Pentel on the word ''advertising,'' making black dots on the napkin. ''It's the grunt work down here that makes the tip higher and wider.''

Our conversation had started earlier in the afternoon in the older of Goodyear's two main buildings on East Market Street. We had talked about the downside risk of not protecting brand equity and about how to make advertising a cost-effective use of corporate assets. This is increasingly difficult as media costs escalate and consumer media options multiply. VCRs, cable, and independent stations are cutting into consumer viewing time, leaving national advertisers scrambling for ways to make an impact on target audiences.

Relieving the Squeeze

''Advertising must increase a product's value in the minds of consumers to protect the price at retail.'' With that comment, Jim DeVoe summarized the deep concern of corporate America. ''This is just as important for durables as it is for package goods. But it ain't easy.'' Jim smiled and held out his arms in frustration as he described the *unbearable squeeze:*

DeVoe's iceberg, sketched on a cocktail napkin, puts distribution at the base, advertising above the water line. The grunt work below the surface pushes the tip up higher.

transaction prices caught between escalating media costs and the higher cost of materials, manufacture, and distribution. The squeeze makes it hard for manufacturers to maintain share of voice in a category. The stakes are high. Those who are outshouted are usually doomed to a shrinking market share.

Through the years, Goodyear has done a good job at every level of the iceberg. To maintain value the company invests $250 million a year to research new products and improve on the old. All this for a product that is, as DeVoe puts it, "a rubber patch the size of your palm holding your car on the road." Goodyear's aggressive investment in support of brand equity is calculated to enhance the consumer's perception of Goodyear value. "We simply have to keep perceived value at the top of the list," he told me, "despite escalating media costs and the great pressures they impose." As a result, the brand that was No. 1 in 1925 is still the leader

Goodyear has sold known value and superior quality from the outset. This ad, from the early 1920s, talks of a man who buys a make he has never heard of at a so-called "discount." The other buys a Goodyear Tire, nothing off. "Who drives the better bargain?"

WHO DRIVES THE BETTER BARGAIN?

Two men, let us say, buy tires. One, thinking wholly of price, buys a make he has never heard of, on the strength of a so-called "discount." The other buys a Goodyear Tire, in a straightforward transaction, nothing off.

Who drives the better bargain?

Maybe the first man doesn't know that the list prices on certain tires are fictitiously high, precisely to allow for the "discount" he receives.

Maybe he doesn't know that in case of trouble his adjustment will be made on the basis of this high list price, with consequent disappointment to himself.

Maybe he doesn't know that the price he paid for his unknown brand tire is actually or almost as much as he would have had to pay for a Goodyear.

Maybe he doesn't realize that a company like Goodyear, with its immense and economical production, can make and sell good tires as cheaply as anyone.

The man who buys the Goodyear Tire buys a reputable product, of known value and superior quality.

He buys a tire sinewed with genuine long-staple cotton, armored with best quality rubber, embodying the most efficient construction yet devised.

He buys a tire famed the world over for long and economical mileage, distinguished everywhere for freedom from trouble.

He buys also the pledge of the dealer to give him the kind of service that will get out of that tire all the mileage built into it at the factory.

When you buy tires, think of these two men.

Ask yourself, *who drives the better bargain?*

GOODYEAR

Copyright 1922, by The Goodyear Tire & Rubber Co., Inc.

today. It joins an impressive group of brands that have maintained a leadership position for more than six decades:[1]

Swift bacon	Prince Albert pipe tobacco
Eveready batteries	Gillette razors
Nabisco biscuits	Singer sewing machines
Kellogg breakfast cereal	Crisco shortening
Kodak cameras	Ivory soap
Del Monte canned fruit	Coca Cola soft drink
Wrigley chewing gum	Campbell's soup
Gold Medal flour	Lipton tea
Life Savers mint candies	Goodyear tires
Sherwin-Williams paint	

The 1987 *Yankelovich Monitor* report underscores the market value of established brands. The extensive *Monitor* lifestyle survey tells us that today's average shopper is a pragmatic and professional consumer who is frustrated by product failures and corporate negligence.[2] If he finds a brand that satisfies him, which is rare, he's likely to stick with it. He is always out to "beat the system," buy on deal, get the best for less; yet, when in doubt, the consumer wants the established brand. *Consumers go to the familiar,* not out of nostalgia or emotion, but *as a guide to competent consumption.*

Time, Money, and the Squeaky Wheel

In supermarkets, shoppers don't have much time to think. Faced with 22,000 items, people can't devote much time to analyzing new products or deciding on which familiar ones they'll buy. About 70 percent of the time they don't know what they want until they get to the appropriate shelf. This underscores the value of the package and of the advertising that makes it stand for something.

The trick is to build a quality product, establish top-of-mind awareness for the product in its category, then throttle back to keep the brand name alive in the consumer's memory. "At that point, a little advertising 'tweak' now and then may be enough to hold the unaided awareness you need," DeVoe commented.

With 440 advertising dollars chasing every man, woman, and child in America each year, it's hard to build awareness from scratch. Airways, cable, and the printed page are as crowded as supermarket shelves. A $12 million national advertising budget, for example, means that an advertiser has a nickel to spend per person. To put it another way, with a $12 million war chest, you can get your 2 cents' worth in just 2½ times a year, enough to buy seven or eight exposures per capita. Of course, most advertisers segment the market in order to reach a smaller target group of consumers with greater frequency. Still, it takes millions to mount a national campaign and to sustain it long enough to build unaided brand recall and establish understanding of the brand's competitive benefit.

That's why an established brand has the advantage. Even then, it isn't easy to stay "King of the Hill." The unbearable squeeze has managers looking for ways to hype sales in the short term. Dollars are siphoned away from long-term brand-building strategy and poured into promotions that are, essentially, short-term pricing tactics.

"People have to make numbers," DeVoe observed, "so they go to retail promotion."

I agreed, thinking about the advertising dollars I'd seen diverted into deals and promotions. It seems much more logical to put money behind something that will produce an immediate return. For many managers, advertising is a strange, unmeasurable activity that may or may not work. On the other hand, it's easy to get trapped into applying grease to the squeaky wheel. And the retailer squeaks every time you see him. The friendly retailer is the brand's worst enemy—the great homogenizer of all brands. In durables, he'll switch the consumer to controlled or private labels, or other brands with wider margins, to make an extra buck. With package goods, retailers are even more inclined to bite the brands that feed them. In so doing, they are shaking the distribution system, which is the base of DeVoe's pyramid.

The reason, of course, is the retailers' own battle for survival. Many chains are closing unprofitable stores, dropping regions, and changing their warehouse systems. Casting around to find ways to recoup, the chains have noticed the golden eggs resting on their shelves. "Why shouldn't the golden goose pay more for the privilege of putting its wares here?" they ask themselves. So they squeeze the goose. Retailers are finding all kinds of ingenious ways to extract bribes and fees. One use of this new source of revenue is to build the brand image of the store. Over the past ten years food store advertising has risen from .7 percent of sales to 1.3 percent to a current level of $3 billion. It's working for grocers. Store customers are loyal: 72 percent of all food purchases are confined to a single store.

The Battle for Turf

Supermarket shelf space is the most precious American turf since Gettysburg. The average market has 36,000 square feet of selling space. When new products come in, old ones are tossed out. *USA Today* carried a dispatch on this phenomenon from the front lines:

> Every inch counts. The result is a war over turf: product makers
> battling grocers—and fighting each other—to win and keep their
> spots in the supermarket. But what used to be a civilized little war is

becoming a high stakes melee. Trying to capture just a little more
market share from novelty-loving, brand-fickle shoppers, companies
are cranking out new items rapid-fire. They're storming the supermarkets to get in—and to knock their competitors off the shelf. And
grocers, watching their shelf space grow more valuable, reap the
spoils: merchandise discounts, advertising support and cold hard
cash.[3]

Because chain store buyers view suppliers as profit centers rather
than as partners, they now often charge an admission fee, push money, or
warehouse "slotting allowance" for the privilege of squeezing onto their
crowded shelves. Then, if the product doesn't move, they charge the
manufacturer a "de-slotting fee" to scoop up the unsold brands and take
them home. Can you imagine the insult this adds to injury? Martha T.
Moore continues her dispatch in *USA Today:* "Retailers say slotting
allowances defray their costs in bringing in a new item. Ralph's, a 127-
store chain in southern California, spent $20 million in 1987 adding 10,000
items and dropping 7,000, says president Pat Collins. Slotting allowances
covered about 60 percent of the cost.''[4] This isn't much comfort to smaller
brand manufacturers who just want to go about their business selling
existing products. However, *without consumer pull-through, and a hefty
category share, the brand is at the mercy of the retail trade.*

Retailers require case allowances, charge for display space, and
sometimes even levy a fee on manufacturers for the privilege of making a
new product presentation to the store's buying committee. This grab-bag
attitude stems from historically lower retailer profit margins, which average 3 percent or less, compared to margins of up to 20 percent for well-
run manufacturing operations. But many small companies operate on
thinner margins and can't stay in the game as the ante is raised. Two of
our food accounts have already dealt themselves out of the brand-building
game. The retailer greed squeeze, added to the cost of raw materials,
proved too much for them. Many others are folding their hands or
dropping out of brand competition and putting production into private-
label goods. Soon only the fittest, with solid category share, will survive.

Sounding the Alarm

Chain store money-grubbing practices now take up to a half of the $19
billion currently spent on trade deals. Consumer promotions add $60
billion more, further eroding consumer advertising budgets. In 1975, one
out of five purchases was made because the consumer had a coupon, or
because the product displayed a reduced price, or as the result of a variety
of other sales promotion techniques that translate into a perceived price
break. Today, nearly half of all sales are made that way. Customers are
being trained to buy on price. The relationship between brand-develop-

ment spending and promotional spending has changed in just a few years from a ratio of 60 to 40 to one of 30 to 70,[5] leaving some established brands rusting on the side of the road like abandoned automobiles on a New York City freeway. In effect, the world is turning back a hundred years to the time when commodities, not brands, filled the shopping basket.

Our outspoken advertising guru, David Ogilvy, addressed the subject in a "Sound the Alarm" speech to the "50th Anniversary Luncheon of the Advertising Research Foundation in New York on March 18, 1986:

> Any damn fool can put on a deal, but it takes genius, faith and perseverance to create a brand.
>
> The financial rewards do not always come in next quarter's earnings per share, but come they do. When Philip Morris bought General Foods for five billion dollars, they were buying brands.
>
> There used to be a prosperous brand of coffee called Chase & Sanborn. Then they started dealing. They became addicted to price-offs. Where is Chase & Sanborn today? Dead as a doornail.
>
> I have a habit for prophecy. Listen to three paragraphs from a speech I made in 1955:
>
> "The manufacturers who dedicate their advertising to building a favorable image, the most sharply defined personality for their brand, are the ones who will get the largest share of market at the highest profit.
>
> "The time has come to sound an alarm! To warn what is going to happen to brands if so much is spent on deals that there is no money left to advertise them.
>
> "Deals don't build the kind of indestructible image which is the only thing that can make your brand part of the fabric of American life."[6]

This is a passionate argument, but it is often ignored by the troops in the trenches. I told Jim DeVoe about the book I was writing to help marketers understand how advertising fits into the scheme of things: how promotions and dealing can live side by side with advertising so that established brands won't go down the drain; when to use advertising and how; and when to fold the tent (which is the subject of our next chapter).

Divide to Conquer

Dinner was over now, and it was time for brandy. Jim DeVoe made two final observations. "Time was, when costs per thousands were low, you could throw money at consumers," he said. "Now, with higher media costs, commercial proliferation, and media fragmentation, you have to segment markets carefully." Brands that became mighty staples in every household owing to national reputations built on the basis of cheap national media are now being marketed region by region and even locally because today's national media costs are so steep. In 1986, for example, according to *Business Week,* national advertisers spent $6.5 billion on local TV ads, an increase of 8 percent, while their spending on network TV rose only 3 percent, to $8.5 billion. These high media costs put an even greater emphasis on creative innovation in advertising to make the bucks go farther. Advertising must capture the consumer's imagination while it gets attention.

"It's getting tougher to be noticed today," DeVoe continued. "Consumers have been raised on television entertainment. They're demanding and cynical and very much aware of their options. Manufacturers need to keep putting the quality into the product. You guys in agencies must enhance the product's value for us to be able to sell it at a fair price."

Sum & Substance

Established brands are difficult to dislodge if they are protected by consistent advertising. The consumer is pragmatic. A satisfied consumer is likely to reorder unless another brand in the category is equally familiar and offers a unique advantage. Low price alone is not enough to dislodge a brand leader fortified by perceived added value. Sometimes this truth is overlooked by marketers caught in the squeeze between manufacturing costs and retail price points.

Retailers are now finding all sorts of imaginative ways to extract price concessions from their manufacturer-suppliers. These demands increasingly draw available dollars away from brand-building advertising. As familiarity falls, the brand's pull-through power is lost along with market share. Faced with sales quotas, managers often resort to short-term promotional tactics, which further drain away resources previously used for long-term advertising strategy.

Higher media costs call for creative innovation to make advertising linger in consumer minds and so bridge the gap between fewer insertions. With national media costs prohibitive for many brands, markets must be targeted through regional strategies in order to marshal the weight and impact necessary to influence share. But the greatest need is for managers to understand advertising's power and to have the will to deploy it.

To be effective, both the product and the advertising must be different to attract the interest of an inundated audience. As advertising surrounds the brand with a unique mystique, it sets it apart from other products in the same category to give it added value. This doesn't happen overnight. It takes repeated exposures to form a lasting impression, encourage trial, and prompt repeat sales.

·3·

Hostage Brands

Virtually everywhere in the world, manufacturers are abdicating control of their businesses to retailers.

—Norman Berry, Chairman/CEO,
Ogilvy & Mather

Each year the nation's canners meet at a glittering resort somewhere in North America. The way things are going, next year some may have to pass up the trip. In the late 1980s, the people who make those cans of beans and tins of meat you see in the supermarket are in trouble. Many are in the grip of the unbearable squeeze that Jim DeVoe and I talked about. In May 1987, the canners got together at the Greenbrier in White Sulphur Springs, West Virginia, to see what they could do about it.

Like Akron's Diamond Grill, the Greenbrier is a value-added experience. The brilliant white package is wrapped in green rolling hills surrounded by blue mountains. Inside the magnificent, rambling structure, with its jutting wings and columned central facade, a splendid room is yours for $250 a night, breakfast and dinner included. It's well worth the price, especially at company expense.

This year, the canners brought a list of nagging concerns along with their golf clubs. Our client, Pete Peterson, president of Bunker Hill Foods, had invited me and several others to address some bothersome issues: commodity versus brand thinking, retailer "hostaging," electronic couponing, slotting allowances and fees. I was invited because Pete had read in *Adweek* a summary of Ogilvy's comments (see Chapter 2) on the dangers of commodity thinking. It was the "Sound the Alarm" speech. Peterson wanted me to embellish the subject and to urge the canners to step up brand advertising before their products reverted to commodities—faceless items sold the way the corner grocer once offered flour, sugar, and soap out of a barrel.

I'd talked with Pete about our experience with a regional potato chip brand, Snyder's of Hanover (Pennsylvania). Snyder's marketing director,

Bruce Cutting, had sought out our agency because he was a brand builder. Bruce had been hired away from Procter & Gamble, where, as a brand manager, he had learned the value of an established consumer brand franchise. For him, advertising was a strategic resource. He wanted innovative, consistent brand advertising to build preference, mystique, and price stability over the long haul. That was his long-term strategy. He viewed promotion as a tactical resource, a pricing tool, a way to force distribution, get displays and tie-ins with the selected chain programs. As is true of most food companies, he budgeted roughly 15 percent of sales for promotion and broke out another 5 percent for consumer advertising.

Bruce expected advertising to expand the base of loyal Snyder customers by making it the brand of choice. He felt we could bring to bear enough clout in selected markets to allow this regional brand to break through the clutter and build both share of mind and market share in the potato chip category. His boss was skeptical about the value of advertising. The Snyder brand was buffeted about in a category where most products were trapped in the low price cellar; no brand had a clear consumer franchise, and greater retail sales resulted only from broader distribution forced by short-term dealing.

When a competitor, Eagle Snacks, found facings diminishing or hard to come by, it bought shelf space. In other words, Eagle paid the retailer ''rent'' to squeeze its products onto the shelves. In this way, Bruce told me, slotting allowances were introduced into the snack food business. However it started, the practice spread like a virus from chain to chain, from market to market. Chain buyers know a good thing when they see it. The slotting practice is now standard for most categories. For Snyder's, the unforeseen expense added an extra million dollars to its budget, and it broke the back of our client's resolve to advertise. Bruce left the company. Snyder's decided to forgo advertising to finance this and other forms of retailer blackmail. The brand became an unwilling hostage of the trade.

How a Brand Falls Hostage

I planned to deal with this experience in my talk. A few weeks before the meeting, I had called Keith Jones[1] of the Summa Group, promotion consultants of Nielsen Marketing Research. I wanted to get some additional information on retailer hostaging. Jones had personal experience of the pitfalls involved when a brand is no longer under the manufacturer's control. Before joining the Summa Group, he directed marketing for Duffy-Mott and watched retailers take his apple juice brand hostage. This experience led him to a systematic study of brand hostaging and to his creation of the Brand Hostage Index© as a way to deal with it. To my surprise, Pete Peterson had gotten to Keith Jones before I did. ''I can't give you all my good material,'' Keith laughed. ''I follow you on the program.'' We decided to compare notes, instead, so each talk would complement the other.

Keith Jones is a tall, bespectacled yuppie type who observes lifestyle trends by noticing what's happening in food stores. He offers up all kinds of fascinating information, such as the fact that condoms are the fastest-growing new item in food stores, and that another baby boomlet must be under way because disposable diapers have grown into a $2 billion business.

He told the group how a brand is taken hostage:

> Once volume under deal exceeds 90 percent, the brand is no longer under your control. The brand's bargaining position with the trade is lost. Your brand is now a hostage. Usually, about 65 percent of most products are sold on deal, but a good chain buyer can beat this number by using scanner data and computer-based forward buying. Then, by diverting product from warehouse to warehouse, the aggressive chain moves toward 100 percent.

In other words, the manufacturer loses control when the product is always sold into the trade at a discount. A chain uses low prices to polish its thrift image. It gets price breaks by holding a gun to the manufacturer's head, then takes all the credit for offering low prices to its customers. Meanwhile, revenue-starved brands fall into a commodity trap. To meet short-term goals, promotions are expanded and advertising is reduced. Without advertising, loyal customers are lost and control of the brand is handed to the retailer. Without loyal customers, the product sits on the shelf until the retailer calls the manufacturer in and charges a fee to have it removed. This is the fate of a hostage brand. Price, rather than value, is the rule of the game.

Vive la Difference

I told Keith my Snyder's story, and, to my surprise, he agreed with the company's decision to drop advertising. "The key is always market share," he said, "and *the key to share is a distinctive product difference, or being there first as one of the pioneers in the category*. At 20 percent share or better, the brand has the clout to influence chain behavior. When brand managers focus on profits, rather than share, share falls, trade costs rise, advertising is reduced, and trade pressures increase." As he described the downward spiral, I thought of Ogilvy's Chase & Sanborn example. Other brands came to mind as well: Schlitz, Bon Ami, Ipana, and Fluffo, to name a few that became promotional footballs. All the king's horses can't make them leaders again.

"I suspect potato chip consumers are trained to buy on price," Keith continued. "When that happens, and the customer can't distinguish a product difference, advertising might increase top-of-mind awareness, but the product won't gain the share needed as long as the retailer controls price."

He told me his own apple juice story. "We tried to advertise our way out of the box, but failed to gain share. This is typical for hostages, whether it's tuna, cake mix, dry pasta, or apple juice. You can't break out when the retailer controls price and consumers buy low because they don't see product points of difference. We stopped advertising juice until a line extension of unique-tasting blended juices could be introduced. With a distinctive benefit to talk about, advertising paid off."

Advertising can create a personality for the brand. Many products with strong category market share have done this over a long period of time. As discussed in Chapter 2, Crisco, Kellogg's, Del Monte, Lipton, and Swift all lead their categories, and have done so for sixty-five years. These pioneer products are much like others in their respective categories, but these brands have strong distribution, the base of DeVoe's pyramid, and have sustained customer loyalty and market share over the years by maintaining share of voice in their respective categories. Faced with leadership brands savvy enough to protect the consumer franchise, second-tier brands find it hard to move up in the category while retailers do what they can to pull them down.

Consumers stay loyal because they trust the quality of an established brand. With dozens of items on their shopping lists, they don't have the time or inclination to stop and think about impulse purchases—they just make them. Because leaders have consumer clout, retailer shenanigans can't do them much harm.

It's another story for a new brand or a weak brand without a clear product difference. Only with a distinctive difference can the hill be won. For example, sales of unpopped popcorn popped along at a predictable level until suddenly they tripled to a half billion in five years, heated up by microwave ovens—a brand-new category since 1980. There is always room for new products that strike the consumer's fancy or fill a need (in this case, speed and convenience).

Even established products can add value by giving an old song a new arrangement. Jello did it with chocolate pudding by calling it chocolate mousse and tacking 30 cents onto its retail price. Keith agrees that the best escape from being held hostage is to find a unique product benefit. "That's when advertising makes all the difference," he said. "Swanson's TV Dinner was a low-cost product. So what did Campbell's do? They targeted weight-conscious working women with a low calorie dinner that could easily be heated in a microwave oven. They gave it an upscale name and package. Campbell's glop is much the same as Swanson's, but it sells for twice as much."

Campbell's is an innovative marketer. In response to higher national media costs and retailer pressures, the company is now tailoring its products, advertising, promotion, and sales efforts to fit different regions of the country—and even individual neighborhoods within a city. By developing products that appeal to various regional and ethnic tastes, Campbell's seeks to boost share by offering appealing product differences.[2]

Brand Ransom

Finding a product difference and romancing it is one sure way to avoid being held hostage by the trade. I asked Keith if he had any other suggestions.

"Well, you can ransom the brand."

"Ransom?"

"Yes, ransom. Pay the price. You can give up sales and market share by cutting back on deals. Trim your sales. Reduce your product line. Give up distribution. Back your strongest items. Concentrate on smaller regions. Advertise where media weight makes a difference. Build share in manageable markets."

"That sounds pretty dramatic," I said. "Does it really work? You're talking about cutting into plant capacity. There are mouths to feed, payrolls to meet."

"You have to have deep pockets. But if you have a strong brand, you must protect the consumer franchise. You can't cheapen the brand."

I asked for an example. He told me about Heinz pickles. Heinz was once the leader; now it is No. 3. "Instead of 57 varieties, most chains carry only three or four Heinz products," Keith said. "Some don't stock Heinz at all. What remains of the Heinz brand are items which have the most brand loyalty. Heinz gave up almost half its business to improve margins and regain control of its franchise.

"There's another way," he continued. "You can overlay existing trade deals with coupons. This will give you a price advantage over competition. You'll get better retail cooperation with displays. The brand will be featured in retailer advertising. Tropicana did that to stave off P&G's new Citrus Hill orange juice. That strategy works if you have staying power and deep pockets."

Ransoming is expensive, and it's also risky.

Value Positioning

In his speech to the canners, Keith talked about *value positioning*. He used Barbasol shaving cream as an example. Barbasol rolled back the list price to an everyday low, positioned between private-label and premium brands. This strategy got the product out of the deal game. Over an eight-year period, its market share doubled from 9 percent to 19 percent. To afford value positioning, it cut the package cost by eliminating the cap. It replaced its sales force with brokers and distributors. "Of course, value positioning is a one-way street," Keith observed. "Barbasol can never again command a premium price, nor can new products be launched under the brand name."

Holding the Bottom Line

A few months after the meeting, Pete Peterson lost the brand battle at Bunker Hill. Despite his best intentions and desire to maintain customer loyalty through steady brand advertising, the company could not afford to maintain a competitive category share of voice in its key markets. Slotting allowances sliced too deeply into his profit margin. The Farm Fresh chain fired the first volley, extracting fees for products already in the warehouse. Then A&P joined in, charging fees for products already in the stores. As Bunker Hill's competitors in the canned meat category held the line on low prices, margins disappeared, forcing advertising cutbacks to an occasional newspaper ad featuring coupons, a sop to the trade.

"We just can't stay in there," Pete said. "Even the big boys are feeling the pinch. Campbell's cut staff 10 percent, General Foods dropped 2,500, and there's a blood bath at Pillsbury."

In 1988, Young & Rubicam's president, Peter Georgescu, noted the manufacturer's slide. "There is a steadily accelerating, steadily frightening trend in our marketplace . . . toward what I call 'commodity-ness,' " he said. "And in the commodity marketplace, only one thing matters: price."[3]

Y&R should have a good perspective. In 1988, it was at the top of all the nation's agencies, with the most domestic billings. It represents Colgate, General Foods, Gillette, and Kraft, to name only a few. Georgescu told fellow ad executives in Chicago, "On the client side, there is greater concern with the short term than I have ever seen before in my 25 years of experience. There is concern with this month's sales, this period's share, this quarter's bottom line, this morning's stock price . . . as never before."

With even well-heeled major marketers with an established share scrambling, a regional marketer like Pete's Bunker Hill brand has little choice, especially when beef prices put on a squeeze at the other end. But it is sad to see a brand with a loyal following forced to fall hostage to retailers, with no resourceful MacGyver to engineer an escape out of cast-off chicken wire, no rich Daddy Warbucks to come up with the ransom. For the future, Bunker Hill will hold onto the customers it has through value positioning, and meet overhead through low-margin private-label production. The big boys will slap their own labels onto Pete's output and fight the brand battle for market share on the high ground, while retailers wheel up the artillery and try to bring them down from behind.

Sum & Substance

The other day, a former food broker told me why he quit the business. "When you have to buy your way in, its time to get out," he said. Consumers aren't aware of the infighting that goes on in the no man's land between the factory and the cash register. The food business is separated into "them" and "us." From the manufacturer's point of view, the "thems" are out to drive down price until there is no money left to sustain brand loyalty among consumers. The stores view their suppliers as fat cats with big margins, while theirs are a puny 3 percent or less. Since the fat cats want shelf space, they can damn well pay for it, they feel, so that "we can make some money."

In this scenario, the little cats pay up or drop out unless consumer loyalty kicks in as an override. The control flash point is 20 percent category share. Below that level the brand is hostage to the trade. Above it, brands have the clout to influence chain behavior. Consumer loyalty is the key, and brand uniqueness (or the perception of added value) is the essential ingredient. Shoppers buy the familiar, and retailers stock to serve customer desires. Shoppers reach out for brands with quality they can depend on. Or they turn to new products with something added that makes the product taste better, faster, easier to use, look nicer, smell sweeter, feel softer, whatever. The brand and its label conjure up these things automatically if advertising has adroitly planted this information in consumer minds. Price and deals alone won't build this mystique. The aura comes from steady, consistent advertising over time.

·4·

The Hat Trick

The marketing people who are responsible for introducing the product get all wrapped up in the service and forget all about the customer.

—Al Ries and Jack Trout, in *Positioning*

Back at the turn of the century, advertising agencies weren't what they are today. They were space sellers. Newspapers and magazines paid them a commission to sell ads. Even though agencies now represent advertisers instead of the media, the commission system continues. It is an anachronism that is often criticized, but it has helped stablize agency pricing through the years. Even in the late 1980s, when fee arrangements are sometimes more appropriate than the usual 15 percent commission, agencies compete on the basis of merit, rather than price.

To help sell the white space, agencies began to hire writers and artists to do the ads for customers. That led to close agency-advertiser relationships, which gradually changed the nature of the business. The space brokers became advertisers' agents instead of media agents. Now, advertising agencies are citadels of creativity, the spawning ground for ideas, the makers of mystique. To many, the modern advertising agency is a shining symbol of our successful, free-enterprise society. To others, what agencies do is hucksterism.

In those early days, however, agency ad making was only an incidental service ranking along with the paper, pens, blotting paper, and ink the brokers sold or bartered to publishers in exchange for space. Lord & Thomas, one of the nation's three largest agencies at the time, had one artist who took home $25 a week, and a writer who worked mornings for $15 a week. He earned another $15 working at Montgomery Ward during the afternoons.[1] Although the wages were reasonable, the small staff gives you some idea of the low importance agencies placed on the creative process back in 1901.

Two men—a young bookkeeper named Claude Hopkins and a former

Canadian Mounted Police officer named John E. Kennedy—changed the nature of the advertising agency business forever.

Claude Hopkins: Voice of the Consumer

Hopkins writes about his early career in *My Life in Advertising*. In the 1880s, many companies did their own ads, either hiring their own staff copywriters or using free lancers, as needed. One of these, John F. Powers, was then considered the dean of advertising. When Powers worked for John Wanamaker, he was paid $12,000 a year, a fabulous salary in that era which made him "the model and ideal of all men who had advertising ambitions."[2]

One day Powers was assigned a project by the Bissell Carpet Sweeper Company, where Claude Hopkins worked as an assistant bookkeeper. Hopkins was not impressed with the tack Powers took. "He never gave one moment to studying a woman's possible wish for a carpet sweeper," Hopkins observed. "There is not one word in that pamphlet which will lead women to buy." So he asked his boss to let him try his own hand.

Claude Hopkins had persuasive instincts. Even before he wrote his first line of copy, the man David Ogilvy calls "the father of modern advertising" knew that *the only way to sell is to appeal to the interests of the consumer*. It is something many writers never learn. Hopkins wrote about the advantages the customer would take away from the product rather than about what the manufacturer had put into it. His first effort at copywriting produced rather awesome results, bringing in 1,000 orders, the first Bissell had ever received by mail.

Although Hopkins continued with his bookkeeping, he sensed the power of the pen, and his mind caught fire with the possibilities in sales promotion. Focusing his thoughts on carpet sweepers and the women who used them, he came up with a new product idea—another instinctive move, this time in the direction of product differentiation. He gave the new sweeper line a *dominant value point*.

As a boy, Claude Hopkins had been a forestry buff. On his hikes through forests, he looked for samples of different woods, and in this way came to know a great deal about different grains and colors. Now, as a young man eager to succeed in his first job and anxious to use his new powers of mass persuasion, he put this knowledge to good use for his employer. Build Bissell carpet sweepers in twelve distinct woods, one in each wood to the dozen, he suggested. They should run from the white of the bird's-eye maple to the dark of the walnut, and include all the colors between.

This proposal was considered absurd by the mechanics who built and sold the sweepers. Equally opposed were the directors of the company, all of them ex-salesmen. One, the inventor of some new devices, suggested: "Why not talk broom action, patent dumping devices, cyco bearings and the great things I have created?" Hopkins tried to make the man understand what the idea was all about: "I am talking to women. They are not mechanics. I want to talk the things which they will understand and appreciate." At the time, sweepers were gathering dust in showrooms across the country. Even so, Bissell agreed to build 250,000 in twelve fine woods. Hopkins wrote the advertising. The response was overwhelming. The stock was sold in three weeks. With this success, Hopkins left his bookkeeping job and launched into a full-time career in advertising.

In 1907, at the age of 41, Claude Hopkins joined Lord & Thomas, where Albert Lasker, the agency's owner, paid him $100,000, the equivalent of $2 million a year, to apply his magic. His innovations were many: trial offers, test marketing, copy research, brand image. In 1967, thirty-five years after his death, he was inducted into the Copywriters Hall of Fame. At that time Hopkins was lauded as an advertising immortal. "The Quaker Puffed Wheat package still carries Hopkins' slogan, 'Shot from guns,' " the citation stated. "His sell goes marching on. Hopkins was the man who discovered 'film' for teeth (for Pepsodent), the beauty appeal in soap (for Palmolive), moneyback guarantees and coupon testing."[3]

Claude C. Hopkins, advertising pioneer and innovator, was a cautious man who based his work on fundamentals, but nonetheless produced breakthroughs that fathered modern advertising.

Obviously, Claude Hopkins was much more than merely a clever wordsmith. By considering each sales problem from the customer's perspective, he came up with innovations to make the sale take place. He never consulted managers or boards of directors about his work because he felt their viewpoints were "distorted." But he did consult customers. Their reactions to the campaigns he devised, he felt, were the only ones that counted.

Hopkins realized that agencies must represent the consumer. "The maker of an advertised article knows the manufacturing side and probably the dealer's side," he said, "but, this very knowledge often leads him astray in respect to consumers."

One of the most respected copywriters at the present time is Tom McElligott of Fallon McElligott in Minneapolis. Soon after he began as a writer, Tom asked a New York book search firm to find him copies of Hopkins's books *Scientific Advertising* and *My Life in Advertising*. He paid $60 for both volumes. "It was, without a doubt, the smartest investment I ever made," Tom says. Hopkins taught Tom to represent the thinking of the consumer. In a speech he made recently, McElligott quoted Hopkins: "I never had the sympathy of an advertiser in my life," Hopkins wrote. "Still, I respect them for their position. They desire to exploit their accomplishments, just as I do. But they represent the seller's side. I must represent the consumer. And those conceptions are usually as far apart as the poles."

In advertising style and approach, Hopkins and McElligott are also as far apart as the poles, a reflection of the very different times in which each entered advertising history. What both share is a healthy respect for the customer's point of view. McElligott, commenting on the Hopkins quote, said, "As Hopkins knew sixty years ago, smart advertisers don't pay agencies for comfort. They pay for objectivity. For a fresh perspective. For insights into the consumer point of view that they perhaps wouldn't otherwise get."

John E. Kennedy: Salesmanship in Print

Hopkins was preceded at Lord & Thomas by John E. Kennedy, a muscular six-footer with a handlebar mustache who had been a Canadian Mounted Police officer. Kennedy got his job at Lord & Thomas by offering to tell the agency's president, Albert Lasker, what advertising really was. To him it was obvious the agency didn't know. "Advertising is *salesmanship in print*," he said, and to Lasker this revelation was like discovering the world was round, after believing it was flat.

Kennedy learned his advertising craft while working for Dr. Shoop, the patent medicine man. To find out what housewives thought, he would go out and sit on a park bench and engage them in conversation. Their

John E. Kennedy, the former mounted policeman, strode into Albert Lasker's life at Lord & Thomas and taught him—and the world—that advertising is "salesmanship in print." Lasker said he was one of the "handsomest men I ever saw in my life."

Source: John Gunther, *Taken at the Flood,* © 1960, Harper & Row Publishers, Inc.

input gave him the insight needed to address the woman's point of view with his copy.

His first campaign at Lord & Thomas was for the 1900 Washer Company, a client so disappointed with advertising that its managers were about to abandon it altogether. Lasker showed him the ads that hadn't worked: "Don't be chained to the wash tub," one headline read. "You are getting old before your time. Your life and health are being ruined." "This is all wrong," Kennedy told Lasker. "You are speaking negatively. Every woman doesn't feel chained to the wash tub; lots of women might enjoy it. You miss her entirely. Second, the average woman is put in the position of a drudge. She won't want to admit she has been reduced to such bestial servility."

Kennedy worked out an ad with a positive appeal, using a free trial offer. The headline proclaimed, "Let this Washing Machine Pay for Itself." The copy described what the machine would do from the point of view of the woman who used it:

> When you revolve the tub, the clothes don't move. But, the
> water moves like a mill race through the clothes. The paddles on the
> tub bottom drive the soapy water through the clothes at every swing

of the tub. Back and forth, in and out of every fold, and through every mesh in the cloth, the hot soapy water runs like a torrent. The machine must have a little help from you, at every swing, but the motor-springs and the ball bearings do practically all the hard work.

Years later, in a talk to his staff, Lasker described what happened to the washer company: "They were spending $15,000 a year and going to quit—[but] showing you the power of advertising—within four months, out of receipts, they were spending $30,000 a month, and within six months were one of the three or four largest advertisers in America, and within eight months were doubling, trebling their plants."[4]

Kennedy had understood the customer's point of view and expressed it, thus unleashing the power of advertising.

The Agency's Role

The agency's job is to represent the consumer to the client. The client's job is to make, distribute, and market the product. Some agencies act as an extension of the client's marketing department. That's wrong. The agency is an extension of consumer thinking, an interpreter, the client's consumer ally, the essential link with the market. To do this job, the agency must understand which appeals work and which may backfire. Obviously, the only way for the agency to do this is to take the trouble to talk to consumers. The agency must know in advance which product benefits will influence trial.

Doing the Hat Trick

When I was in high school and college, I was a fan of *Printers' Ink,* an advertising trade magazine. I continued to read it every week until it went

Kennedy told Lasker, "There just isn't one thing about this advertisement that isn't wrong if you want to sell goods. You are speaking negatively. Every woman doesn't feel chained to the wash tub."

Kennedy's ad accentuated the positive. It cost $715 to run, pulled 1,547 inquiries in the first seven days, and ultimately produced 3,000 at a cost of 24 cents each. This and other Kennedy ads turned the company around, according to Lasker.

Let this Machine do your Washing Free.

There are Motor Springs beneath the tub.

These springs do nearly all the hard work, when once you start them going. And this washing machine works as easy as a bicycle wheel does.

There are slats on the inside bottom of the tub. These slats act as paddles, to swing the water in the same direction you revolve the tub.

You throw the soiled clothes into the tub first. Then you throw enough water over the clothes to float them.

Next you put the heavy wooden cover on top of the clothes to anchor them, and to press them down.

This cover has slats on its lower side to grip the clothes and hold them from turning around when the tub turns.

Now, we are all ready for quick and easy washing. You grasp the upright handle on the side of the tub and, with it, you revolve the tub one-third way round, till it strikes a motor-spring.

This motor-spring throws the tub back till it strikes the other motor-spring, which in turn throws it back on the first motor-spring.

The machine must have a little help from you, at every swing, but the motor-springs, and the ball-bearings, do practically all the hard work.

You can sit in a rocking chair and do all that the washer requires of you. A child can run it easily full of clothes.

When you revolve the tub the clothes don't move. But the water moves like a mill race through the clothes.

The paddles on the tub bottom drive the soapy water THROUGH and through the clothes at every swing of the tub. Back and forth, in and out of every fold, and through every mesh in the cloth, the hot soapy water runs like a torrent. This is how it carries away all the dirt from the clothes, in from six to ten minutes by the clock.

It drives the dirt out through the meshes of the fabrics WITHOUT ANY RUBBING, —without any WEAR and TEAR from the washboard.

It will wash the finest lace fabric without breaking a thread, or a button, and it will wash a heavy, dirty carpet with equal ease and rapidity. Fifteen to

twenty garments, or five large bed-sheets, can be washed at one time with this "1900" Washer.

A child can do this in six to twelve minutes better than any able washer-woman could do the same clothes in TWICE the time, with three times the wear and tear from the washboard. [Continued.]

This is what we SAY, now how do we PROVE it?

We send you our "1900" Washer free of charge, on a full month's trial, and we even pay the freight out of our own pockets.

No cash deposit is asked, no notes, no contract, no security.

You may use the washer four weeks at our expense. If you find it won't wash as many clothes in FOUR hours as you can wash by hand in EIGHT hours you send it back to the railway station, — that's all.

But, if, from a month's actual use, you are convinced it saves HALF the time in washing, does the work better, and does it twice as easily as it could be done by hand, you keep the machine.

Then you mail us 50 cents a week till it is paid for.

Remember that 50 cents is part of what the machine saves you every week on your own, or on a washer-woman's labor. We intend that the "1900" Washer shall pay for itself and thus cost you nothing.

You don't risk a cent from first to last, and you don't buy it until you have had a full month's trial.

Could we afford to pay freight on thousands of these machines every month, if we did not positively KNOW they would do all we claim for them? Can you afford to be without a machine that will do your washing in HALF THE TIME, with half the wear and tear of the washboard, when you can have that machine for a month's free trial, and let it PAY FOR ITSELF? This offer may be withdrawn at any time it overcrowds our factory.

Write us TODAY, while the offer is still open, and while you think of it. The postage stamp is all you risk. Write me personally on this offer, viz.: R. F. Bieber, General Manager of "1900" Washer Company, 92 Henry St., Binghamton, New York.

out of business sometime in the 1960s. The feature I enjoyed most was a column called "Copy Clinic." It was written by a copywriter using the psuedonym Aesop Glim. Old Aesop Glim wrote about the Hat Trick. The Hat Trick has influenced my approach to the advertising business ever since, although the phrase itself was more appropriate when wearing a hat was in fashion. This is what he said.

> The Hat Trick consists of getting up off your chair, putting on your hat and going outdoors. You're on a hunt for facts—the facts as to what the prospect wants, in terms of the product or service for which you are about to write some copy. On this hunt, you talk with present users (if any); with the kind of people who ought to want the product or service; and with the men or women who have been most successful in selling this product or service.
>
> When you come back, you enjoy two new advantages. First, you know something your fellow workers don't know. This is impressive—and no mean asset in and by itself. Second, you know something you didn't know before. Entirely by your own efforts, you have dug up some facts.[5]

This was Aesop Glim's moral: *mate what the product offers with what the public wants.*

In my own first job in advertising, I was assigned to research. This means that I did the Hat Trick for copywriters. I went out to talk to people about the product. The writers would read my reports, then base their copy on my findings.

I went to hardware stores for Black & Decker to talk to salesmen about power tools. Why did they recommend a particular brand? What did they like about Black & Decker? How about the competition? For customers, my questionnaire was simple. I was after the *who, when, where, how,* and *why.* I would learn that such things as the heft and feel of the power drill's handle were more important competitive advantages than details about horsepower. The sensation of drilling a hole in wood or steel said more about the motor's power than any technical jargon could. Speed, coupled with the sensation of power, was another effective argument to get people to use a power tool instead of a manual drill.

I went door to door giving housewives products like Crosse & Blackwell soup or Musselman fruit pie filling. Then, a week later, I would go back to find out how they liked it and why. Or, if they didn't, why not? Was it too thin? Too thick? Too sweet? Too tart? Did the fruit have a natural flavor? As advertisers, we would start with some preconceived ideas about the appeals to use. The consumers would confirm or reject them. Users of a product are an unending source of information, much of which finds its way into advertising appeals.

When the agency really knows what the consumer thinks, it is charged with inner power. Sure knowledge guides the mind to forceful creative solutions. It also enables account executives to get breakthrough work approved by skeptical clients.

The very first campaign my new agency did, in 1965, applied the Hat Trick principle. A. H. Robins assigned us a product called Donnagel-PG. Kids take it to stop diarrhea. It is a prescription product because it contains paregoric. This means our customer was the doctor, and somehow we needed to get him to prescribe Donnagel instead of competing brands.

Robins had been running ads telling the doctor how the product worked. So did the competition with their products. All advertising in the category was straightforward and technical, reading like pages from a medical textbook. This is a mistake many business-to-business and consumer advertisers make: they do "me too" advertising. If you question this, pick up any trade publication and leaf through it. You'll find plenty of familiar faces. Robins and its competitors canceled each other out with look-alike advertising. Market share was static.

We needed to know why some doctors prescribed Donnagel-PG and others did not. So we did the obvious thing. We went out and talked to them. What we learned was not so obvious; in fact, we made a remarkable discovery. Doctors prescribe Donnagel because children like the taste, not because it has therapeutic advantages over other products. Kids don't like medicine as a matter of principle. Doctors, on the other hand, are dedicated to treating them to help them get well. Because Donnagel tastes good, it overcomes a major initial hurdle. Donnagel is like Mary Poppins with her "spoonful of sugar makes the medicine go down." Donnagel offers something better than sugar: It has a pleasing banana flavor.

Monkey Business

Here was the idea; we would concentrate on Donnagel's pleasing banana flavor. How could we do this in a memorable way? Monkeys like bananas. We would use them to dramatize the product difference. We asked pediatricians what they thought of the idea. They were amused.

The client, however, was skeptical. "Monkeys? We can't do that. We're selling medicine. This is serious business." But we knew that doctors would approve and that the series would get attention in the crowded medical journals. "This is medicine for children," we replied. "There is no disease, it's a condition this product will relieve. Monkey business is O.K."

Generally, it's a bad idea to use whimsy to promote serious products, especially medicine. When a patient's health or life is at stake, there is little humor in the situation. But here, because we were dealing with a less serious problem, monkeys were as appropriate as a pediatrician's framed pictures of Mother Goose or Mickey Mouse.

Our strategic position would be: The banana flavor in Donnagel-PG masks the taste of paregoric, so children will take it without complaint. Sometimes an agency takes a position like that and makes it the whole campaign. When that happens, the advertising becomes one-dimensional. For advertising to interrupt and work its magic, it must convey the position in an unexpected, memorable way. It must move to another threshold, enter a magical dimension. It must be the event Harry Jacobs was asking Ogilvy about. For Donnagel, lovable chimps did it. They became surrogate kids. Kids who loved bananas.

Our monkeys were so crazy about Donnagel-PG that one of the models got constipated from licking the cap. We sent out giant mailing cards using slick photographs, scheduled four-color magazine ads in pediatric journals, and mailed product samples in boxes with chimps in color on the wrapper. Our theme line was:

Kids think it's the bananas.

Every pediatrician or general practitioner in the country soon knew Donnagel-PG was the antidiarrhea product with a banana flavor that masks the taste of paregoric. Sales doubled the first year and the brand soon climbed to the top share in its category. Today, almost a quarter century later, no piece of mail or advertising goes out for Donnagel-PG without a monkey on it. The product's banana flavor is an everlasting *dominant value point*.

Somewhere embedded in the customer's mind is a fact or belief about every brand that can be converted into a memorable idea by skillful advertising practitioners. With an idea that captures the distinctive product difference, you hold the key to brand leadership in the product category.

Sum & Substance

In advertising, the only opinion that counts is the reader's or viewer's. All things great and beautiful flow from this source: sales, share, brand loyalty, ad budgets, the sales manager's job. Considering the importance of this expert opinion, isn't it remarkable how often it is ignored? Sometimes advertising approvals are given by novices ignorant of advertising's power, by people who can't tell a good ad from a bad one. That's bad enough, but often agencies create advertising without bothering to first find out what goes on in the head of the brand's user. They know when an ad is smart, slick, and sensational but have no idea whether the customer really cares about what's being emphasized. That kind of ad can win an award without winning a single customer.

Now that I've castigated tinkerers in both camps, let me state how it ought to be. Start by finding out what customers really want from the product both from the utilitarian and from the psychological point of view. For instance, they may want a smooth, quick, easy hole in the wall, not a long list of facts about how well a power drill is engineered. But even this

This monkey meant serious business for A. H. Robins in 1965. The approach dramatized Donnagel-PG's banana flavor. The monkey motif continues to be used to this day as a reminder of the product's dominant value point.

is an assumption; the point is, you won't know for sure until you ask. That's the agency's job, and clients should refuse to pay them if they don't take the trouble to find out.

This takes extra effort. You've got to get out of the office and talk to people. The search is always for a dominant value point of difference between this product and another, for the point of difference that will influence trial. Then the advertising can be as clever as you can make it. Clever to make it easier for people to remember—not the ad itself, but the brand and its dominant value point.

·5·

How to Deal With Creatives

Every creative act involves . . . a new innocence of perception, liberated from the cataract of accepted belief.

—Arthur Koestler, *The Sleepwalkers*

Harry Jacobs has been my partner for the past ten years. During that time he has also been the benevolent dictator of the creative department at The Martin Agency. Harry preaches that every ad must not only have style but must also be based on a well-thought-out strategic position. After that, it is up to the creative team to find an idea to carry it into a third dimension where the message can find a life of its own in the mind of the beholder. For this to happen, it must convey a familiar truth in an unfamiliar way. Here is where the right side of the brain comes into its own.

Harry and I first met thirty years ago when he was a young art director at Cargill & Wilson. We were both influenced by Al Cascino, who, in the late 1950s, was the outstanding creative director in the South. I remember Al as a pixieish, balding, inventive little character who would see the humor in every situation, but who was strictly professional when it came to producing advertising.

On my first day with Cargill & Wilson, Bob Wilson showed me around the two-story townhouse the agency then occupied on Second Street near Main in Richmond. We went into the conference room, where papers were scattered and crumpled in a jumble on the table. We had just started looking at ads pinned to the corkboard wall when the source of the mess burst into the room talking and arguing, hands flying. Al was in a heated discussion with a copywriter over whose idea should prevail. Al, the art director, felt he was right. Manning Rubin, the writer (later creative director at Grey), insisted that he had the answer. This dynamic tension produced sinewy advertising with plenty of substance.

In my previous advertising agency job, writers and art directors had been physically divided by three floors, and mentally separated by the

account executive. The writer wrote and the art director rendered what
was left of the copy after the account executive had edited it. Al saw to it
that things were different at Cargill & Wilson.

Two Halves Make a Whole

I realized later why it takes a creative team to create great advertising.
Each member of the team brings a fundamentally different side of the
brain to the table. Both are needed.

When you observe the brain from the top, it resembles the two halves
of an opened walnut. The right and left hemispheres are divided by a
valley down the middle and connected by a cable called the corpus
callosum, a mass of 200 million fibers bundled like a telephone cable. As
one writer describes it, "Ideas crackle across those wires—an almost
tangible arc of activity, back and forth, back and forth, as an idea and its
implementation enhance and encourage each other."[1]

The contribution of the left hemisphere is to provide sequential,
analytical, objective, and verbal thought. Our educational system favors
and rewards this type of logical thinking while tending to inhibit the wild
and random thoughts produced by the intuitive right hemisphere. Those
with logical tendencies are often outstanding students, at the head of the
class. But this also means that many emerge from the system with their
wild and colorful butterflies locked in a cage. It may also explain why so
many business executives feel uncomfortable dealing with creative people.
At a meeting with the agency, left- and right-siders come to the table with
different points of view, with mental orientations that spring from separate
sources.

Of course, right-side thinking often manifests itself in unusual behavior as well as in penetrating insight and off-the-wall ideas. In the sixties,
this sometimes meant long hair, beads, and barefoot creative types in
threadbare jeans. In advertising agencies, managers have to learn to take
the good with the bad—that's the price you pay for right-side thinking.

The right hemisphere is artistic. It enables us to recognize visual
images, color, shapes, positions and to appreciate music. It is the source
of style and rhythm. Those dominated by it are seldom perceived as
normal by those whose lives are regulated by the left.

You may have noticed that writers are often easier to deal with than
their artist counterparts. My founding partner, George Woltz, was a
brilliant art director and conceptual thinker. On occasion, he was also
impossible to reason with. It was not unusual for him to stamp around in
a rage sweeping all loose objects from his desk. In meetings with clients
he would remain impassive, saying not a word. Later, when their train
had left and we were still at the station, his frustration and anger would
erupt at the myopic vision of the rational souls God had put into the
bodies of clients.

When George Woltz (on the left) and I founded our agency in 1965, we brought together a balance of left-side and right-side thinking. George was an art director who had a brilliant way with words. I wrote copy and managed the agency and its clients.

To do the job, the writer calls on the discipline of the logical left. Because of this, writers sometimes think like account executives and clients—a distressing fact for them to hear, I'm sure. Left-side thinking is used to develop strategy and tactics. Management types respond to reason. That's why they appreciate the writings of copywriters like Ogilvy, Hopkins, and John Caples, who offer the comfort of rules and guidelines.

Attracting Bees With Honey

The left side of the brain takes a clear, rational approach to a business that is otherwise highly intuitive. The logic deployed by client managers, who draw their thoughts solely from the left side, can stifle the creative muse. They can devastate insecure creative types just by uttering a discouraging word or by hinting their disapproval through body language. The wise client, when he looks at layout and copy, realizes that he is dealing with cherished creative offspring and takes care not to rile the mother bear. In a meeting recently, a food client felt uncomfortable with the approach being presented to him. "Look," he said, "I was trained as an accountant. I know how to put together a leveraged buyout. You are the advertising experts. But I feel in my gut you've missed the point that will sell my product." He knew how to deal with creatives. He didn't emasculate their work. He simply put their thinking on the track that would make the advertising even better. "Suggestions" should be subtle and diplomatically made. Like the client who said, "You should employ some mud wrestlers here so you'll know how my customers talk."

I'm not suggesting that the client should be a wimp. Creatives like a person who works with them and challenges their thinking, but doesn't stifle it. This is the best way to get enthusiastic followers in a creative department. The sympathetic and insightful client has the best talent in the agency lobbying the creative director to get assigned to that account. It is smart business. Ideas must soar to lift a brand above others in its category. Enlightened managers realize this, and loosen the reins so as to give their advertising creative leverage.

Inner Voices

Company managers tap into the right side of the brain themselves. Running a business calls for large doses of creativity as well as a steady diet of logic. Some seek innovative solutions to complex problems by resorting to yoga or by staring at the test pattern on the television screen. This lulls the left and frees the right. How often have you jumped from bed after a half sleep to make notes of incredible ideas that would never see the light in the harsh reality of day? That's the timid voice of the right side of the brain talking while the formidable taskmaster over on the left is asleep.

Henriette Anne Klauser explains how the left-right division affects writing: "When it comes to writing, the left brain thinks it knows everything. The fact is inescapable: language, verbal and written, is a left hemisphere specialty. More than ever, Mr. Know-it-all is going to kick sand in the face of any suggestions that the right brain might haltingly make."[2]

The writer must keep grammar and punctuation in mind and remember how to spell. Such mental gymnastics demand orderly thought. Reason is needed to make a persuasive point. The narrative moves forward logically. But then, as the work progresses, the mind grows heated. Words and ideas begin to flow. Inspiration springs from an unknown source. It is, in fact, the intuitive right pumping ideas into the conscious mind. Later, when the dust settles, the logical left will be brought back in to do some ruthless editing. Sometimes work slips through without it. The uncomfortable client then has a choice: to be a hard-ass and kill it, or to do some fast, creative thinking on the spot to find a way to send the writers and art directors back to do even better.

The Artist Becomes a Full Partner

Because the writer was king in most advertising agencies through the 1950s, advertising grew up as a left-side discipline. Advertisements were conceived in the mind of the writer, who then tapped them out on an old Underwood. The artist was called in after the fact to dress up the copy. This kind of advertising was easy to approve. It was comfortable, safe, dull. It was much easier to be a client then. Ads were reasonable, not wild and strange.

Sometimes, it takes an almost conscious effort to switch on the uninhibited right hemisphere with its imaginative flights of fancy. When the artist and writer became a team, this method of creating work changed and so did advertising. In the campaign development stage, the two now engage in a free flow of ideas, subconciously suppressing "Mr. Left," the critical editor, the way brainstorming groups did in agencies in the mid-1950s.

One day early in 1962, I first learned the difference between the left and right sides of the brain. I had finally persuaded Everett Bond of the Chap-Stick company to visit the agency to hear a capability presentation. Jim Cargill and I showed him some case histories, but what intrigued him most was a presentation by Al Cascino. What he had to say was a surprise to Cargill and me, as well as to Bond. At the time, Chap-Stick lip balm had far and away the dominant market share, but it faced an assault from an array of competitors, and Bond was looking for unusual advertising to attract the attention of users to keep them loyal to the brand.

When it was his turn to speak, Al didn't show ads, as he generally did. He discussed the left and right sides of the brain. He showed charts with triangles, squares, and arrows leading into the left side and then exiting in an orderly manner. "This is your input," Al said, looking at Bond and pointing to the various shapes entering the brain like obedient animals boarding Noah's Ark. "This is also data from research and customer interviews," he continued. "We want all the logic, statistics, and product advantages you and the account team can give us. But don't expect your ads to be logical. In some agencies, the ads come out like this": He then pointed to the neat line of triangles, squares, and arrows exiting the left side of the brain. "That's not the way we do advertising here. At this agency, we use the right side of the brain." Out tumbled a crazy jumble of shapes like clowns and acrobats upstaging all other performers in a circus. He then presented examples of the agency's work, selected to prove his point. "Give us your account and you'll see advertising you've never imagined for Chap-Stick."

Bond assigned us the business, and Al made good his promise. Our success with Chap-Stick led us to other accounts in the health and beauty aid category.

The writer/art director team method of working broke with the copywriter-dominated past. Although the Cargill agency had been structured this way since the mid-1950s, duality thinking came into most agencies in the early 1960s, when a creative revolution swept through advertising like Sherman burning his way through Georgia.

Doyle Dane Bernbach, which later bought the Cargill agency, fired off the first recorded shot in New York with a campaign for a small bakery: "You don't have to be Jewish to love Levy's." The photo showed the lined face of an American Indian smiling as he took a bite of a sandwich made with Levy's Jewish Rye bread. This campaign stirred things up on Madison Avenue mainly because it was so visible to the New York ad community. It was displayed on posters at every subway stop.

Meanwhile, down South, Al Cascino and his assistant, Harry Jacobs, had been creating unusual advertising for banks, beer, apple sauce, and smoking tobacco. They surrounded themselves with other art directors and writers whose inherent inclination was to create bold, provocative, stylish, and witty advertising. They thought that way naturally and readily broke all rules, if necessary, in order to be fresh and inventive.

How the Creative Team Works

By the time the writer and artist sit down together, their left sides have computed research data and they've taken an active hand in drafting the position statement and in devising the creative strategy. By now they have lived with the product to learn about its unique advantages. All this input gives them a fix on the directional thrust to take. What is sought now is a simple, straightforward, honest idea and a brilliant, unexpected way to express it. Together they seek a dramatic moment.

The writer and designer need to know not only what the consumer considers important about the product or service, but why he is likely to use it. This is the stage when research has tremendous value. All this left-side input is essential so that the meaningful point of difference can be dramatized by free-wheeling right-side thinking. But the wise client doesn't insist on a rigid interpretation of research data. This takes away the spark that ignites consumer fires.

Right-side thinkers are valuable allies for any company that wants to stretch its advertising dollars. While these free spirits can't be allowed to go unchecked, they can't be reined in either. They must operate under loose guidelines provided by a tightly drafted strategy statement. It's a delicate task to channel creative energy down a productive path, but it must be done for advertising to be effective. Since brands have a "person-

Bill Bernbach insisted the product name should be changed from *Levy's Real Rye* to *Levy's Real Jewish Rye*. New York ate it up. The poster campaign ran for many years in the New York City subways. Reprints were popular items in bookstores.

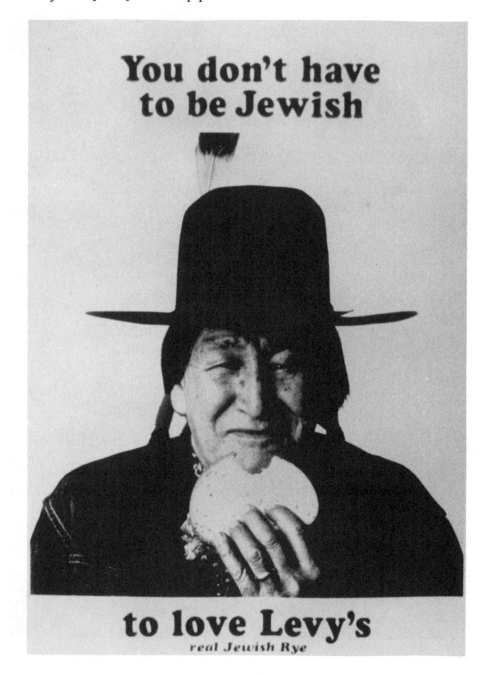

Three creative revolutionaries meet in 1973 to discuss the new partnership between Doyle Dane Bernbach and Cargill, Wilson & Acree: Jerry Torchia (on the left), Harry Jacobs (both now with The Martin Agency), and the late Bill Bernbach (center).

ality,'' ask your team to think of your product in human terms. For example, here's what a typical product might require of its creative team:

1. I have a valuable point of difference. Please direct your efforts to making the customer understand what it is.
2. Do not let your imagination stray from this central point.
3. Make my advertising profoundly different from anything ever displayed by my competitors.
4. Use language my customers will understand; they are not as sophisticated as judging committees.
5. Give me human qualities. A sense of humor. A warm voice. I want consumers to know we're soul mates, so touch their emotions. I can help bridge life's little difficulties and give them something they can't get from anyone else.
6. Demonstrate my value difference in a graphic way so people will remember it.
7. I already have many loyal customers. They know what I offer and like it. Surprise them by all means, but don't confuse them. Be sure my tone of voice is familiar because, to them, I'm an old friend. If you believe my personality is disagreeable, change it gently, a step at a time. Let's not zero-base the advertising.
8. With all that said, don't hold back. I'd be proud to win a Clio or a Stephen Kelly award.

Some of these requests may seem strange to you at this point. But as you read on, you will see why I made them.

Sum & Substance

Any creative undertaking draws inspiration from the right side of the brain. At the idea stage, it's best to let inspiration flow without blocking it by inhibiting judgments. Editing comes later, when the left side of the brain kicks in, somewhat disdainfully, to scoff at silly, irrelevant ideas that have wandered far from strategy or strayed from the point at hand.

In advertising agencies, artists and writers sit down together with strategy statements pinned to the wall. Next to that are benefit points identified through consumer interviews. The task at hand is to find a compelling, inventive way to bring that strategy and those benefits to life. They seek a dramatic moment.

In the old days, and even in some agencies today, a writer simply sat down at the typewriter, flanked by product catalogs and a work order, and began to think and write. What came out was usually on strategy. It was logical. And clients loved it. They got to approve the kind of ad they'd do themselves if they had the time or the talent. And coming out of the Depression and World War II, when goods were in short supply, and later, when product innovations made everything we owned obsolete, it was fairly easy to move consumers.

Now things are different. Every man, woman, and child under 50 has been raised on entertainment. They've seen the wonders of Sesame Street, Disney, Lucas, and Spielberg. They've rapped and flash danced. Advertising is a reflection of the culture of the moment, and the best advertising leads it. But it doesn't lose sight of the selling point at hand.

·6·

Ideas Start Where the Buck Stops

The higher up the advertising decisions go in a company, the better the advertising.

—John O'Toole, CEO,
Foote, Cone & Belding

It is natural for a good CEO to delegate responsibility and to hold managers accountable for results. However, the brand franchise is the essential link with customers, the lifeblood of the business. Protecting it should not be delegated. The brand's personality reflects the company's culture and heritage. Like the flag of a nation, the brand unfurls, evoking emotions and past associations. Through the years, enduring brands come to stand for practices, employee attitudes, and customer expectations, which the current chief executive should continue—or modify only with the greatest caution.

Sometimes the pressure to achieve short-term goals will result in practices that conflict with the long-term interests of the brand—for example, pricing strategies that cheapen the brand; promotions that substitute for brand advertising and thus abdicate share of mind to competitors; or changes in the product itself that make it unfamiliar to long-time users. When this happens, the public becomes confused, forgetful, or disillusioned, and brand loyalty is lost. The involved CEO can prevent this potential disaster, and, as the leader, take risks resulting in dramatic payoffs.

While still in his youthful mid-50s, John O'Toole departed as chairman and CEO of one of the nation's largest advertising agencies, Foote, Cone & Belding. John had become frustrated by the tendency of large corporations to avoid risk taking in advertising, to accept only that which can be measured and projected by laboratory experiment. Like his early predecessor, Albert Davis Lasker (who quit Lord & Thomas while simultaneously turning ownership over to Messers Foote, Cone & Belding), he yearned for the days when tycoons called the shots and took risks—

tycoons like George Washington Hill of American Tobacco. As crusty and flamboyant as the titans might have been, they were fiercely involved at every step in shaping communication; and because they ran things, they were free to take the kind of intuitive risks that build brands.

In his parting speech as chairman of the AAAA, John said,

> There is evidence that American business, including major advertisers, does not place the same importance on advertising as we do. There is evidence that they regard it as playing a relatively minor role in increasing their volume and profit. And there's evidence that they look upon it as too unpredictable, too ambiguous in its effect, to rely upon.
>
> We must do all we can [he told his fellow agency executives] to involve the top management of our client companies in setting advertising direction and standards and in final approval of major creative work. Great advertising involves risk and only at the top is one rewarded for taking risks.[1]

A Brand Called "Colonial Williamsburg"

Carl Humelsine was a CEO who ran Colonial Williamsburg the way Captain Kirk ran the Starship Enterprise, always in command. He invited the views of his top lieutenants, listened carefully, then made the decision. To a man, they accepted it, without argument or further discussion. When it came to advertising, Tom McCaskey was his Spock. Don Gonzales was his Dr. McCoy. Together they presided over what is possibly the best-known travel attraction in America.

I first encountered Carlyle Humelsine in 1965, when our new agency was one of several invited to make presentations before the State of Virginia's travel advertising committee and he was chairman of the over-sight board appointed by the governor.

On that occasion, we presented a campaign using four-color photographs in a two-page spread format. One of the ads showed the faces of children in extreme close-up, their noses pressed against the window of a wigmaker's shop in Williamsburg. A powdered wig was in the foreground, slightly out of focus. The children were looking at it with eyes wide, their expressions a mixture of amusement and awe. It was an emotional way to sell history, one of Virginia's four primary appeals, but we used the word "perukemaker" in the headline, and the board members didn't know it meant someone who makes wigs.

The campaign was such a departure, our agency so new, and the board so logical that it decided not to take a chance and stayed with the incumbent. Instead of advancing a bright new image, the state continued to grind out black and white ads extolling Virginia's history, beaches, mountains, and attractions. (Three years later, however, we got another

Carlyle Humelsine (on the right) and Mrs. Humelsine greet Emperor Hirohito when the Japanese royal family visited Colonial Williamsburg in 1975. They also hosted many dignitaries ranging from Walt Disney to President Johnson and Queen Elizabeth.

chance and won the business with the enduring campaign, "Virginia is for lovers.")

Our disappointment was softened by Carl Humelsine's support for us behind closed doors. About a week later, I got a call from Colonial Williamsburg's director of advertising and travel marketing, Tom Mc-Caskey. "Carl tells me you have some fresh ideas," he said, "I'd like to meet you." Naturally, the next morning I was in his office in Williamsburg's colonial brick administration building just off Merchant's Square.

Tom started working for "the restoration" in the early days, soon after John D. Rockefeller advanced the seed money to convert a tacky twentieth-century town into an eighteenth-century village. Williamsburg was restored faithfully, seventy million Rockefeller dollars later, down to the last handmade nail, to just what it had been in the time of George Washington, Thomas Jefferson, Patrick Henry, and George Mason. The restored area stretches one mile and about four blocks wide from the Wren building on the campus of William and Mary College, dating from 1695, to the rebuilt Capitol at the other end of Duke of Gloucester Street. In between, the quiet street is free of automobiles. Sheep, ox carts, ducks and geese roam along with the tourists past craft shops, a printer's shop, the Palace, the Armory, restored colonial houses, taverns, gardens, and the Village Green. Off to one side, two blocks away, is the Williamsburg Inn and the Lodge, festooned with ponds, bowling greens, tennis courts, and a Robert Trent Jones championship golf course on which Jack Nicklaus posted the eighteen-hole record for the lowest score.

The town is both a fine resort and a living history lesson. Costumed villagers interpret the significance of the events that took place at the time of the American Revolution. They use anecdotes as well as facts to help the visitor learn how people lived and worked in colonial times. They teach history from the consumer's point of interest. The experience gives more than a million visitors a year insight into the customs, furnishings, architecture, and horticulture of eighteenth-century America.

Tom spent some time explaining all this to me. He showed me the ads Williamsburg had run through the years in the *Reader's Digest* and *The New Yorker* to foster an appreciation of all this while at the same time generating hotel reservations. The ads were handsome, but static, and lacked story appeal. In my opinion, they did not capture the emotional side of what Williamsburg had to offer. However, this observation was left unsaid because it is presumptuous for one agency to comment on the work of another without knowing all the factors that led to the chosen execution.

Tom agreed to pull together a meeting with the executive staff so that we could submit a proposal along with our ideas for Williamsburg's advertising. He called Humelsine's secretary and the date was set for three weeks later.

Advertising Is Three Parts Preparation

For the next two weeks we lived and breathed Williamsburg. By studying sample hotel reservations and all available market information provided

My early effort for Colonial Williamsburg was a Humelsine favorite. It drew off-season visitors to Williamsburg after the crowds were gone and the hotels could use the business. The mile-long Duke of Gloucester Street delivers on the promise.

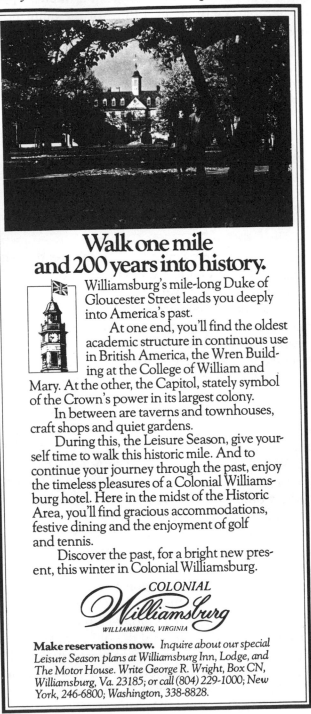

by hotel sales, we pieced together an accurate picture of visitor demographics. We commissioned a telephone survey to measure public awareness of Williamsburg. I expected to find it up around 90 percent. Instead it was surprisingly low. Only about a third of the adult population could accurately identify what Williamsburg was and in which state it was located. Clearly we had a great opportunity to build attendance.

My partner, George Woltz, and I spent a week roaming the streets, gardens, and oyster shell paths of the colonial town, talking with tourists, shopkeepers, waiters, blacksmiths, and wigmakers. We learned how eighteenth-century craftsmen made shoes, fabrics, baskets, bonnets, bread, clocks, candles, and cabinets. We took every tour, studied every book, read every annual report.

And One Part Inspiration

When the day came for the presentation, we were ready. The meeting was scheduled in the Goodwin building conference room for 8:30 A.M. on the first Thursday in January. We were there at 7:00, rearranging furniture, setting up the two carousel slide projectors, rehearsing, checking the reel-to-reel tape machine. The copy was recorded for the dramatic reading that would accompany our slide show of the layouts.

By 8:20 the troops had arrived: Tom McCaskey; his assistant, George Wright; Don Gonzales; Rudy Bares, who headed hotel operations; and several others. At 8:35, a silence descended. The coffee cups were empty. The pleasantries were exhausted. It was time to begin.

The grandfather clock ticked in the hallway. Where was Carl Humelsine? A secretary came into the room and gave Tom McCaskey a pink telephone slip. We all looked at Tom expectantly. The bad news was that Carl Humelsine had a cold and wasn't coming into the office. The good news was that he would hear the presentation in his dining room at 9:30.

That was good news? George and I looked at the maze of equipment, the well-orchestrated setting. This was long before the agency had a skilled technician to help set things up. Well, advertising is a service business, so you do what has to be done. We packed up and loaded everything into my Buick station wagon and drove a few blocks over to Humelsine's framed house on Duke of Gloucester Street near the Palace Green. It was a beautifully restored colonial building loaded with antiques. In the dining room, we gingerly moved the old English silver candlesticks, the Waterford glasses, and Chinese porcelain to make way for the slide projectors. We rearranged the Hepplewhite chairs. The group reassembled just as I plugged in the tape recorder and George was raising the aluminum arm to hook up the movie screen. We were ready.

Carl Humelsine entered the room dressed in pajamas, a bathrobe, and slippers. His nose was red, and his eyes were watering. He looked like a glum basset hound, and was in no mood for small talk. Silently he motioned for us to begin.

The slides built a case for the six appeals of Williamsburg as we saw them: its historical significance and the town's ability to illustrate the life and customs of colonial America, its crafts, its furnishings, its architecture and gardens. The copy sent chills down my spine as the melodious voice of the narrator extolled the importance of Williamsburg and positioned it right next to Athens as a source of thought and erudition. With the minds of Jefferson, Washington, James Madison, Patrick Henry, and George Mason at hand, I felt it was a fair comparison. I could feel the presentation going well. The audience was fascinated. When we were finished, we opened the curtains and everyone turned to Carl Humelsine. This was the moment of truth, the culmination of three weeks' work on little sleep. What would he say?

Moment of Truth

He thought for a moment. Then he looked me squarely in the eye and said, "You claim too much. Williamsburg was important, but not as important as you have stated. Significant events took place in Philadelphia, Valley Forge, and Boston. You make it sound like the Revolution was conceived, fought, and won here. We did not give birth to the nation, we only assisted in the delivery." He turned to Tom McCaskey. "What do you think, Tom?"

My earlier euphoria was a miscalculation. Things hadn't gone as well as I imagined.

Tom came to our rescue. "Well, putting Williamsburg in the same league with Athens is a bit much," he said dryly. Nervous laughter broke the tension. "You are right that the claims are sometimes overstated, Carl, but this is a fresh approach. We haven't told the story of Williamsburg this way before and I believe we should. It will appeal to visitors and convey our mission to a broad audience."

"I like the idea of featuring the various appeals of Williamsburg," Don Gonzales offered. Don was vice-president for public affairs and a chief guardian of Colonial Williamsburg's traditions and image. "The copy can be toned down, but I like this approach."

Humelsine solicited the comments of everyone in the room. By and large, they were favorable. Humelsine listened carefully, and when everyone had had his say, he lapsed into thought. Finally he said, "Here's what I want you to do. Tom, Don, Rudy, I want you to get together and draft a white paper. Inventory what we offer. Define what can and cannot be said about our program. Put down objectives and guidelines. This paper will be the who, what, where, how, and why of Colonial Williamsburg. It will guide all future communication. When that's done, let's review it, refine

This ad came along twelve years later. It has the Jacobs' touch. It appeared in full color to promote The King's Arms, Christiana Campbell's, and Chowning's taverns. Shown here is The King's Arms. The place is there now. If you're interested, call ahead.

it. Then we'll call these people back in to see if they can make advertising to reflect what we stand for.''

Here was a wise and thoughtful man. He cared about his brand and what was said about it. He understood advertising's power not only to inform but to mislead if handled incorrectly. Through the next fourteen years of our relationship, until he stepped down as chief executive, he took the time to review every campaign, to challenge the agency by asking hard questions, to reject and accept, and always to make sure that what was said accurately reflected a place where patriots once debated the concept of democracy and where people can come today to have a good time finding out about it.

Sum & Substance

Middle managers want to be top managers and this means that they are very careful not to make mistakes. An agency is trouble coming in the door, especially when it is one with bright irreverent ideas. Every ad submitted is regarded as a potential bomb that could shatter a promising career.

Top managers have moved from being doers to thinkers by skillfully avoiding land mines. From the executive suite, the horizon is not limited to a department or a division; it includes the industry at large and the world in general. People in the rooms at the top are paid to be inventive, to move the company forward at a profit, to be conservative with costs but liberal with ideas.

When it comes to advertising, the chief executive should do one of two things: (1) approve the advertising and listen to the rationale directly from the agency, or (2) remove fear from the lives of the middle managers to whom they delegate the approval authority. If the second alternative is chosen, they should choose decision makers imbued with the spark of right-side thinking and then give them the right to take risks.

·7·

Story Appeal

If you want the drawing to help tell a story, then I will do that for you.

—Norman Rockwell

Two years later, in late January of 1968, Carl Humelsine and Tom Mc-Caskey took me to lunch at the Williamsburg Inn to discuss ''an exciting project.'' Colonial Williamsburg was restoring four buildings at a cost of several million dollars. These would be added to the exhibition program the following summer.

One would be the Wren building, designed by the great London architect Christopher Wren and built in a wilderness in the 1690s. There would be a tavern, a silversmith's workshop, and, finally, a fine colonial house built by Peyton Randolph.

From the discussion at lunch, I gathered that Peyton Randolph was an important colonial patriot, although I had never previously heard of him. I found out later that he was one of our most influential early leaders. As president of the First Continental Congress, he was featured on the ''most wanted'' list by the British. In 1775, the militia paid him the tribute of calling him ''Father of our Country.'' But he died a short time later, and George Washington inherited both his job and the title.

Carl and Tom wanted ads that would give people a reason to come back to Williamsburg, and, by romancing these new exhibitions, we would take the crowd pressure off some of the other well-established attractions like the Capitol and the Palace.

They gave me a fat document containing a minute history of each building down to an inventory of its furnishings and tableware. It had been compiled painstakingly by the archeology department working with historians. There was only one hitch. We couldn't use photographs because the buildings were still being renovated—and construction sites aren't very interesting.

Artwork usually isn't effective in travel ads. People like photographs because they show in advance of the trip what to expect. We were faced with the task of making the campaign interesting, but how could we do it when there were so many limitations?

Artful Solution

A few days later, I was sitting in my office when Libby Meggs, a young art director just out of art school, came in with a brilliant idea for making the ads dramatic. Some right-side thinking was about to convert something potentially dull into a campaign with the penetrating force of story appeal.

"Here's our idea," she said. "We have to use drawings, but they can't be just any old drawings. There's no interest in that. We want Norman Rockwell to do them—drawings like these." She opened up a big book of a Rockwell retrospective and showed me some pencil sketches he had done while on vacation in France. They weren't in his usual style. They were much more casual—loose, free, sketchy.

My first worry was the cost. Rockwell was bound to be expensive, and we had budgeted only $250 for each illustration. My second concern was, would he do it?

At Libby's insistence, I called him then and there. I knew he lived in Stockbridge, Massachusetts, so I called the information operator.

"*The* Norman Rockwell?" she asked. Obviously, she was based in Boston. A Stockbridge operator would have been more blasé.

"Yes, the artist."

"Well, here's the number." From her tone of voice, I knew she was as surprised as I was to learn his number was listed.

Norman Rockwell answered on the first ring. He was in his studio, at the back of his house, working. I introduced myself and told him about the Williamsburg project. My thought was, we would send him photographs so he could draw the buildings in his studio. "Drawings like you did on vacation in France," I suggested, "like the ones in your new book—the loose, sketchy ones you can dash off in no time at all—they must be fun to do." I was selling hard.

Rockwell was unimpressed. And he was busy. "I'm working on an illustration of astronauts. Lots of heads. Takes lots of time. After that I have enough assignments to keep me busy for a year." He sounded weary.

"Maybe you'd like to take a few days off," I suggested. "A vacation, like the one in France. Williamsburg is a great place to take a vacation."

My random shooting made a direct hit. There was a long pause. "Is it warm down there in Virginia? It's awfully cold here in Stockbridge. Do you have snow?"

"No snow. It doesn't snow much in Virginia. It's so warm I played golf in my shirtsleeves last Saturday." That was the truth.

"Well, we've had snow on the ground since Thanksgiving, and I'm tired of it. Let me talk to Molly."

The next day I got a call from George Wright, Tom McCaskey's assistant at Colonial Williamsburg. Rockwell had called to find out the name and number of the advertising agency because he'd lost the scrap of paper with my number on it.

"What's this all about?" George wanted to know. "This has caused quite a stir here."

I explained what we had in mind. He thought it would be just fine if we could afford it. He reminded me what we had in the budget. Just then the receptionist came in to say that Rockwell had called while I was on the line. "He was so cute," she said. "He introduced himself and said he was an illustrator and that you have an assignment for him. As if I didn't know who he was!"

Rockwell always made it clear that he was an illustrator rather than an artist. "Andrew Wyeth is an artist," he told me later in that honest, upbeat, incredulous schoolboy way he talked. "And do you know, someone once traded one of his paintings for one of my illustrations? Imagine that!"

When I called him back, I found he had already made air reservations and would arrive in Richmond on Sunday afternoon.

"Molly says it's cold up here so we're coming to Williamstown." He confused the name Williamsburg with that of Williamstown, Massachusetts, just north of Stockbridge. He never did get it straight.

"But we haven't talked about your fee." I was somewhat overwhelmed by the turn of events.

"How much have you got?" He was in a jovial mood and refused to let money get in the way of it.

I didn't have the nerve to tell him. So I said vaguely, "Our total budget to run the ads is only $200,000."

He laughed. "That's enough! We'll see you at the airport."

Rockwell in Williamsburg

We met the plane at Richmond's Byrd Field on a gray, overcast Sunday afternoon in early March. Snow flurries were predicted. It was cold. From the waiting room we watched the passengers unload. Soon the crowd thinned. There was no Norman Rockwell. We were sure he'd missed the connection. Since the news that Rockwell was coming to Virginia had gotten out, a newspaper reporter was with us. He worried about having no story to write, while I worried about the weather and Rockwell's reaction to it. I was afraid I'd be accused of false advertising.

Soon, a little, white-haired lady popped out and started down the ramp sideways, left foot first on each stair. She was followed by the

familiar lanky frame and craggy face we'd seen so many times in photographs. He was wearing a hat and Harris tweed jacket and carrying a
raincoat and wooden paint box. He had a cold pipe in his mouth.

The couple quickly crossed the ramp and came into the building. The
little lady was Rockwell's wife of two years, Molly Punderson. She was
about his age, which I knew to be 74. Molly was full of pep and enthusi-
asm, one of those bright, quick, inquisitive people you meet so rarely who
are interested in everything and ready to try it all. Her energy carried the
calm and gracious Rockwell along in its wake. I could see why he
consulted her about this assignment. "It's warm here in Virginia," Rockwell remarked. By then we were on the second floor of the terminal. The
heat was turned up on this chilly day, and much of it had risen from the
floor below. It was hot. After the interview, we whisked them away in a
heated station wagon for the forty-minute drive to Williamsburg. Along
the way, George Woltz explained the four layouts. Illustrations of the
buildings were to be at the top of the page, the copy below. Libby's layout
showed simple, impressionistic sketches of the buildings. And we talked
about the sketches Rockwell had done of the farm dwellings in France.

The roadways into Williamsburg are planned to move the motorist
quickly into the eighteenth century. I took the Colonial Williamsburg exit
off Route 64 into a protected, landscaped route past the Information
Center and Motor House. Then we turned right up a hill past a windmill
into an earlier world. Traffic is forbidden on Duke of Gloucester Street,
but the streets on each side can be used by cars. We drove past the Peyton
Randolph house. Rockwell looked at it for a minute, then remarked, "My,
there are a lot of windows. I hate to draw windows. Have you noticed how
many windows there are in the houses here, Molly?"

Later, George looked at the layouts and commented, "I guess Rockwell doesn't do windows."

Williamsburg had arranged for the couple to stay in one of the Inn's
colonial cottages near the King's Arms restaurant, where we all went to
dinner. It was a colorful sight to see a costumed colonial waiter tying a
huge napkin around that scrawny neck. That was a memorable moment, a
span of two centuries of Americana coming together in a single instant.
After dinner we dropped the Rockwells off at their cottage and set a date
to see his first drawing on Tuesday afternoon. We would meet in the rear
lobby of the Williamsburg Inn, where there was a pleasant fire. It also
would be quiet. The lobby was seldom used by hotel guests.

On Monday, Jack Woodson, a Richmond illustrator of some renown,
called to ask if he could meet his hero. Woodson worked in a style similar
to Rockwell's. His work told a story and it was beautifully rendered in
painstaking detail. I told him about our Tuesday meeting and invited him
to stop by.

On Tuesday, Jack arrived just as Rockwell was showing George and
me his sketch of the Peyton Randolph house. Woodson was loaded down
with his own illustrations, and the two artists immediately found common

Norman Rockwell and his wife Molly pause in the warmth of Byrd airport in Richmond. He told a reporter about the rigors of sketching presidential candidates from life. He looked forward to his assignment in Williamsburg because the buildings didn't move.

ground. They went over to the sofa by the fire and spent the next twenty minutes going over Jack's work.

This was fortunate because we had a problem with the Randolph illustration. Rockwell's sketch wasn't anything like the layout that had passed muster through several client approval channels. The point of the ad, of course, was to show off the house. For most of his illustration, Rockwell had focused on the branches of a crape myrtle tree. With this drawing, all you could see were corners of the house poking out at each end. Then he had added a new element in the foreground. He had drawn a pencil portrait of Peyton Randolph, curly peruke and all. It was wonderful, of course. But it wasn't the same ad.

"What do we say to him, George?" Woltz was an art director, and a good one, but that day George was operating solely with right-side brain cells. He was of no logical help, but he did see humor in the situation. "He damn well took care of the windows, didn't he?"

Tense Moment

Finally, Woodson shook hands and left. Rockwell was ebullient. "Woodson is really good. Did you see that wonderful stuff? And, you know, he really likes my work!" He seemed surprised and genuinely flattered. Rockwell had an amazing humility about him, as if he were completely oblivious to his fame and incredible talent. Then he asked how we liked the drawing.

"Well, Norman . . ." (on Sunday, Rockwell had insisted we call him Norman) "it's very good. Of course we knew it would be."

He could tell something was wrong.

"What's the matter, don't you like it?"

"Well, there are two things different, two things we didn't expect. You have a drawing of Peyton Randolph here in the front, and the layout didn't call for that. Of course, it adds interest and I'm sure we can get that approved, but we didn't expect that, you understand, and the client doesn't expect that either." Then to take the edge off and stall for time, I asked, "How do you know what he looked like?" I thought he might have made him up.

"I got his picture out of a book in the library," Rockwell said with a sigh of impatience. He wanted the other shoe to drop. "You said two things."

"You see, the Williamsburg people are very proud of the house and they want people to recognize it. The advertising will make it famous so people will want to see it. But with all those branches . . ."

Now he seemed more hurt than impatient. He was always the gentleman. His reply was pleasant, not curt or sarcastic. He expressed an honest opinion. "I thought you wanted sketches like I did in France. My

Rockwell's interpretation of the assignment was a shock when I first saw it. It didn't resemble the layout, which called for only a rendering of the building. But the Peyton Randolph portrait brought the ad to life.

**This is the Peyton Randolph House.
You remember Peyton Randolph,
don't you?**

200 years ago, he was one of our most influential leaders. Today, he is one of the least remembered.

He was President of the First Continental Congress, Speaker of Virginia's House of Burgesses, Attorney General of the Colony.

In fact, Peyton Randolph presided over nearly every important legislative body in Virginia during the years just prior to the Revolution.

He was also featured on the "most wanted" list of the British.

In 1775, the militia paid him a tribute calling him Father of Our Country. (He died shortly after that and the title went later to his friend George Washington.)

But he left behind a handsome two-story house of warm paneling, marble mantles and heavy walnut doors.

Today this is one of Williamsburg's most distinguished original houses.

Beginning July 1, it will be one of four historic buildings to be added to the Colonial Williamsburg exhibition program.

Come and see the surroundings where one of our early leaders lived and worked.

And you'll always remember him.

COLONIAL
Williamsburg
VIRGINIA

Where to stay: Williamsburg Inn, from $24 double; its Colonial Houses, from $15 double. The Lodge, from $14 double. The Motor House, $18-$20 double. For information, color folder or reservations, write Betty Fisher, Box C, Williamsburg, Va. 23185. Or call Reservation Offices: New York, CIrcle 6-6800; Washington, FEderal 8-8828; ask operator in Baltimore for Enterprise 9-8855; Philadelphia, Enterprise 6805; Westchester County, Enterprise 7301; Essex County, WX 6805.

impression of the scene. There is a fine tree in front of the house, so I drew it. You see, if you just want an accurate drawing of the house, you can engage an architect. He will render a fine elevation. But, if you want the drawing to help tell a story, then I will do that for you. That's what I've done. By adding the portrait, I'm helping you tell the story about the person who lived there.''

He was right, of course. The drawing had drama the original layout lacked. It brought the advertisement to life. It gave it an added dimension, memorability, and stopping power. By injecting story appeal, he gave the message extra distance. This was proved later when the ad appeared.

Starch Readership scores went through the roof. The phone calls for reservations doubled. Our cost per inquiry went down to less than $2. Telephone follow-up conversion studies showed that the ads paid for themselves five times over in hotel use alone.

"Come back Thursday," Rockwell said at last. "We'll see what can be done."

Erasing the Problem

The next morning at about eleven, I got a call from Don Gonzales in Williamsburg.

"I hear you're giving Rockwell a hard time." He seemed amused. "I understand you don't want pictures of people in the ads."

"The layouts you approved don't include them," I reminded him. "But they improve the ads so I told him to go ahead."

"That's good," said Don. "Tom and I have talked it over. If he wants to put people in, let him do it."

I was surprised that the client already knew about our problem, so I asked, "How did you know all this?" I had an eerie feeling Gonzales was clairvoyant.

He laughed. "Williamsburg is a small town," he replied, leaving it at that.

Later I learned what had happened. Molly had gone out that morning to see the town. Most people would go to the Information Center, buy a ticket, and take a tour. Not Molly. She knocked on the door of the first house she came to. It was meticulously restored, but, like many in the restored area, it was a private residence. "I'm Molly Rockwell," she told the lady who answered. "My husband is here on an assignment. He's out doing an illustration now, so I came to see the houses." She was invited in, and over tea Molly explained the problems her husband was having with the advertising agency. As soon as she left, Don Gonzales got the call. Ten minutes later, he called me.

On Thursday evening we met in the Rockwells' cottage. Molly and Norman had arranged refreshments. They were on a table in the corner of the room shrouded by several white napkins. On the mantle over the fireplace, two flat rectangular objects leaned against the wall. They too were hidden from view by napkins draped carefully over the front and tucked around the edges.

Norman greeted us with a huge grin. He was excited, and pleased with himself. "Which do you want first? Refreshments or the unveiling?" "The unveiling," I said. "Then we'll have a toast." With a flourish, face beaming, he removed the first napkin, and looked around quickly to see our reactions.

The Peyton Randolph drawing was mounted inside a white cardboard frame. It was perfect. It was just as it was before except that Rockwell had erased some of the branches to let the suggestion of windows and an outline of the house show through. The house could now be clearly seen. Although the sketch was impressionistic, the Peyton Randolph portrait would make it familiar to all as the work of Norman Rockwell.

"Do you approve?"

"Yes!" and we all clapped.

"Which signature would you like?" He showed us two styles: script and outlined block letters in upper and lower case. We chose the latter.

Then he unveiled the second drawing. It too was in a white cardboard frame. He had mounted the drawings using Band-Aids brought along in his suitcase. This pencil sketch was for the ad featuring the James Geddy silver shop. Instead of the exterior called for by the layout, he had drawn an interior view showing a huge fireplace in the background with a fire glowing inside. Colonial fire tools were hanging from the brick chimney. In the foreground, a carefully drawn portrait depicted James Geddy holding a candlestick in one hand as he put the finishing touches on it with a pick held in the other. The young craftsman who worked in the shop had posed for him, and Molly had taken photos Rockwell later used for reference. The illustration was a perfect complement to the copy:

200 years ago, James Geddy fashioned
neat silver work here. Just as we do today.

James Geddy lived and worked in a two-story house on the edge of Palace Green, a little removed from the center of activity in Williamsburg.

So he wooed customers with resourceful salesmanship. "The walk may be thought rather an amusement than a fatigue," he advertised in The Virginia Gazette.

And his customers must have been amused, for they came to Geddy for teaspoons and tongs, spurs and shoe buckles, buttons and brooches and brandy warmers.

The handsome Geddy house is one of four original eighteenth-century buildings recently added to our exhibition program.

Come see how a colonial silversmith lived, and watch artisans work just as they did 200 years ago.

We think you'll still find it rather an amusement.

The call to action urged the reader to phone for reservations. Listings of the hotels and their rates were also shown in small type.

It was time to celebrate. Like a matador flagging a bull, Rockwell swept the napkin from the table top to reveal a tray full of Coca-Cola and a basket of potato chips.

Rockwell Strikes a Bargain

Later, during dinner at Campbell's Tavern, I noticed the waiters eyeing Rockwell. Usually, they were blasé about celebrities. They had served everyone—presidents, kings, movie stars, and movie makers like Walt Disney. Rockwell's star quality was something different. His drawings and illustrations through the years had found a special place in the hearts of

The layout called for an exterior of the Geddy silvershop. Rockwell disregarded that notion, much to my surprise, and proceeded with this interior view. He was right. The craftsman working midst his surroundings was infinitely more interesting.

Rockwell ran out of time and completed these two illustrations after returning to Stockbridge. He worked from photographs taken by Molly at each site. Featured are Wetherburn's Tavern and the Wren Building.

most people in this country. Soon, one of the waiters came up and asked him for his autograph. He graciously complied; in fact he went a step farther.

Turning his menu over, he quickly sketched a little white dog with black spots. Then his flashing pencil tied a string to its tail. A can was tied to the end of the string. The waiter was delighted. Frankly, I wanted one of those drawings myself, but didn't ask. A few years ago, I noticed a Norman Rockwell souvenir shop in Vermont and stopped to look around. The proprietor was selling key chains with a similar drawing reproduced on a plastic tag. The original drawing was hanging on the wall. I asked how much he had paid for it. "$2,500," he replied.

That was $2,500 more than we paid for the four illustrations (Rockwell completed two more from Molly's photographs after he returned to Stockbridge). We finally got around to discussing the subject of fee on the last day of his stay.

"I'll tell you, David. I'm making so much with the Famous Artists' School, most of what you would pay would go for taxes anyway. I don't need the money. But Molly and I did need to get away from the cold. If you want, you can take care of our expenses. That will do just fine."

The Kelly Awards

Each year the best magazine campaigns in America find their way to the Waldorf-Astoria to be appraised, like so many perfect Miss Americas, in a show named in honor of the late Stephen E. Kelly, former publisher of *McCall's, Holiday,* and the *Saturday Evening Post.* When he was president of the Magazine Publishers of America, Kelly promoted the idea that creativity is the key to sales results in magazine advertising. This became the principle behind the MPA Kelly Awards.

In 1988 Harry Jacobs was one of the judges. Although the show is only seven years old, it ranks alongside CA and the One Show as those most important for creative people. It also gives $100,000 to the winning creative team.

When Harry walked into the suite the Waldorf had set aside for the judging, he was struck by a kaleidoscope of color mounted on easels stretching thirty yards against the walls on both sides of the room. These were the campaigns that had successfully run the gauntlet in five cities, where screeners had narrowed down the 278 original entries to the 48 now on display. "The campaigns that made it to the Waldorf were striking," Harry said. "Handsome, well done, not a dog in the lot."

Harry and seven other judges were given scorecards and asked to go to work. Their job was to rate three factors: (1) graphics and design; (2) headline and copy; and (3) fulfillment of objectives. Based on scale of ranking for each, 23 would be eliminated and 25 would remain. One would be the Kelly winner. Price Waterhouse tabulated each scorecard and kept the winner's identity secret for a month until the date of the Kelly Awards luncheon. The judges, together with a thousand others at the ceremony and hundreds more watching by satellite, were kept guessing until the last minute.

When the winner was announced, an Ogilvy & Mather team walked off with the check with all the zeros for the third time in seven years. Their winning campaign was for the American Express Green Card. The best editorial photographer in America, Annie Leibovitz, took shots of Tip O'Neill, Ella Fitzgerald, Tom Seaver, Ray Charles, and skater Eric Heiden in fascinating poses. Each told a story as surely as Norman Rockwell's sketches did for Williamsburg. Although the copy was limited to a single line (for example, "Tip O'Neill, cardmember since 1973"), the photo and the subject shown embody a lifetime of story appeal calculated to involve the reader.

In fact, all 25 semifinalists in this year's contest had an interesting story to tell. "There is an appeal of intrigue and mystery embodied in the execution of each one," Harry told me. "They are all classics, like Ogilvy's eyepatch for Hathaway, or the ticking of the clock in the Rolls-Royce ad. You can run them now, or ten years from now, and they will work just as well."

From the time each of us was a child, we've loved a good story. Tell one in advertising and people will read your message and love your product.

Sum & Substance

Every ad should have story appeal. You are probably familiar with slice-of-life advertising, a style now somewhat discredited, which usually features two housewives talking together about a detergent. The problem with this technique is that it lacks inherent drama, and the situations dreamed up seem phony. This is an example of story telling that hardly meets the definition of drama, "a literary composition that tells a story, usually of human conflict, by means of dialogue and action."

John Pepper, president of Procter & Gamble, showed a collection of his company's commercials to the AAAA at its 1988 annual meeting. He pointed out which ads worked and which didn't. Invariably those with a fresh, new story line were the most successful in building market share. Of all the spots produced by this largest of the nation's advertisers, a commercial for the cold-water detergent Cheer received the most vociferous applause. As it came on the screen, it was greeted the way fans react when their favorite performer sings a well-known hit. You may remember it. A man in a tuxedo cleans his handkerchief in a cocktail shaker full of ice cubes while the voice of an opera singer provides all the audio. It is a new and different way to sell soap. It is inventive. And it tells a story in an interesting and entertaining way. It is a sharp and welcome departure

Who can turn the page without pausing to inspect this photograph of Wilt Chamberlain and Willie Shoemaker? Certainly the Kelly judges didn't pass it up. They picked this Ogilvy campaign for American Express best in the nation in 1988.

Wilt Chamberlain Cardmember since 1976
Willie Shoemaker Cardmember since 1966

from the dreary dramas of dirt removal we are all accustomed to yawning at.

As you relax with a copy of *Time* this evening, or sit down mindlessly to watch television, note which ads interest you the most. See if a vivid minidrama unfolds in those you favor. A story is easier to remember than facts or fluff, and it's hard to be dramatic without an element of drama.

▪8▪

Did You See the One?...

*To be called "great," advertising . . . must get
talked about. It must be so audacious that it gets
written about in the newspapers, discussed in
supermarkets, worried about in boardrooms or
even joked about on talk shows.*

—Peter Cornish, group creative director,
N. W. Ayer

Try this experiment. Walk into a room filled with strangers, none of whom are in advertising. Ask them about advertising campaigns, and see which ones they talk about. It is a sobering experience. Companies spending millions of dollars to tell people about their products or services find they have made very little impression. With some advertising, when it is out of sight, it is also out of mind.

People will mention one or two campaigns. Maybe even three. As part of your experiment, when a specific campaign is mentioned, check to see how much money was spent on it. Was it money or imagination that led to its being remembered? The California Raisin spots, for example, were the most popular in America in a year when the budget for them was only one percent of that spent for the spots that ranked fifth.

Advertising given added life through word of mouth can jump a brand several notches in its category, while competitors spending much more can lose ground. It all gets back to unaided recall. The product named first will be the first off the shelf. If distribution is pervasive enough, it will also be the category leader.

The mind works in mysterious ways. The trick is to capture consumer imagination by taking the reader or viewer beyond strategy and style into a magical dimension. Every great advertisement incorporates all three. Remember Brylcream's "Greasy Kid Stuff"? Volkswagen's "Lemon"? Avis's "We're only No. 2"? These ads jumped to top of mind, and would have even without optimum media levels and skillful execution of reach and frequency. They entered the magical third dimension that triggers word of mouth. Like a good joke, a great idea quickly makes the rounds.

"When advertising gets talked about," Peter Cornish writes, "it multiplies the effect of the media budget. It becomes a part of our culture, like 'Where's the beef?' 'Try it, you'll like it' or 'Reach out and touch someone.' It also creates a reservoir of goodwill toward the brand that will sustain it during periods of product problems, adverse publicity or intense competition."[1] Talk is cheap, but it can be worth millions.

Start With an Idea

Advertising doesn't have to be created for national television to have this quality. A recent two-page color spread for protective North work gloves is an example of trade advertising entering the third dimension. A small, creative agency in Providence, Rhode Island, Leonard Monahan Saabye, did it by showing a wet sponge cut out into the shape of a hand. The photo spans both pages. The headline reads, "This is what your hand looks like to most toxic chemicals." The agency took a mundane product and turned the advertising for it into a talked-about event in that industry.

In 1984, Hal Tench, an inventive art director and conceptional thinker, came up with a talk-provoking ad for our client, the Electro-Motive Division of General Motors. At the time, railroads had thousands of locomotives in storage, and trade publications were full of ads with photographs of trains on trestles. With your hand over the logos, all the ads looked alike. Hal put a four-color photo of an old locomotive upside down across two pages, but not just for effect. The ad told an economy story by pitching fuel efficiency. Railroads can save millions in the long run by trading in their old fuel guzzlers for new models. Mike Hughes provided the headline and copy: "You could lose $40,000 waiting for an old locomotive to die a natural death." *Adweek* named it one of the ten best magazine ads of the year, it was written about in numerous advertising publications, and it became the talk of the rail industry. It preconditioned the railroads for the GM salesmen who came to call. Prospects listened, and invested millions in new locomotives at a time when there was virtually no interest in buying new equipment.

The Knothole Gang

In the earliest days of television I learned that advertising that can generate talk multiplies sales. I was a broadcast writer/producer when most of the commercials we did went on the air live. One of my first assignments was to write and produce the *Esskay Knothole Gang,* a 30-minute show sponsored by Esskay Hot Dogs. It was transmitted live from the playing field at Baltimore's Memorial Stadium before every Oriole home game.

Happy Felton, a promoter, had approached the agency with the idea. Hot dogs and baseball were naturals. He had lined up a former baseball

A product demonstration with a twist. It gets you where it hurts. This ad for North protective work gloves by Leonard Monahan Saabye gets right to the point of product advantage.

THIS IS WHAT YOUR HAND LOOKS LIKE TO MOST TOXIC CHEMICALS.

It's been said that ignorance is bliss. Unfortunately, when you're handling dangerous materials, that bliss can be rather short-lived.

You see, despite their rugged appearance, hands need protection. But, it isn't just a matter of providing a pair of gloves. The gloves have to be designed for the particular situation.

It takes expertise to do that in today's industrial environment. And that's exactly what we offer at North Hand Protection.

A good example is what we're doing in gloves that resist permeation. We're the only producer of industrial gloves of Butyl and Viton® elastomers. These two formulations provide the best protection against many toxic chemicals.

Even these gloves, however, aren't always appropriate. That's why we produce different gloves, such as Nitrile Latex, for a variety of other chemical applications. So no matter what you're working with, we can deliver the best protection possible.

As a matter of fact, we offer the same level of quality in our industrial gloves as the U.S. Government demands in the gloves we supply for protection against chemical warfare agents. You'll find no other manufacturer can match North's capabilities.

But industrial hand protection doesn't end with chemical resistant gloves. And neither does our expertise.

We were leaders in developing the coated knit glove. This innovation performs so well that it's becoming the industry standard. And while everyone else was cutting and sewing their gloves, we began knitting them on machines to eliminate the seams and make our gloves more comfortable. This also gives them longer life and added value.

It's easy to see why industrial workers should put their hands in North gloves. Before they put them in anything else.

We'd like to tell you more. Contact North Hand Protection. 4090 Azalea Drive. P.O. Box 70729. Charleston, SC 29405. (803) 554-0600. North Hand Protection products are sold through authorized distributors.

NORTH
Hand Protection

star pitcher, Bobo Newsom, to be the host. Bobo was a big, husky man with thick wrists and a broad smile. His tall, athletic frame was then running to fat, giving him a somewhat disheveled look, like a giant sack of potatoes in a white Oriole baseball uniform.

Bobo interviewed Little Leaguers before the game. We gave the kids official Oriole caps, as well as Esskay T-shirts, but just being on the show was compensation enough. For each game, we put up a portable set near first base. It looked like a wooden fence with big knotholes in it. "Esskay's Knothole Gang" was scrawled boldly on the boards like graffiti. The show opened with a wide shot of the fence, then zoomed to a close-up of a knothole, before cutting to Bobo and the boys with the playing field in the background. At the close, the camera peered through the knothole at Bobo near first base, then pulled back to reveal the fence and the title.

Bobo asked each boy his name and how his team was doing in Little League play. Then he would say, "How'd you like to meet Mickey Mantle?" "Yeah, yeah!" Their faces beamed as they looked at each other knowingly. The kids were already excited to be on the show and down on the field just a bunt away from their heroes warming up on the infield. The stands began to fill with the thousands of spectators whose laughing voices and cheerful shouts created a discordant backdrop of sound to further charge the excitement of the moment.

Into this dramatic scene would stride a baseball legend like Mantle, Yogi Berra, Ted Williams, Al Kaline, or Bob Lemon. It was almost too much for a twelve-year-old. For the viewers at home, it was great entertainment—often better than the game itself. The show was the talk of the town. Other advertisers used greater reach and frequency with their product-oriented advertising. Yet "The Knothole Gang" lifted its sponsor into another dimension of awareness. It tied Esskay into baseball, putting it right in there with motherhood and apple pie. It gave the product personality. Photos of Bobo were used in store displays, and his store visits became celebrity appearances. Esskay soon had the best-selling hot dogs in Baltimore.

Virginia Is for Lovers

Nearly twenty years ago, we were invited to pitch the Virginia travel account. That was in the late 1960s. A campaign we created almost by accident changed the image of a state and its citizens' view of themselves. It became part of Virginia's folklore and shows signs of continuing forever as an important ingredient in tourism advertising. It stirred talk, along with hearts and minds.

We had been influenced by the "Pepsi Generation" commercials, which were relevant to all ages. Virginia's travel market was aging. To compete successfully with other states, it was necessary to attract young married couples, with children. To do this, we needed a campaign that would appeal to that audience without turning off the older bread-and-butter market. Pepsi had done it. How could we?

The creative team closeted itself with research data, competitive advertising, and this mandate. Soon a young copywriter, Robin McLaughlin, who was then making about $100 a week, emerged with a campaign idea. She showed me an ad featuring Virginia's historical attractions. The headline read, "Virginia is for history lovers." The idea was to vary the headline with each ad. "When we feature beaches," she said, "we'll change it to 'Virginia is for beach lovers.' " I wondered if the approach might be too limiting. Each ad would deal with one subject, whereas the underlying appeal of a Virginia vacation is the diversity of things to do and see.

My partner, George Woltz, agreed and his solution was simple. "We'll just drop the modifier and make it Virginia is for lovers."

We made the presentation in October in a hearing room at the State Capitol before a board committee of the Department of Conservation and Economic Development. Most were bureaucrats and appointees in their 50s or 60s. While they didn't know much about advertising, they knew a great deal about politics, coal mining, and oil distribution.

At this point in the twentieth century, the younger generation was practicing "free love," but the committee was still easily shocked. To the members, the word "lovers" conjured up something illicit vaguely reminiscent of the writings of D. H. Lawrence. Despite these reservations and their basic conservatism, however, they were intrigued. They went along with our agency and the theme, and soon most of America knew "Virginia is for lovers."

Perhaps the phrase was softened by our argument that the word "lovers" was firmly rooted in Virginia history. "Of course, Virginia is for lovers," I told the committee. "The very first romance leading to matrimony in this country took place in Virginia, the very first honeymoon. You may recall that was in 1608, when a young maidservant named Anne Burras met and married John Laydon, a carpenter, in the thatched and log chapel at Jamestown." At this point, I presented a layout of an ad for bridal magazines showing the couple in full color. "As this ad shows," I continued, "it was by no means the last Virginia honeymoon. John and Pocahontas Rolfe, George and Martha Washington, Tom and Martha Jefferson all honeymooned here. The evidence is clear: Virginia is for lovers."

Four Words That Spawned a Million

Much to our surprise, the four words had an almost magical quality right from the start. We were hard pressed to understand why. Sometime later,

The big idea sometimes catches the public fancy and enters popular culture. The quality that does this is hard to identify. When we did this first "Virginia is for lovers" ad in 1969, we never dreamed the phrase would still be alive twenty years later.

Virginia is for lovers.

Antique Lovers. See treasures like this figurehead from Newport News' Mariners Museum. Or search for treasures on your own. The nation began right here, so we had antiques before some spots had settlers.

Home Lovers. Come to Mount Vernon and see the first First Lady's kitchen. (Though with all the help she had, it's not likely she spent a lot of time standing over a hot hearth.)

Food Lovers. We have an oyster bar that stretches for miles and miles. It's called the Chesapeake Bay. We've also got clams and hams and peanuts and delicious mountain apples. Come on. Indulge yourself.

History Lovers. This is where history happened. Bring the children to Jamestown and Williamsburg and visit America's past. You can live in the present any old time.

Beach Lovers. Come visit our wide, white beaches. You can sail, swim, fish, ski and surf in the Atlantic. Or just soak up sun on the soft, silver sands.

For free 100-page booklet and brochures on your travel interests, visit, write or call VIRGINIA STATE TRAVEL SERVICE. Richmond 23219, 911 E. Broad St., phone (703) 770-4484. New York 10020, 11 Rockefeller Plaza, phone (212) 245-3080. Washington 20006, 906 17th St., N.W., phone (202) 293-5350.

This advertisement appears in the following publications: Cosmopolitan, April, 1969; Mademoiselle, April, 1969.

Richmond News Leader columnist Mike Houston put his typewriter fingers squarely on one plausible explanation: "It stops just short of its real meaning to present an intriguing picture, implying notions that are not expressed explicitly."

Maybe so when viewed in limbo on a button or a T-shirt, but the ads themselves were innocent enough. We bent over backwards to qualify the meaning of the word "lovers." Any reader would soon see we were talking about lovers of history, of beaches, mountains, and so forth, with no suggestion of anything naughty out of deference to our conservative client.

The ads ran in sixty national magazines, dozens of newspapers, and on radio and television. The approach was squarely on target. Virginia jumped to an 8 percent lead over other states. More than 20 million tourists visited Virginia in 1970, and 500,000 wrote, visited, or called Virginia Travel Service offices in New York, Washington, and Richmond to get brochures and maps before leaving home. Tourism became Virginia's second largest business, topping a billion dollars (it is a $6 billion industry today). As the phrase caught on, it spawned dozens of imitators (including "I love New York"). It gave a Virginia vacation the highest top-of-mind rating in the nation. With a 32 percent unaided recall, Virginia led all states; Florida, using a bigger budget, was second, with 23 percent share of mind. As you might expect, with highest awareness, Virginia also became America's most popular travel destination. By the end of 1971, Virginia ranked more than twice as high as any other state for "intent to visit." Pent-up intent led to a rapidly expanding tourism industry during the 1970s and encouraged two major theme parks to locate in the state with start-up capital investments exceeding $200 million.

This is heady stuff. Think about it the next time somebody wonders whether an intriguing advertising idea can really make a difference. This is especially true when the idea is compelling enough to generate word of mouth.

Who's Got the Button?

It did take more than ads alone to make "Virginia is for lovers" the best-known travel slogan in the United States. It took a combination of advertising, publicity, merchandising, and, most important of all, the powerful force of word of mouth. The talk started in San Diego in late 1970 at a meeting of Discover America travel organizations. Just for fun, I took along a couple of hundred "Virginia is for lovers" buttons to pass around. We made these especially for the meeting, at agency expense, because the state government opposed getting into the novelty business. Stuart White, the travel commissioner, turned down several merchandising ideas calculated to give the campaign slogan greater mileage. Buttons were one of them.

At the meeting, I noticed a plethora of bumper stickers and buttons from various attractions laid out in great piles on the registration table. My supply was so limited I simply wore the button and kept some in my pocket to give away when asked. The reaction was amazing. Soon my 200 buttons were gone, and virtually everyone at the meeting had "lovers" buttons pinned to their blouses and lapels. Frankly, I was flabbergasted.

Why such great appeal? Charles "Mike" Houston's theory of an intriguing notion inexplicitly expressed was a major part of it. But there was more. It was also the time when Erich Segal's *Love Story* was a best-seller and Book of the Month Club selection. The peace demonstrators were proclaiming "Make Love, Not War." Perhaps *The Commonwealth Magazine* had it right when it wrote in its July 1971 cover story:

> It turned out that the timing was a masterstroke. The new theme
> anticipated and then coincided with a change in the national mood, a
> sweeping return to—*Love*. It began to make sparks at a time when the
> country's young and old alike were taking a closer look at our ills and
> coming to the conclusion that only by a greater effort to understand
> and love one another could there be an end to riots, mistrust, vio-
> lence, disaster.

This is philosophical stuff. My own theory is that the public was intrigued to see a governmental body, a state name, with all it represents—shipyards, industry, beaches, mountains, people, farms, George Washington, and Thomas Jefferson—linked with the shocking word "lovers." But it didn't matter what it meant. The people of Virginia felt good about being on the side of love and lovers.

When I got back to the office, I got a call from Stuart White. "I need some of those buttons you took to San Diego," he said somewhat sheepishly—eating crow since he had steadfastly opposed all recommendations to produce buttons, shirts, or anything else with the phrase on it. Stuart thought the theme was undignified. He much prefered the quiet, sedate, warm, and fuzzy sell of the previous campaign, "the Face of Virginia," and others that had preceded it during his thirty years in government service.

"There aren't any buttons left," I told him. "I gave them all away."

"I've got to have them. I need them tomorrow!" Stuart sounded slightly desperate. Governor Linwood Holton had heard of the reaction in San Diego and wanted some for the Republican Governors' conference in Sun Valley. We rushed through an order. Again, the buttons created a major stir. Governors are people too, it seems, just like delegates to travel conventions. Holton made sure he wore one for an interview on the *Today Show*. It became a topic of discussion overshadowing more important (and long-forgotten) matters on the conference agenda. An AP wirephoto release put Holton and his button on front pages across the country. This national exposure kicked off a fad along with numerous follow-up stories.

Washington's *Sunday Star* for January 17, 1971, asked this question next to a photo of the button on the front page:

> What is round, displays a red heart on a black background and says, "Virginia is for lovers"? Ronald Reagan knows. In case you don't, it's the new lapel button issued by Virginia's state government as a lure for added tourism. Holton's staff credited the button with causing the GOP governors to schedule their next meeting in Williamsburg. According to this account, California Governor Reagan, proudly displaying his button, said, "If Virginia is for lovers, let's go."

Novel Ideas

All of a sudden "lovers" T-shirts became a hot item. Demand had been stimulated, during 1970, by our television commercial featuring, among other things, a lovely young woman named Debbie Shelton wearing one on the beach. As luck would have it, a few months later Debbie entered a beauty contest and won. The contest was of some significance: She was named Miss U.S.A. People remembered seeing the shirt in the commercial, and requests poured into the travel service, much to Stuart White's frustration. He steadfastly refused to get the state involved in such unseemly matters, so the shirt Debbie wore was the only one in existence. We decided to print up some at agency expense.

Back then, we hadn't had much experience with T-shirts. I had recently joined the Young Presidents' Organization, and at a YPO meeting in Puerto Rico, I met somebody who did. His name was Bill Pannill, of Pannill Knitting Mills, so I asked if he would make some for us. I found out later that his company is one of the largest T-shirt and sweatshirt makers in the country. Although ordinarily the company only processed huge volume orders, Bill did us a favor. As small as our order was, we stretched our financial resources to come up with the money needed to buy 5,000. John Boatright, the account executive, then took them around to department stores, where they were snapped up immediately. We soon reordered. By April we had sold 60,000. That year we made more profit on T-shirts than we did on the advertising business.

Meanwhile, demand for the buttons began to snowball. The state ordered 1,000, then 5,000. By June 1971, 100,000 had been distributed, along with 50,000 bumper stickers. By year end, more than 350,000 buttons were sold or given away, and the figure soon topped a million.

Most of the news stories were unsolicited. Reporters scrambled to find an angle. Whenever celebrities came near Virginia, someone stuck them with a button. Bob Hope loved it. So did Agnes Moorehead and Helen Hayes. (Later, in 1978, Elizabeth Taylor sported one as she campaigned for her then husband, John Warner, during his successful bid for

Usually a product is put into production and demand is created. In this case, demand came first. "Lovers" buttons and stickers rolled out like dollar bills at the mint.

the U.S. Senate.) Governor Holton kept popping up wearing the T-shirt, displaying a 4-by-6-foot afghan, wearing the button on *Meet the Press,* and showing it proudly to Ronald Reagan at the National Governors' Conference in San Juan. That AP photo hit the wires in September 1971. The governor also proposed a "Virginia is for lovers" commission to compete with the Kentucky Colonel citations given to citizens who demonstrated noteworthy achievement. Taking note of this, on July 14, 1971, Shelly Rolfe of the *Richmond Times-Dispatch* wrote:

> One clearly does not dally when the governor has made a command decision. High octane thinkers were consulted. Best brains were put to work . . . including a delegation from the agency that in what manifestly was a stroke of genius minted "Virginia is for lovers." The deed has been done. The citation that commissions the bearer as a Virginia Lover has been wrought.

Larry Bonko of Norfolk's *Ledger-Star* had an idea: "The time has come to change the words on the Virginia seal from *sic semper tyrannis* to *Virginia is for lovers.*" This was on September 10, 1971, a year and three days after he had written, "The slogan suggests there is Sodom and Gomorrah in the Blue Ridge foothills. I have been keeping my eye on the Richmond bureaucracy ever since I discovered a semi-exposed bosom on the state seal. It is right over *sic semper tyrannis.*"

On toll roads, uniformed coin collectors wore the button. When the General Assembly convened in January 1971, it was sported up and down the hallowed halls of Mr. Jefferson's capitol. This important event was pictorially reported across eight columns in the *Times-Dispatch.* A pro basketball team, The Virginia Squires, who that year became the ABA titleists, wore "Lovers" sweatshirts as warm-up jackets. George Allen, coach of the Redskins, wore a button at a press conference announcing the move of the NFL team from the nation's capital to Fairfax County, Virginia. The slogan popped up on postage meters and stationery. A television star, Peter Haskell, came to town to be grand marshal of the National Tobacco Festival. He fell in love with the "lovers" button and, along with love beads, wore it everywhere, including to the Festival Parade, where he also flashed the peace sign to the crowd of 175,000. The next year, actor John Forsythe was grand marshal, but he didn't want to wear a "Virginia is for lovers" sweatshirt. Asked if he would, he said, "Oh, no. I'm too old for that kind of stuff." Even so, his photo with the shirt and tobacco princesses popped up in print across the country.

The advertising strategy behind the theme wasn't lost on reporters. *The Roanoke Times,* for Sunday, August 8, 1971, under a headline identifying the slogan as "more than a passing fad," wrote, "The motto is happily sported by small children licking popsicles and sedate statesmen swinging golf clubs. The idea appeals to the old. The idea appeals to the young."

In 1970, it was novel to see an ad slogan on novelties. By 1973, "Virginia is for lovers" had appeared on just about every novelty item you can imagine.

Later, the state licensed novelty manufacturers to make every kind of item imaginable: coffee cups, bumper stickers, tote bags, coasters, key chains, and beach towels, as well as T-shirts. "Lovers" items became a multimillion dollar business.

Twenty years later, the theme lives on, having survived a generation of change, five governors, and two intervening advertising agencies. (We were reappointed in 1987 after a seven-year hiatus.)

"Lovers" novelty items continue to be popular Virginia souvenirs. Of course, ad-theme novelties aren't so novel today. But they were when the first "lovers" items accidentally edged onto shelves. They extended the life and value of the campaign and, along with the press coverage, brought Virginia share of mind in the travel business it couldn't afford to buy. Now, alongside "Virginia is for lovers" T-shirts, you'll find a variety of Spuds McKenzie items or sweatshirts and beach towels emblazened with California's Dancing Raisins. Even Burger King's abortive Herb the Nerd campaign produced $250,000 in T-shirt sales.

The Magical Dimension

Half of what we learn is forgotten within the first sixty minutes. When your advertising gets talked about, it lodges in the public consciousness, reverses the "curve of forgetting" (see Chapter 9), and pushes awareness back up off the chart. Media dollars are leveraged far beyond the reach and frequency the advertising schedule can deliver on its own. Word of mouth also piques the interest of reporters and editors. They write about what people talk about. Every advertising campaign should shoot for this magical third dimension.

Sum & Substance

Advertising muscles its way into our daily lives by buying admission to all the time slots where our attention is likely to be focused at any given moment in time. It is there from drive time through prime time.

Through the media, those who create advertising have unique access to the public. A great opportunity is lost if ideas fail to capture popular imagination. If you can get people talking, you'll get them buying.

This means that the advertising must touch emotions, relate to trends, or reflect topical interest. Usually a popular concept is related to the mood of the moment, but it doesn't borrow interest—it leads interest into new avenues of thought. Somehow, through some magical juxtaposition of words, a clever phrase becomes an exclamation mark to punctuate life. (Remember "V for Victory" or "Kilroy was here"?) Like a yellow smiley face, the latest fad enlivens the day. "Where's the beef?" "Try it, you'll like it," and "Virginia is for lovers" all did this. Often these ideas move into the public consciousness to a degree far beyond the expectations of the writers and artists who dreamed them up. They were popular accidents.

Advertising doesn't have to be aired nationally to pique interest and hype sales. Our theme park client, Kings Dominion, in fierce competition with Busch Gardens, was helped by a phrase buried in body copy that sparked interest regionally. A commercial promoting a new rollercoaster, called "the Grizzly," showed an old, wise prospector warning a tenderfoot about an ominous "monster" who lived in the forest. "It's a bad bear, boy" became a phrase that delighted teenagers who repeated it up and down the long lines waiting to take the ride. That year Kings Dominion broke all previous attendance records.

The point here is that advertising should be developed with more in mind than merely getting the selling strategy across. As the campaign material evolves, be sure it is seeded with phrases and ideas calculated to pollinate the public fancy so that the primary message has a life beyond what the client has paid for.

·9·

Personality Is Permanent

If you run a brilliant campaign every year, but change it every year, your competitors can pass you with a campaign that is less than brilliant—providing he does not change the copy.

—Rosser Reeves, chairman,
Ted Bates, in *Reality in Advertising*

The only constant is change. Nowhere is this more true than in advertising. All the best creative teams in agencies throughout the country go to work each day committed to creating brilliant advertising. They search for ideas and techniques never expressed before.

The quest for ''breakthrough'' work usually means an abrupt break with the past, a dumping of all that has gone before.

The best creative people are attracted to agencies that (1) encourage risk, (2) push to the outer limits of the envelope, and (3) eliminate any fear of failure. A continuation of an established campaign is out of sync with this attitude. The best creative people want to reinvent the wheel to make it slicker and faster and better as they go about putting their own stamp on the hubcap. They should. They wouldn't be creative if they didn't.

Talented teams do their best work for advertisers who also want breakthrough campaigns to multiply the value of their media dollars by getting high attention at low cost. These clients want to double or triple market share and are willing to encourage creative risks to reach that goal.

The best clients, from the agency point of view, are creative soul mates. They understand that the most talented art directors and writers work for the joy of the process, and to see their work in print or on the tube. They urge them on.

Once a campaign is established, most clients tire of it, as do their creative counterparts in the agencies. Subsequent work becomes routine. They see elements more often than they could ever hope to expose to readers or viewers. They see layouts, copy, storyboards, revisions, filming, rough cuts, editing, final prints and proofs. They make presentations to management, salesmen, directors, staff. By the time the advertising appears, it is so familiar that they long to see something new. They are anxious for a new campaign development to begin. Consumers, of course, only get bored if the message is dull to begin with, or when they are subjected to the same commercial seven or eight times during a two- or three-week period.

With advertising agency writers and art directors, there is a natural tendency to want to move on to the next breakthrough, to do it better, to find the Holy Grail. As soon as the work is produced, they're ready to try something different. But, whereas the agency team can usually find satisfaction by moving on to do work for another company, the original client is stuck with an established campaign that now bores him. New ads in the series don't help; they seem "more of the same." The client begins to wonder if the agency is as creative as everyone thought it was. This is not so much a problem with the advertising manager, who is usually an advertising professional. It's more acute at other levels—in the field, in the executive suite, and in the board room. Over time, pressure builds for change.

Don't Change the Subject

There is always pressure to "change" advertising. Meanwhile, consumers who are basically indifferent and involved with more important matters, forget who is doing what for whom.

Even when the client is committed to the campaign, there is pressure within the agency to change it. When the creative team comes back to extend the campaign, or to address new market realities, its fundamental instincts are to do something new, to break with the format, style, and theme dreamed up last year.

Jim DeVoe has the seven stages of advertising framed on his office wall at Goodyear:

> Enthusiasm
> Wild elation
> Disillusionment
> Panic
> Search for the guilty
> Punishment of the innocent
> Promotion and honors for the nonparticipants

The first three phases always occur. Creative people want to spend their lives at stages one and two. But when a new job is handed them, they look at what was done before and immediately move to stage three, which often results in stages four through seven as sales decline.

The "newness" bias is refreshing and stimulates the atmosphere in advertising agencies, but unless it is modified and channeled, it can be counterproductive to the long-term success of the brand.

Personality Is a Buoy, Not a Dead Weight

Great brands are built over a long period of time with advertising that is faithful to product personality. Brands, like people, project a personality. The advertising is what gives it to them, along with packaging, signage, service, and product trial. Volvo, Ford, Chevrolet, and Dodge all conjure up different responses from consumers, drawn from their own experience and what they've seen and read about the products through the years. A Mercedes and a Maserati cost the same, but their images are different. They appeal to different kinds of people. The product has a personality to start with; advertising enhances and magnifies the image and makes it familiar through repeated impressions.

Recently, I shared an airport limousine with two used car dealers. Their conversation sheds light on the consumer's perception of added value in automobiles and the perceived quality of American craftsmanship.

"People buy an American car, go around the block, and come back complaining," said the first. "They buy a foreign one and they're happy."

"Yeah," agreed the second. "I had a Corolla stick shift with the nose bashed, tires bare. I sold it to this guy. He fixed it up. Fixed the fender. Comes in once. The speedometer is going bananas—back and forth, like a windshield wiper. He says it doesn't bother him a bit, but would appreciate it if I'd fix it. If that'd been an American car, he'd a been all over me. I don't know what it is. They buy a foreign car, they're happy."

"You are right about that. Used to be everybody wanted a Cadillac. Model would change and people would line up. Now its Mercedes. That's where it's at."

"Yeah. People like Mercedes. That's where it's at."

Why is Mercedes "where it's at" today? How did Cadillac lose the mystique that meant the "best" in the automobile category? The standard started in 1914 with the advent of its new high-speed V-8 and an advertisement, "The Penalty of Leadership," which ran just once in the *Saturday Evening Post*. The leadership image enhanced by obvious craftsmanship gave this car a quality mystique that flourished for fifty years. Then Cadillac started coming out with different models to match various market segments. No longer was the "rose" "a rose is a rose": It was in fact much like a Buick, a Chevrolet, an Oldsmobile. To drive Cadillac's image back into preeminence, General Motors recently dropped the brand's mid-level price models, which had confused the brand image, and started again to concentrate on building cars for the luxury category.

What the manufacturer does to change or maintain a product's personality has as much to do with consumer perception as does the advertising for it. Both should be modified when a change for the better is indicated, but they should not be abruptly whipped around.

Call Up Familiar Echoes

Norman Berry, creative director at Ogilvy & Mather, believes there are values in many brands that have been tossed away. "If you can find those 'roots' you can revitalize brands," he told an advertising audience recently. He used the example of Duracell batteries, which in the early 1980s ran a memorable commercial featuring a little pink rabbit powered by the product.

Berry resurrected the pink rabbit mnemonic in recent Duracell commercials. It was obvious to him that a favorable association with the product remembered by the audience should be a springboard for something even better. If the audience didn't forget the rabbit, why should the agency? "I believe we should resist the temptation to change great campaigns," he said. "It is astonishing that a manufacturer turns over a brand, the most valuable asset he has, to a brand manager without telling him he has handed him an investment of millions of dollars worth of value spent in a franchise built over years with his consumer. Further it is astonishing he will allow that same person the power to change a campaign because it isn't 'his.' It is equally ridiculous for an advertising agency to allow a 'new creative group' to do the same thing."

After the meeting, over glasses of Chablis, I asked him how ingrained that point of view was in his approach to advertising. How does he keep creative people motivated when they must stick everlastingly to an established campaign?

The answer is that tone and product personality and faint echoes are the constants. Everything else is a variable when a replacement campaign is developed. "If the advertising has made a favorable impression in the past, people are confused when commercials take off in an entirely different direction," he said. I asked what he would do if handed a new account. "I would look at prior advertising as far back as reels and proofs can be found," he replied. "I would look for familiar echoes, something that helped set the product's personality. Then I would call up that echo in the light of present objectives."

I have found that creatives can make their own mark, do something completely different, and find a refreshing and relevant application essential to getting attention in the marketplace without sacrificing continuity. They don't do this by reworking the same old thing. But they must keep in mind that a product with an established customer franchise also has a residue of personality. This must be reflected in each new assignment they tackle.

Once established, and favorably accepted, a brand's personality is permanent. It must not change at the whim of every creative team.

Remember the pink rabbit powered by a Duracell battery that kept rapping the drum? Millions of people do. That's why Duracell reached back and used that familiar "echo" years later in new advertising.

Keith Reinhard, a former copywriter who is now chairman of DDB/
Needham, says, "When a customer identifies with the personality of a
product, and finds its behavior attractive, he transfers that personality and
behavior to himself by buying and using that product. It's like putting on
a badge and wearing it proudly."

That truth is shattered when the brand's personality is split or
splintered through a total departure in advertising. This is sometimes done
when advertising is asked to depart from theme so that it can deal with a
special situation. Some advertisers couldn't care less about image; they
want the ad to sell something, to pay for itself every time out, as it does in
direct response advertising (direct mail or telemarketing). Even when this
is the object, care should be taken to consider the long-term effects. Brand
mystique accrues by projecting a consistent personality over time. The
quotable David Ogilvy synthesized this point in a speech to the AAAA
back in 1955.

> What would you think of a politician who changed his public person-
> ality every year? Have you noticed that Winston Churchill has been
> careful to wear the same ties and the same hats for fifty years—so as
> not to confuse us? Think of all the forces that work to change the
> personality and image of the brand from season to season. The
> advertising managers come and go. The copywriters, the art direc-
> tors, and the account executives come and go. Even the agencies
> come and go. What guts it takes, what obstinate determination
> to stick to one coherent creative policy, year after year, in the face of
> the pressures to "come up with something new" every six months.[1]

Perhaps the greatest challenge to a creative person is not coming up
with a new approach but finding fresh and innovative ways to build on an
established campaign. This is a true test of creative maturity and patience.
It is more immediately gratifying to start from scratch, to disavow the old
and invent the new.

This has always been true of artists. The best look for ways to break
with the past. They want to start tradition, not follow it. For example, in
1863, Manet painted *Déjeuner sur l'herbe* to revolt against the idealized
esthetics favored by the art establishment of his day. It was an audacious
act. Instead of the cherubs and nude goddesses demanded by tradition
and popular taste, he painted a picnic scene in which the men are fully
clothed in the dress of the day, but a female companion, in the foreground,
is nude. The public was shocked. Napoleon III was outraged.

One critic, Théophile Thoré, was not as scathing as the rest. He saw
something in this new art that the others had missed: It is "odd and crude,
yet sometimes exactly right, even profound. Things are as they are,
beautiful or ugly, distinguished or ordinary. . . ." In other words, it is
honest. As advertising must be. The painting and the furor set the stage
for Monet, Cézanne, Picasso, Matisse, Pollack, Rauschenberg, and War-

hol to push to the outer limits of the envelope, to produce what they regarded as honest expressions of their creative muse.

Artists would rather revolt than render. The ideal is to be both revolutionary and honest. In advertising, this must be done without revoking brand personality and consumer expectations.

Titus Moody

In the early 1950s, David Ogilvy borrowed the Titus Moody character from the Fred Allen radio show and made him the star of Pepperidge Farm commercials. The homespun character was played by Parker Fennelly, a radio star who died in January 1988, at the age of 96. Fennelly was popular for his portrayals of old Yankee characters. He played Titus Moody on both radio and television, and I remember how the laughs started to roll out even before he began his routine. His classic opening line, "Howdy, bub," was enough to bring down the house. He was a comic icon like Charlie McCarthy, and if he'd been made of wood he would be in the Smithsonian. (Although Fennelly retired as Pepperidge Farm's spokesman at the age of 85, the commercials and the character continued with a new actor in the role.) Legend has it that Ogilvy was awakened from a deep sleep by this dramatic idea.

Ogilvy wanted the personality of the brand to project the homey quality of old-fashioned home cooking. "In effect, [Titus Moody] did for packaged bread and cookies what Ralph Lauren did for English country wear," commented *Adweek* in 1988. The magazine was apparently surprised by the current popularity of the character. "He's suddenly trendy," the article tells us. "These days, we seem to have a new media phenomenon: Geezer Chic."[2]

Somehow the writers and artists have found a way to breathe new life into a campaign that's older than they are. Titus and his horse-drawn white wagon have endured thirty-five years thanks to the staying power of successive creative teams at Ogilvy and their willingness to follow the precepts of the agency founder to consider every advertisement as "a contribution to the complex symbol which is the brand image." What started as a tiny bakery company in New England at the time the first commercial appeared is now a massive company and the most successful part of the Campbell Soup Company.

There is a compelling reason why each new advertising campaign should draw on the echoes of past successes and serve as one more building block in the solidification of the brand. It is the same reason why campaigns to follow should be fashioned with similar material.

People forget. They are human. They do not have Mr. Spock's Vulcan mind, with its facility for total recall, which became so familiar to viewers of *Star Trek*.

How Quickly We Forget

A hundred years ago, Hermann Ebbinghaus, a German philosopher and scholar of independent means, set about a two-year task to learn how the mind stores information and retrieves it. His experimental study of human memory revolutionized the field of cognitive psychology and demonstrated that half of what we learn is forgotten within the first sixty minutes. He did it by memorizing lists of nonsense syllables. Each word on his list contained three characters, a vowel sandwiched between two consonants, words like *wak, seg, mur* (not unlike brand names dreamed up by a computer). His "curve of forgetting" is still an authoritative reference for students learning the psychology of memory.

Some scholars have challenged his findings on the grounds that nonsense material does not represent a real-life situation in which prior experience makes it easier to learn. One of these was F. C. Bartlett. In the 1930s, he conducted memory experiments using stories—and these are much more relevant to advertising. Here's the first paragraph of one of the stories, followed by how it was played back by one of the subjects after fifteen minutes, and, then again, after four months.

> One night two young men from Egulac went down to the river to hunt seals, and while they were there it became foggy and calm.

Ebbinghaus shows us that half of what we learn is forgotten during the first hour. After eight hours there is another 10% drop. Then retention fades so that after a month we remember less than a third of the original material.

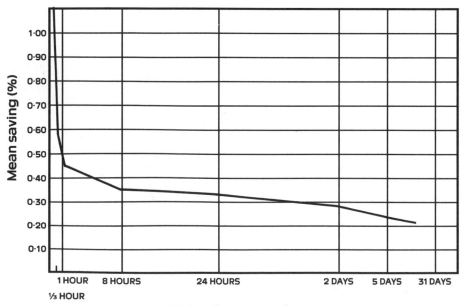

The Psychology Of Memory

> Then they heard war cries, and they thought "Maybe this is a war-party." They escaped to the shore, and hid behind a log. Now canoes came up, and they heard the noise of paddles, and saw one canoe coming up to them. There were five men in the canoe. . . .

Here is the recall after fifteen minutes:

> Two young men from Egulac went out to hunt seals. They thought they heard war cries, and a little later they heard the noise of the paddling of canoes. One of these canoes, in which there were five natives, came forward towards them. . . .

And recall four months later:

> There were two men in a boat, sailing towards an island. When they approached the island, some natives came running toward them. . . .

The subjects were required to learn the stories as a student would a lesson while studying for an examination. It was not a question of catching them during a station break with a pithy message from the sponsor. Bartlett noted that as time passed there was a tendency to shorten the passage. Details were lost. The subject's attitude was important: "In trying to remember a passage, the first thing the subject tends to recall is his attitude toward the material. The recall is then a construction made largely on the basis of this attitude, and its general effect is that of a justification of the attitude."[3]

Memory "Bites"

In advertising, we seek to shape attitudes. Some details will be remembered, most will be forgotten. What we want is for the consumer to remember the brand and what it offers and to have a positive attitude about trying it.

I've tried a memory experiment of my own during half a dozen speeches. I ask the audience what moment is most memorable from three films they've seen: *Chariots of Fire, High Noon,* and *From Here to Eternity.*

What do you remember? Stop for a minute and think, before you read on.

In *Chariots of Fire,* it is "running on the beach." This exuberant scene, overlaid with the extraordinary, synthesizer score composed by Vangelis, creates an emotional moment that is indelibly implanted on the synapses of the brain.

In *High Noon,* it is the ticking of the clock as the minute hand approaches 12. The tension builds to the climactic gunfight as we see the anxious faces of the protagonists and hear the whistle of the noon train with the killer on board. Again music makes all the difference.

In *From Here to Eternity,* it is the couple embracing in the surf: an erotic and emotional moment as the ocean pounds furiously over their bodies.

All three of these responses stem from human emotion: joy, fear, sex. All told, the three segments take only 60 seconds on the screen. The three films run a total of 5 hours and 43 minutes. Bits and pieces from the remaining 342 minutes are remembered, of course, but these three scenes, which can be edited into a single minute, set the tone for all the rest. They make a vivid case for the value of a dramatic moment, for the use of emotion, and for the skillful manipulation of sound and scene. These moments shape our attitudes toward each film. They establish its unique personality.

If sequels were planned, where would a new *High Noon* product be without the emotional echo of the ticking clock, or another *Chariots of Fire* without the Vangelis score, or a *From Here to Eternity* without that pounding surf?

Why Start From Scratch?

Long after the details are lost, people vaguely remember impressions of what they saw, heard, or read. For example, do you remember the name of Walter Mondale's running mate in the 1984 presidential election? According to a recent poll by The Hearst Corporation, less than half of America did by 1988. Despite the millions in media weight, television appearances, photos on the covers of *Time* and *Newsweek,* and pervasive election coverage by the media, the name Geraldine Ferraro was lost from conscious memory by 52 percent of the public. The indelible impression that was undoubtedly made on the billions of synapses of the brain four years earlier was now hazy. An attractive woman candidate, to be sure, the first to aspire to high office. The face, the voice—that you remember, but what was the name? It wouldn't take much media exposure to boost unaided awareness back to high levels.

The same is true of brand name recall and familiarity with its selling proposition, provided the advertiser doesn't start from scratch to establish a completely new personality. If the brand has merit and a strong franchise of acceptance, why start again with what would be essentially a new candidate?

Brand personality is permanent. Lose it and lose the franchise.

Sum & Substance

Advertising campaigns are spawned and quickly abandoned on the client's doorstep. It's not that they are unloved. Creative teams are simply anxious to move onto the next challenge. They often find it very tedious to render new ads for an old campaign. Many clients join them in wanting something new. They suspect that an agency is lazy if it fails to produce a new campaign every year. So every year, new campaigns replace the old, and impact and staying power are lost. It is advertising served up by dilettantes to amateurs.

Consumers are indifferent bystanders. The mental notes they take of advertising are soon forgotten unless the product's personality and advantage points are tirelessly reinforced. There is too much clamor for their attention for them to tire of a specific advertisement. It won't happen unless they are bombarded by the same commercial, incessantly, over a short span of time.

A good campaign that's working can continue for years. Fine tuning can make it better, but even as the emphasis changes, the elements people remember from past campaigns should be retained to jog hazy memories. A melody, a character, a phrase, a graphic look—whatever worked and is remembered should be brought up again and again. These echoes link the product with past experience.

We must do whatever we can to nudge memory. Recent experiments by Kevin Keller, a marketing professor at the University of California at Berkeley, suggest that it is even a good idea to put elements from ad campaigns on to the package itself. When this is done, his findings show, there is an 18 percent advantage in positive brand evaluation and a 10 percent advantage in purchase intent.[4] This may be the ultimate way to provide memory cues and complete the loop to reinforce the personality of the brand.

▪10▪

A Brand Is Born

Whenever possible, we introduce a personality into our ads. By making the man famous, we make his product famous.

—Claude Hopkins, copywriter

In the early 1970s, Frank Perdue produced more live chickens than anyone else in the country, about a million a week. He also had a processing plant and an abiding desire to expand retail distribution into supermarkets, where big processors, like Holly Farms, dominated the poultry cases. At the time, chicken was a commodity product that was sold unlabeled in the same way that sugar and flour were in the last century. Perdue changed all that with his familiar blue label. Now, half the chickens sold in the United States carry brand names.

The Perdue story is a good example of a consistent product personality. It paid off in its eleven-state distribution area. Don Mabe, a thirty-year Perdue veteran and current CEO, estimates that the brand controls a fourth of the category and 8 percent of the market nationwide.

In 1971, Frank Perdue's desire to step up promotion directly to the consumer prompted him to shop around for a new advertising agency. After about six weeks devoted to the project, he narrowed his list from forty to nine to one. His selection was Scali, McCabe, Sloves, our partner agency in the "creative confederation" that Sam Scali and Marvin Sloves have put together around the world.

Somewhere, Perdue had learned that it is a good idea for a chief executive to have plenty of direct contact with the person who writes his ads. For this reason, he wanted an agency where the writer on his account was a partner and, therefore, likely to stay with him as he built his business. He also wanted the best writer he could get. He had heard Ed McCabe was the best, and since Ed was also a founding partner of Scali, McCabe, Sloves, he had found what he wanted. His second requirement was to have assigned to his account, Sam Scali, one of the best art directors in advertising (which is why Marvin Sloves wanted him to help start the agency in 1967).

During their first visit to the Eastern Shore, where Perdue Farms is based, Scali and McCabe were impressed with Frank Perdue's dedication to quality. They noticed the care he took feeding and raising his birds, his passion for cleanliness, his methods for making them plump and healthy, including feeding them marigold petals, which raises the xanthophyll level to give them a golden hue.

They wanted to find a way to impart this quality story to consumers. How to say it without saying it? Just stating "Perdue stands for quality" leaves little to the imagination. There is no memory value, no story appeal, no credibility. It sounds like a big brag. The best way to make a point about quality, reliability, experience, or service is to demonstrate it through an arresting idea and then leave it to consumers to draw their own conclusions. What evolved is a good example of the "indirect" selling technique. It lets consumers discover quality benefits for themselves rather than bluntly and dully relating them.

When we were in Venice at a Scali confederation meeting, Frank Perdue was there as a featured speaker. I noticed he was introduced as a "tough client." This was said with some affection and a great deal of respect. Obviously, Perdue is as demanding of his advertising agency as he is of his own employees and himself. There are no compromises.

After his speech at the Bauer Grunwald Hotel, we adjourned for luncheon on the terrace next to a canal. I asked him if he had been a "tough man" before his television commercials made him out to be one. Perdue is cast as a tough man who raises tender chickens. I wondered if the pattern had been cut to fit the cloth. He assured me he has always been uncompromising in his basic beliefs, the pursuit of his goals, and the quality of his product. He said this in an unsmiling way that convinced me he meant it.

A Tough Man

This uncompromising toughness did not go unnoticed by Scali and Mc-Cabe on their first visit to Perdue's farm. It became the hook on which to hang the quality story. It was a way to make the claim meaningful to the public.

The idea came to both men very late in the first night of their Eastern Shore visit in 1971. After the tour of the farm and processing plant, the agency creative team went to dinner with Frank Perdue to discuss the assignment. After dinner, as they were returning to their hotel, the three drove by the Perdue plant, where on a tall metal pole the American flag was flapping in the heavy breeze sweeping east from Chesapeake Bay. It was almost midnight.

Ten years into Perdue's "Tough Man" campaign, newspaper ads like this supported television and the enduring idea that an uncompromising Frank Perdue goes to any extreme to give his chickens a soft life. The payoff is a tender meal.

It was too dark to see it, but Frank Perdue was turning red. They knew his temper was near the boiling point. He asked his companions to wait in the car while he went into the office to make a telephone call.

About twenty minutes later, the plant manager drove up wearing pajamas, a raincoat, and shoes without socks. His confrontation with Perdue was icy; sheepishly, the plant manager lowered the flag, folded it neatly, and stored it away for what remained of the night.

In the car, Scali and McCabe looked at each other and agreed, "There's a tough man."

Perdue was destined to be the first corporate head to become a TV star by appearing in his own commercials. The casting couldn't have been better. On the screen, he is reminiscent of a chicken with his thin neck, beaked nose, and squawky voice. He clucks about quality. Off the screen today, at 67, he is tall, tanned, and vigorous, a man who takes care of himself, as healthy as his birds.

An Enduring Personality

The first print ads and television commercials laid out a basic selling position that hasn't changed since. The first commercial shows Frank Perdue in his shipping department. He's wearing a hard hat and talking to the camera. Behind him, workers are loading boxes of chicken for shipment.

Here's what he said:

Some of my people think I should freeze my Perdue chickens. Then we wouldn't have to stay up at night packing them in ice and shipping them out fresh.

But, I'm not interested in less work. I'm interested in fresh chickens. After all the trouble I go to raising perfect chickens, I'm not about to foul them up at the last minute, and if any of my people don't like the hours, they can go to work for somebody else.

This is no country club outfit.

Super: It takes a tough man to raise a tender chicken.

Fifteen years later, the basic position remains the same, as does the tone and style of language. It is pure Frank Perdue, talking the way he talks. Here's a recent example. Frank Perdue is inspecting a large tray of golden, yellow chickens. One of them is white.

What we've got here is a rare bird: a white Perdue chicken. I don't know where we went wrong. Maybe it caught a cold. Maybe it went off its feed. All I know is, that somewhere along the line, it got fouled up and lost its golden, yellow color. It also lost its right to wear the Perdue name tag. Occasionally

*one of my chickens disappoints me. But, I make sure of one thing. It will never
disappoint you. (He tosses the reject into a waste bin.)*

Super: It takes a tough man to raise a tender chicken.

What do these two spots tell you about Perdue chickens? That a
tough, persnickety man has your interests at heart. He raises quality,
tender chickens. You can count on the Perdue label. Nine out of ten
people can now recall the Perdue name and this selling proposition without
prompting.

What does it tell you about Perdue advertising? It says that Frank
Perdue realized, instinctively, that the higher up the advertising involve-
ment in a company, the better the advertising; that he had advertising
professionals working with him who understood, as he did, that once you
have a winning campaign you don't change it.

Annual revenues at Perdue Farms have increased from about $60
million, when the first commercial appeared, to nearly a billion today. The
media budget has grown from about $200,000 in 1971 to a figure exceeding
$20 million today. Perdue now processes 6 million chickens a week.

Frank Perdue is older, of course, and what's left of his hair is gray.
But that's about all that has changed. As the spots above demonstrate,
the advertising hasn't changed. The dramatic changes are in the balance
sheet.

Sum & Substance

The Perdue story illustrates the point made in the previous chapter.
Customers are passive and indifferent. They are not advertising aficiona-
dos. They gravitate to the familiar. Minds focus on a brand's image after
repeated exposures over a long period of time. Advertising must play to
this reality.

The Perdue campaign is an advertising classic because it meets two
classic criteria. First, *it is inventive*. Every ad in the series is clever.
Consumers delight in seeing what Perdue will come up with; each is
loaded with benefits that viewers can assess from their own point of view.
Second, *it is predictable*. The advertising doesn't shift gears, leaving us to
wonder who the sponsor is. Each ad builds on the one that went before.

·11·

Television Is Entertainment

Each commercial found the comic essence of a business problem and solved it in 30 hilarious seconds.

—Bob Garfield in "Ad Review," *Advertising Age*

Back in the days when today's yuppies were merely a gleam in their parents' eyes, television was both live and lively.

As a child, I marveled at my own image on the tiny screen as the camera swept the crowd at the New York World's Fair (the one in 1939). That was entertaining, but it wasn't entertainment: it was technology. As a teenager, I watched the first telecast in our town from a vantage point on the street outside an appliance store window. Nearly 200,000 American homes had television at the time, but mine wasn't one of them. Unfortunately, I grew up before television did. I was out in the world working in an advertising agency by the time a black and white set arrived in my home, the same year television arrived in 21 million other homes. Television and I came of age together. It was time to switch off the radio and tune into *What's My Line?*, Gary Moore's *I've Got a Secret, Liberace, The Ed Sullivan Show,* and the McCarthy hearings. They were all great entertainment, especially George Welch, Roy Cohn, and the rest of Joe McCarthy's cast in the Senate hearing room.

Soon after that, I started working on the other side of the screen. This amateur viewer became a professional television writer/producer, and discovered that the best television commercials are also great entertainment.

The television deprivation of my youth was not experienced by more than half of today's adult population: the 73 million baby boomers (now oldsters ranging from 23 to 42). Unlike mine, this generation was raised on television. Television was first the "boomer's" baby sitter, and then, a constant home companion. It shaped tastes and expectations from the cradle up and turned this vast and lucrative market into professional television watchers: cynical, sophisticated viewers who appreciate beauty, taste, wit, charm, humor, imagination, fantasy, heroes, role models. As a group, boomers relate to symbols of enduring value, to heritage, exclusivity, and uniqueness.[1] And the "postboomers" are even more sophisticated, although there are 5.9 million fewer teenagers today than there were ten years ago.

All this is something the advertising practitioner of today will do well to remember. Hard sell, and Madge and Maude in a kitchen talking about their detergent, won't really cut it if the hope is for the brand to jump out of the back of the pack to take the lead in its category. On television, advertising must entertain as well as persuade.

Along with a daily dose of three or four hours of television entertainment, the average American sees thirty or forty commercials superimposed on the 2,000 or so other advertising messages. In most houses a set is on for eight hours a day; that's 88 million television households tuned in fifty hours a week. Each of us will spend a year and a half watching commercials in the course of a lifetime. There is plenty of variety. Each year, 25,000 new commercials appear on the three major network screens. With a beer in one hand and a remote control unit in the other, the consumer is in complete command, master of all surveyed. Advertising that bores or insults the viewer does so to the peril of the brand. The fate is not death, it's zapping: wasted dollars.

Early TV

Back in the early days of television, life was much simpler, as were most things. Television was such a novelty that you could get away with being dull, trite, and even corny. The commercials were usually live, which translated into practically no cost for production. Now a well-produced television commercial costs $75,000 to $125,000 (according to an AAAA survey, the average for a thirty-second spot today is $113,940), with a million or more spent to produce an extravaganza from time to time. Pepsi's New Generation commercial with Michael Jackson is a good example. Jackson's contract alone cost Pepsico $10 million.

In the early days, the time cost wasn't out of sight either. That was long before sixty seconds on the Super Bowl went for $1,350,000. (As the audience is about 90 million, you can flash nearly half the population for $22,500 a second.) In the mid-1950s, *Tonight Show* spots went for about $7,000 for sixty seconds (compared to an average of $121,860 per 30 seconds on networks today); as a bonus, the star would pitch the product. In the fall of 1955, I was assigned to write and produce live Black & Decker commercials on *Tonight* just prior to Christmas.

Tonight was led by the witty and talented Steve Allen. It was a crazy, extemporaneous, ad lib, explosive show where anything could happen and often did, except in the commercials, which were delivered straight up by the host in a "let's-get-it-over-with-and-get-back-to-the-show" way.

The regulars, in addition to Steve Allen, were Skitch Henderson and his orchestra, plus three young singers getting their first exposure to a national audience: Eydie Gorme, her husband Steve Lawrence, and Andy Williams.

There was also a young staff announcer named Gene Rayburn. Rayburn was relatively unknown, and he wasn't the sidekick that Ed McMahon is to Johnny Carson. His job was to do the commercials when asked and to introduce Steve Allen enthusiastically when he came on stage for his opening monologue. Before the show, Rayburn's banter and jokes and engaging personality warmed up the audience, priming it into a roaring monster ready to cheer madly at the slightest witticism. After that, his job was just about done. When the show went on the air at 11:30, he took a seat reluctantly in the front row of the audience and waited for a chance to go back on stage. Usually, though, Rayburn was left high, dry, and off the air. Steve Allen was stuck with the commercials because most sponsors wanted his personal stamp on the product.

Rayburn was quite open about his frustration. He wanted more national exposure. In contrast to this eagerness to be on camera for any reason, Allen seemed bored having to do commercials. He wanted sponsors to use Rayburn. In fact, he urged them to do so when they met in his office during get-acquainted sessions; still, most resisted, opting instead for Steve Allen's implied endorsement. In rehearsal, Allen breezed through the copy, and on the air his delivery was short and sweet. A sponsor was pretty much limited to having his product held up in one hand while Allen peered into the teleprompter and read the lines.

One night I was sitting next to Rayburn in the audience when our commercial came on. "You're crazy not to have me do them," he said. "Look at that! It comes on, then it's over, boom, boom, boom." He had a point. There was no drama. The commercial was a talking head, Allen's talking head, I'll grant you, but except for that, it could just as well have been on radio. The only visuals we used were slides to illustrate how bookcases and partitions could be built using Black & Decker tools. Sometimes we even inserted a film clip to demonstrate the tools in action, but the footage was dull, like something out of a training film. On the other hand, Rayburn could handle a demonstration. He was an accomplished do-it-yourselfer with a workshop at home loaded with tools, including some we had given him.

Then I had an idea. Why not have Allen speak the lines, and let Rayburn demonstrate the product? Maybe we could get the commercials into the spirit of the show.

The next day I went to a novelty store on 6th Avenue and bought five rubber thumbs. Then I went to a lumber yard and bought several 1″ x 6″ boards five feet in length. This commercial would be pitched directly to the novice who had some trepidation about giving power tools a try.

Steve Allen liked the idea of using Rayburn to demonstrate while he did the voice over. He even liked the copy. The spot opened with Allen holding up his hand with a giant thumb stuck on each finger.

Are you all thumbs when it comes to doing handy jobs yourself?

[Laughter]

I'll bet you'd like to use a Black & Decker saw or hand drill, but you're not sure you can do it . . . are you? Let me tell you anybody can. And I mean anybody. Here's living proof.

At this point the camera cut to Rayburn on stage left hunched over the one-by-six, which was extended between two saw horses. *[More laughter.]*

See how easy it is?

Rayburn proceeded to saw the board in two—z-z-z-z-z-zip! Then he reached down to the stack of boards and grabbed another. This time he sawed a fancy pattern. He took his time, stalling to stay on the air. By now, more than sixty seconds had ticked away. The audience cheered.

Allen got up from his seat behind the desk and came over to watch. There was a spare saw on the floor for Rayburn to use in case the first one failed. Allen spotted it, and made a quick decision. He could see the audience had gotten into the spirit of the moment, and as he often did when a skit caught fire, he went with the flow. He asked to try his hand, and sawed the board quickly through. Rayburn selected another board and the two began a race to see who could saw the fastest, leaving the other to hold what remained.

The spontaneous performance lasted eight minutes, while the audience roared. Drum rolls and clashing cymbals punctuated every move.

I figured we got about $50,000 in extra air time.

Gene Rayburn got interested because we filled his need. His interest got others involved: Steve Allen, Eydie Gorme, Steve Lawrence, the public. After that, the performers were more than just accommodating—they wanted to do the commercials. In one spot, Eydie Gorme danced around the stage humming as she dusted furniture with the buffer attachment on a Black & Decker drill. In another, Rayburn showed Steve Lawrence how easy it was to change drill bits. Commercials became part of the entertainment.

Black & Decker jumped out to an early lead in the home power tools market and never relinquished it.

Raising Raisin Awareness

One of the favorite songs of the 1960s was Marvin Gaye's rendition of "I Heard It Through the Grapevine." In the late 1980s, it was a hit again, this time as the sound track for California Raisin commercials. The "Grapevine" turned golden for Priority Records.[2]

It hit the baby boomers squarely on the nostalgia button, and picked up millions of younger fans as well. The finger-snappin', toe-tappin' Claymation raisins danced all the way to the cash register for the California Raisin Board. Raisin sales jumped 9 percent over the previous year during the months the commercials aired. According to *Advertising Age,* raisins, of all things, were one of ten products that made news in 1987. The commercials, produced by Foote, Cone & Belding/San Francisco, are consistently mentioned first by the public in unaided awareness tests. This gave them a ranking near or on the top as the most remembered spots of 1987. What would Claude Hopkins think of that? And of his old agency, which produced them? In television, entertainment works when the product is star of the show.

People Like to See Spots

The Bruzzone Research Company (BRC) regularly investigates commercials appearing on prime time network television to find out such things as commercial recognition, commercial interest, brand name recognition, viewing level, product use, and demographics. To obtain its data, the company sends out photos and scripts of commercials with the brand names blocked out to a nationwide sample of 1,000. It receives replies from about half the sample. Participants who recognize a commercial are asked to check any of twenty alphabetically listed adjectives they feel

Everyone likes to look at Claymation characters. After Will Vindon developed the raisins in 1984, along came Domino's Pizza Noid, Kentucky Fried's chickens that turn into hamburgers, Wendy's singing eggs, and talking lemons for Lemon Joy.

describe it. Ninety-four percent check at least one, and the average is 2.1
adjectives checked per respondent. The findings lay to rest the notion that
television commercials are generally regarded as irritating. And they point
up the fact that viewers find them both entertaining and effective.[3]

Here are the findings for an average commercial:

Irritating	6.1%	Amusing	13.3%
Silly	8.7%	Lively	6.8%
Phony	7.5%	Appealing	12.0%
		Convincing	13.0%
		Informative	18.2%

The Sunflower

My favorite commercial is amusing, lively, and appealing; from the results
we measured, it is also convincing and informative. It was created by
Mike Hughes and Cabell Harris of The Martin Agency for FMC's Furadan
insecticide. When Cabell showed the storyboard to the account executive,
she broke into a sweat and refused to show it to the client. "This is silly,"
she said. "They'll never buy it." I had to agree, it was bizarre. But it was
also squarely on position.

Furadan is effective in controlling pests that feed on corn, alfalfa,
tobacco, and a variety of other crops. This commercial was designed to
promote its use on one of the most obscure of them: sunflowers. Sunflowers grow on about 3 million acres in Minnesota, North Dakota, and South
Dakota. That's not many when you consider that there are 60 million
acres of corn planted in this country.

You may wonder why farmers grow sunflowers. (Do I hear you
saying, "Yes, that's right, why do farmers grow sunflowers?" Well, stand
by. I'll tell you.) Before we were assigned the FMC account, my own
knowledge was limited to those appearing in the Van Gogh painting
Christie's sold for $39.9 million in 1987. For one thing, sunflower seeds
are a health food along with raisins, dried apricots, and tofu. Sunflower oil
is low in polyunsaturated fat, and thus an excellent cooking oil. Some
spice manufacturers mix the seeds with soy nuts, onion, carrot, sweet bell
pepper, and chives to make a crunchy, flavorful salad topping. Because
sunflowers have practical use beyond being subjects for still lifes, or
stirring the senses as a golden display against red barnsiding in the brilliant
light of early fall, it pays farmers to grow them.

Furadan applied at planting prevents damage to a sunflower crop by
merciless enemies such as stem weevils, sunflower beetles, and early
grasshoppers. Most farmers didn't know Furadan did that. The commercial's job was to tell and sell them.

This commercial was risky and the budget was too small to test it.
Farmers, like the account executive, might think it was silly. FMC,

however, is one of those rare clients that is willing to take risks to get share. For that reason, the advertising it gets is consistently superior. It's the kind of account creative people fight to work on, and the fact that it is in the ag business and that this commercial would only be telecast in the towns of Minot, Bismark, and Fargo, North Dakota, didn't matter that much.

The commercial opens with a Warren Beatty kind of a guy in a business suit talking into the camera. He is sincere and earnest. As it turns out, he is also a sunflower.

Let's say I'm a sunflower [he says, as he puts on a sunflower bonnet] and I was treated at planting with Furadan insecticide.

At this point, a disheveled runt of a guy wearing a wilted sunflower bonnet glumly edges into the frame.

Here's a sunflower that wasn't treated with Furadan. Just look what sunflower beetles and grasshoppers did to him. And once those stem weevils got to him . . . well. . .

Gales of laughter greet this odd couple. The healthy sunflower and his wilted sidekick are reminiscent of Abbott and Costello. To see what people remember, I've run recall studies after speeches. This spot is always listed as the high point of my presentation.

Our hero sighs, and punches his wilted friend fondly on the shoulder.

If you were harvesting you'd run right over a little guy like that.

The slight punch is too much for a sunflower in such weakened condition; he coughs, reaches out, and falls to the ground off camera with a loud thud. The camera zooms slightly to a closer shot of the healthy sunflower adjusting his bow tie, as he shrugs knowingly.

So take some advice from a sunflower who knows; use Furadan at planting. It's the best way I know to keep your heads up.

The frame dissolves to a close-up of the package, and an announcer says, "Furadan from FMC."

The client loved it. So did farmers, and so did a senator from North Dakota who showed it to the Senate Agriculture Committee as an example of responsible farm advertising. The readers of *Nation's Business* voted it one of the three best business-to-business commercials in the United States. It won top advertising awards in every exhibition entered. People called the stations to find out when it was scheduled so that they could watch and tell their friends. Even the *North Forks Herald* ran a front page feature. It outscored Wendy's "Where's the beef?" in local popularity.

It was great entertainment.

Best of all, it doubled sales. Furadan was applied to 20 percent of all sunflower acres that year.

Sum & Substance

The best commercials today are minimovies with all the drama, suspense, wit, and O. Henry endings that can be compressed into fifteen, thirty, or sixty seconds. When professional couch potatoes sit back and invite the colorful, flickering, outside world into their living rooms, they want to be entertained. Great television commercials can be both entertaining and persuasive in a way today's adults appreciate. But Ogilvy is right that there is a tendency to get carried away with "show biz" advertising. When commercials do a great job of entertaining but people move on to the next offering without remembering the brand or what it stands for, the sponsor's money is wasted.

This can be avoided by starting with the *dominant value point* and dreaming up an entertaining way to get it across. The Furadan sunflower spot did that: Furadan at planting keeps sunflower heads up. You can find a value message in the raisin commercials too: Eat raisins instead of candy, chips, and all that other junk food. But the spot's primary purpose was to boost raisins to top of mind. It did that for months on a slim national budget, and that's amazing. In the Black & Decker spot, we wanted people to see it was easy for an amateur to use power tools, something only pros had been able to do. The best way to get that across was to demonstrate it, so we did. If Allen and Rayburn could use them skillfully, anybody could.

Television is great entertainment. And great commercials are extremely entertaining.

·12·

No Risk, No Gain

BONSAI, *Bahn sye,* is the art of dwarfing trees. The dwarfing is brought about by a combination of root confinement and starvation. But it is a genuine art. The plants must be starved without killing them.

—Frederick F. Rockwell

In television advertising, a performer's personality can make the difference between success and failure. A delightful accident can be electrifying, while other "takes" of the same scene would have been mundane.

Performers often bring accidents of inflection to a spot, thereby lifting it beyond original expectations. Clara Peller's outraged cry in Wendy's "Where's the beef?" is a good example. It probably took twenty-five or thirty takes to get that one memorable moment.

Sound is another variable. The sound track touches the heart by reaching the mind. Emotions stir to music. Basic instincts are titillated by sound effects synched to sight. What is channeled through the ear excites, saddens, delights, thrills. The mind absorbs, stores, then sends signals to the heart and glands; the pulse quickens and adrenalin begins to flow.

These variables, planned and accidental, suggest why it's hard to prejudge consumer likes and dislikes in advance of full production.

Broadway shows try out on the road before they come to the "Big Apple." Even then they're not sure to succeed. Critics have the power to close down a show after opening night. But critics do not always reflect public sentiment; sometimes, when a show is able to continue, what was panned turns into a hit.

Who can guess what an audience will like in the way of movies, stage plays, television commercials, or a television series? In 1982, the producers of the popular sitcom *Cheers* talked with TV critics about their ideas for a comedy series set in a bar. "A bar?" they said. "Wouldn't that be confining? A romance between a know-it-all college student and her dumb jock boss? Wouldn't that be unbelievable? Would the viewers really want

112

to watch?"[1] Cast chemistry and good scripts made it the hit that continues on the air and in the "top ten" seven years later.

Which just goes to show what critics know. Critics, you will remember, panned Manet, ridiculed Monet, and laughed at Van Gogh.

Critics, clients, and agencies can't predict what consumers will find appealing on an emotional level, and it is their emotional response over the long haul that gives the brand precious added value.

Bonsai or Giant Oaks?

In advertising, the ultimate critic is copy testing, the art of dwarfing advertising inspiration. Testing is an attempt to remove risk from advertising, but by sanitizing copy, it removes advertising's color and texture and punch.

Commercial testing based on a single showing, or done prior to full production, can kill an innovative approach that might jump a brand in its category. Many testing methods are used in an attempt to bring science into what is essentially an art form. People are asked to react to slides, animatics, crudely produced film, ads placed in portfolios. Cameras measure eye movements. Commercials aired once are measured for recall a day later. Sometimes spots are shown in theaters, sandwiched between other commercials, to measure what the audience remembers and what point the spot conveyed. The commercial lives or dies according to the results of this laboratory experiment. In this way, the child of creative inspiration is often cast aside unloved, in an atmosphere devoid of emotion, like the Bonsais grown in a shallow pot.

To be fair, these tests can identify a negative approach that might be counterproductive, and they can show to what degree factual content is likely to be recalled, but they do not measure the intangible, emotional response that builds brands over the long haul. It is the left side demanding left-side answers to right-side subject matter.

One day I was walking along in Rockefeller Center when an attractive NBC staffer asked me to take part in a test. I was ushered into a small theater and my wrists were wired to measure pulse rate changes. Afterward, I filled out a questionnaire. This procedure was being used to predict the appeal of a pilot for an upcoming series, which, as I recall, was something about a creature who lived in a swamp. These methods seem to me as fruitless as the comically failed attempts of early investors to build a flying machine. Of course, you might argue that we now travel in jets, so anything is possible. So it is, but then aviation is a science. Flight of the spirit is another matter. Maybe science will someday enter the creative side of the advertising business to measure the emotions that lead to persuasion, but, in my opinion, it hasn't yet.

Ready-made research is a security blanket for left-side thinkers who

demand statistical logic in a field where imagination must soar. To overtake brand leaders with superior resources, intuition must take the helm.
The people you employ to create breakthrough material must be encouraged to do so, rather than handed their heads after flunking a recall test.
As Lou Hagopian, chairman of N. W. Ayer, said a few years ago,
"Advertising people must be free of fear in order to take risks. New ideas,
different ideas, the kind that make interesting and effective campaigns,
always involve taking risks."[2]

In 1985, John O'Toole, a former copywriter and chairman of Foote,
Cone & Belding, contrasted intuition with scientific plodding in an eloquent address to fellow advertising executives. He noted that the ancient
Polynesians used no navigational instruments. They traveled the sea for
days and nights when clouds obscured the sun and stars. "They encountered unpredictable wind changes and powerful currents," he said. "But,
these neither discouraged them nor prevented them from reaching their
destinations. We need all the compasses, sextants and charts we can lay
hands on for accumulating information, for assembling media plans, and
for developing objectives and strategies. But, from that point on, like it or
not, we have to turn the helm over to the Polynesians if we are to exploit
the enormous potential of advertising."[3]

Most major advertisers navigate by recall tests rather than by Polynesians. DART (Day-after-recall-test) questions people by telephone. To
assemble a sample, researchers screen people to be sure they have viewed
the test commercial the previous day. The interviewer finds out what
consumers remember about the spot, how well the brand name registered,
and whether the strategic copy point came through. Rather than measuring
recall, the test measures the ability of the viewer to *articulate* what can be
remembered. Sometimes DART tests are the only tool agencies use—
which means they may be shortchanging their clients. In his book *What's
in a Name?* John Philip Jones claims that recall testing "discriminates in
favor of explicit copy which communicates concrete, product related
benefits," and against implicit copy, "which communicates less tangible
or more psychological benefits."[4] Recall testing helps perpetuate dull,
inane slice-of-life commercials. It favors irritating formula messages in
which the brand name is mentioned thirteen times (the first time no later
than the first five seconds). Jones continues:

> The question that immediately suggests itself is why ready-made
> research techniques, in particular recall testing, are so widely and
> apparently uncritically employed by many demonstrably successful
> manufacturing companies as a quality control over their advertising.
> Perhaps these advertisers have learned special and sensitive ways
> of interpreting such scores. Perhaps they are attracted by the very
> simplicity of the findings, a refreshing change in an increasingly
> complicated world. Perhaps they do not ask themselves what the
> scores really mean, but accept them in blind faith as prompts to
> action: go or no-go.[5]

Most package goods brands are parity products. The *perception of added value* is often the distinguishing difference. What makes this difference is a composite impression of quality built over time. To the consumer, the purchase of a 6.4-ounce tube of Crest toothpaste or an 11-ounce can of Old Spice shaving cream is a low-involvement decision. No down payment is required, no mortgage is needed. These low-cost, everyday products are selected on impulse when supply is low. Impulse sales are a reflex action resulting from unaided brand awareness.

High Energy Moves the Brand

Because the creation of brand awareness, and desire for the particular product, is a long-term building process, it seems meaningless to devote so many resources to finitely measuring the playback power of a specific commercial. The hill to be assaulted by advertising is the awareness curve, the bayonet is the product point of difference, and the troops used are a series of commercials, dressed with some uniformity, and deployed over a long period of time. Some of these "soldiers" have exceptional emotional energy, like marching raisins or Levi's impromptu vignettes for 501 jeans, which broke new ground while beating category competitors for top efficiency in cost per 1,000 "retained impressions" during 1987.[6] By making the product the focus of attention, these TV "troops" capture imagination—a strategic victory—clearing the way for a fast and cheap assault on *awareness*.

Getting someone to try the product is half the battle. If he does so and likes it, the brand has probably recruited a loyal customer (unless another product with equal appeal offers a better price the next time around). Use leads to satisfaction, confidence, familiarity, and repeat purchases. Because category leaders have "trial" going for them, it takes extraordinary, high-energy commercials for second-tier brands to gain share. Commercials produced to formula, or calculated to beat the DART test, won't do it. It takes advertising with enormous energy calculated to generate publicity and word of mouth about the product and its distinctive difference. A playback analysis of a specific commercial will not identify the "soldier" with exceptional energy. It does not measure the emotion that contributes to a brand's added value. It provides no strategic direction.

Choose Your Risk

Advertisers today can't afford to fall into the "me too" trap fostered by exhaustive testing. To make the bucks go farther, the advertiser should ask for advertising that stands out in the product category like a black sheep in a snowy white herd. My partner, Mike Hughes, recently made a persuasive case for risk-taking advertising in *Pencil Pointers,* the newsletter published by New York's One Club. Talking to fellow art and copy people about the Bernbach heritage of wild, witty, and entertaining advertising born thirty years ago, Mike said, "Then, as now, the toughest job in advertising isn't writing it, art directing it or presenting it: the toughest job is approving it. So the people at Ohrbach's, Levy's, El Al and Volkswagen must have had reservations about approving work like this. They must have discussed the risks involved.

"The risks, back then, were real. After all, these ad managers were entering new marketing frontiers.

"They stuck their necks out, and they were rewarded for it. This strange and wonderful advertising actually worked. Sales soared and brands were established. In fact, a strong case can be made that brands were established more forcefully and more economically than ever before.

"A number of us in the creative business today learned our trade by studying Doyle Dane Bernbach ads. Of course, we work hard to be fresh and different, but we have to acknowledge that most of the time we want to be fresh and different in the same way Doyle Dane was fresh and different.

"We still expect our work to be simple, direct, imaginative, honest, witty and entertaining. Just like those guys did.

"We still expect to win both gold pencils and new accounts when we successfully create ads in the Doyle Dane Bernbach mold.

"That's all well and good.

"But then we make a mistake. We follow the DDB trailblazers one step too far. We tell our clients that to run work like this takes guts. We say that they have to be willing to take risks if they're going to reap the rewards of great creative advertising. We imply, and sometimes even say, that the greater the creative work, the greater the risks.

"And that's crazy. It's even harmful to our business.

"There *are* risks involved in any business endeavor. Just as the most skilled surgeons sometimes lose patients, the most skilled ad-makers sometimes create campaigns that aren't as successful as they should be. Only a fool would guarantee success with every campaign. In fact, in the real world, it's usually impossible to pin success or failure on any one factor, whether it's advertising, distribution, product quality, pricing or anything else.

"But when we pass out dire warnings to our clients, we're not acknowledging this generic risk. Instead we're saying that award-winning advertising is riskier than other kinds of advertising.

"That's simply not so. The safe thing to do is contemporary, award-winning advertising.

"In the process of developing their work, writers and art directors should take risks. They shouldn't be afraid to fall. They should reach and stretch and explore new ideas. And through that process—and through a lot of hard work—they should develop outstanding advertising.

"That advertising works better than any other kind. We can prove it. In fact, it would be wasteful, and maybe even risky, to run anything else."[7]

Logic Doesn't Leverage

Sophisticated customers are not the problem. Young artists and writers understand them better than most people do because they think constantly about how best to commune with them. That's the creative team's job. The conflict between agency and client comes when all this right-side thinking from the creative department confronts the left-side logic of company managers. People close to the product are used to solving real-world problems. They are loaded down with engineering and production and sales considerations. They look at a piece of foolishness in an ad layout and wonder what the hell is going on. They seldom sit around communing with the minds of consumers. They're worried about next quarter's earnings. The agency worries about getting ads noticed.

Smart clients understand that these creative loonies are a tremendous resource and harness their creative energy to the product's advantage. They see to it that the ad has a point, underscores advantages, and isn't so ludicrous as to invite ridicule or lawsuits. After that comes risk that can jump a brand in category share.

Sum & Substance

Skepticism is a given in a relationship that joins successful, left-thinking clients with highly creative, right-side-of-the-brain advertising agencies. The more startling the idea the greater the suspicion that it won't do the job. An idea breaks old molds and shakes new trees. It is, by definition, a hazy perception, a vague impression, a fanciful notion. Will this fanciful notion actually work? That is the question. So research is conducted to find out. But research can't actually do that. It can tell what might backfire—but not whether the notion will strike the public fancy.

A fresh idea threatens the comfort of previously assimilated experience. And when something threatens, it is often killed. That's the fundamental law of survival at work. A number of years ago, a house ad for the J. Walter Thompson agency eloquently took note of this. It was entitled "Death of an Idea."[8] Here is what the ad said:

> It's so easy to say no to it.
> It's so understandable to want to fix it and make it more conventional and familiar.
> It's so reassuring to take the alarming part out of it and smooth the rough edges. And sandpaper it to death.

Oscar Wilde put it this way: An idea that isn't dangerous is hardly worth calling an idea at all.

It's the shocking part, the unknown element that makes an idea an idea in the first place. If you feel comfortable with it from the very first, take another look.

It's probably not an idea.

Most business decisions are made after studying a set of quantitative facts. These facts lead to rational conclusions. Advertising, on the other hand, is the odd ball that defies quantitative analysis in advance. It is a subtle and mystifying force that can be sandpapered into sameness and dullness by excessive testing and second guessing and a desperate attempt to be scientific. By attempting to reduce risk, clients and agencies risk running advertising that will be ignored—and with high awareness essential to the brand's future, that's the greatest risk of all.

· 13 ·

Benefit Testing

"We, over and over again, stress this so-called inherent drama of things because there is usually something there, almost always something there, if you can find the thing about that product that keeps it in the marketplace."

—Leo Burnett, founder, Leo Burnett Company, Inc.

We endured several nights on the road holding meetings in isolated motel dining rooms located deep in the nation's farm belt. It was a frustrating experience. We were here to conduct copy-test sessions for Modown, a herbicide made by our client Mobil Chemical. We had recruited farmers by telephone, using leads from salesmen. This was the third and final session, and we hoped it would go better than the others had. Dinner was over, the dishes were cleared, and the time had come to show the farmers ads and ask for their reactions.

A trained moderator showed the farmers several advertising layouts and read the copy. These were ads for four possible Modown campaigns. It was like a focus group, except that the session was held in one corner of the Holiday Inn dining room instead of a special interviewing room with a one-way mirror.

Suddenly, the farmers stopped being experts on crops and crop chemicals and became advertising critics. Rather than reacting to the substance of our advertising arguments, they began to challenge the copy and layouts in terms of style. They liked the illustration in one ad, but hated the copy. They liked the copy in another, but suggested using an illustration from a different ad. It was a mess. If we were to believe what they had to say, it would be impossible to please them.

The standard method of testing print copy is a portfolio test. In this, respondents are shown a book full of ads, each of which has been tested previously. The new ad you want to test for recall is included and measured against other known performers. We had opted for a focus group setting, in this instance, because rather than recall, we wanted to probe for reactions that would lead us to the most effective appeal. It didn't work. Obviously, we had to rethink our methods.

How to Find the Value Point

We wanted a systematic way to find out what people thought about the product and its alternative appeals *before* ads were prepared. Harry Jacobs took on the assignment of finding a way to do this. We wanted to guide creative thinking rather than stifle it. We knew that if copywriters and art directors developed a technique for their own use it would be embraced, whereas something handed them by the research department would not be. What came back was the test we use to pinpoint the product's most meaningful value point. This method is somewhat more sophisticated than Kennedy conducting copy research from his park bench, or Hopkins talking over ideas with his neighbors, but no more complicated.

It is an effective way of getting target customers to focus on the product and its use, not on advertising executions. The customers identify the brand's *dominant value point* without realizing they are doing it.

In benefit (value point) testing, each appeal is isolated, illustrated, and summed up by a phrase. Display boards are prepared to hold the attention of participants and to keep their thoughts focused on that particular selling idea. A paragraph of text is read by the moderator to amplify the concept.

When it comes to dreaming up possible selling attributes to test, everyone gets into the act: the account executive, advertising managers, salesmen, client CEOs, marketing directors, copywriters, art directors. After reviewing product specifications, studying market research data, listening to salesmen, and talking to distributors, retailers and customers, everyone concerned has a pet theory about the best way to sell the product. The consumer is the final arbiter. His or her emotional response to the product's appeal is what counts.

Without benefit testing, the agency uses its own best judgment or follows the client's lead and proceeds directly to campaign development. Either guess could be wrong. If it is, the campaign would either run without further testing and be a waste of money, or be killed by after-the-fact testing. With benefit testing, we at least know the approach is right before it is read, seen, or heard. The findings lead straight to a copy platform and competitive selling position. This, then, is the basis for work created from the customer's point of view. Ads dramatize what the customer takes away from the product rather than what the manufacturer puts into it.

As we did with the Modown copy test, we called typical consumers and invited them to attend a meeting. Usually we group consumers by age and other demographic characteristics to match the defined target audience. When possible, sessions are held in a conference room with a one-way mirror at one end. Behind the glass, agency and client representatives observe the discussion without being seen. This also leaves them free to make comments without being overheard. When I first saw this type of setup, I thought a privacy mirror was needed to keep the onlookers from inhibiting the participants. Actually, people couldn't care less about having an audience once a benefit board is introduced. They are soon caught up in the subject at hand and become lost in conversation among themselves. Once a Holiday Inn housekeeper burst into the meeting room with her vacuum cleaner going full blast. The group didn't miss a beat. Nothing stops them once they begin.

We like to videotape each session and edit it later to highlight the findings. The scenes of customers discussing the product and its various appeals make compelling viewing for salesmen at sales meetings. It also brings findings to life for decision makers who couldn't fly to Duluth or St. Louis or Los Angeles to view the live performance. Customers, rather than the client or the agency, select the appeals to use in the advertising. It is devastating to see a customer blast away your pet idea. Often, an approach that you felt instinctively would be a winner is blown away. I've had them laughed off the table or simply disbelieved.

Obviously, this is diagnostic, qualitative research, not meant to be projected to the audience universe. However, a pattern soon begins to take shape. The conclusions are usually consistent from group to group regardless of geographic location. We have found that women in London react very much the same as women do in Chicago or Washington. Bankers in New York are not unlike their brethren in Atlanta. Farmers in the delta are akin to their counterparts in California. Teenagers in Baltimore see things the way teenagers do in Greenville, South Carolina. There may be slight differences owing to regional variations in traditions and lifestyles, but the clear winner in our covey of campaign candidates usually emerges. Sometimes, however, the "winner" is a combination of ideas expressed on two or three boards. Secondary appeals can be identified. Copy points can be ranked in order of importance.

New Value-Added Products

The technique often identifies new product possibilities in addition to providing advertising direction. For a bank client, Signet, we found that customers react with considerable emotion to overdraft charges. Bounced checks are a major source of irritation. We used this knowledge to woo checking account customers away from competitors. Our client adopted the policy of calling customers to advise them of overdrafts, providing the customer signed up for the service ahead of time. The advertising dramatized this service by showing an astronaut getting a call from his banker while in orbit. "A phone call instead of a bounced check" became a unique value-added service in an otherwise parity situation. Our client met its six-month goal for new checking account customers in four weeks.

The findings sometimes suggest an entirely new marketing direction.

Lane Cedar Chests

For Lane Cedar Chests, benefit testing was one element in a major research project that led to repositioning the brand. For sixty years, Lane chests had been marketed as a high school graduation gift. The idea had always been for the young girl graduate to have a bridal chest where she could store cherished keepsakes until she married. For years, so the scenario went, she opened her Lane chest lovingly to lock away letters, fine linen, and lace. Lane was marketed as a hope chest, a sweetheart chest, a love chest, and these allusions to romance and romantic expectations worked for generations.

This was not a new idea dreamed up by Edward Lane in 1912. Romance had been associated with cedar-lined chests since the time of the ancient Egyptians. In Europe, during the Middle Ages, a new bride carried her trousseau chest with her when she went to join her husband. Wealthy families commissioned artists, some as renowned as Leonardo, to decorate bridal chests and turn them into lavish works of art.

In America, the Lane Cedar Chest became one of our most enduring and best-known brands; to have one was a deeply rooted tradition in many families. This was clear from benefit testing as well as from extensive, quantitative research. However, times change. Many women now go to college and pursue careers rather than early marriage. They have very little interest in a bridal chest until they graduate from college, and even then practicality seems to go hand in hand with any ancient ideas about love and marriage. When they find themselves out in the world working at a new career and living in a cramped apartment, young women become very interested in storage space. A chest is a handy piece of furniture in which to store blankets and bed linens out of sight when closet space is limited.

Benefit testing showed us how practical and ultilitarian most women are with regard to purchasing a cedar chest. Although emotional feelings about bridal chests are there below the surface, we found that young women, together with their mothers and grandmothers, were intrigued to learn how many different styles are now made in addition to the typical bedroom chest. This told us that there was expanded market for attractive storage furniture for use in other parts of the house. As for timing, high school is out. College graduation, the first apartment, or the time of marriage are in. This has implications for media selection as well as copy approach.

A number of boards were used in the test. Group sessions were held in two cities, one a major northern market, the other a small city in the South. We invited women in two age categories: 18 to 24 and 35 to 54. While tradition was less of a factor in the North, it proved a strong consideration in the South.

Here, in bold typeface, is the statement that was shown to respondents along with a visual of a chest loaded with typical trousseau items. The text was not shown, but was read by the moderator to stimulate thought and discussion. This particular board dealt with tradition.

IT'S NOT JUST A VERY NICE GIFT, IT'S A TRADITION.

It's a tradition with hundreds of thousands of American families. A young girl reaches a special time in her life—her graduation, perhaps, or her wedding—and she's given a Lane cedar chest. It's something she'll keep her most important keepsakes in for the rest of her life. Just like her mother did.

Shown here are some typical reactions. In the North, older women, the most probable gift givers, were likely to respond as the following two women did:

Boards like this with a key phrase are shown to people seated at a table in a typical focus group setting. The illustration is an important element. People pick up on things shown or pick them apart. You learn what's important and what isn't.

It's not just
a very nice gift.
It's a tradition.

"I object to that because the world my daughter is
growing up in and the world I grew up in are
diametrically opposed. It's too soppy sweet."

"I don't think it appeals to young ladies. When they
see tradition, it doesn't mean anything. It brings
back the old hope chest idea, and hopefully girls are
beyond that. They're thinking about going to
college."

However, the young women sampled in both cities disagreed with
these assessments. Typical responses by those who lived in the North
were:

"I like that idea. Neither my grandmother nor my
mother had the tradition, but it would be a tradition I
would have the opportunity to start. If my mother
saw that, she would be inclined to go out and buy it
for me as a wedding gift. It is something I could
keep and remember."

"I think it would be a very good tradition to start."

"I would ask for it to start the tradition or I would
give one to my mother."

And in the South:

"I like that. That's the meaning of the hope chest—
the tradition."

"There's the daughter, the mother, and the
grandmother. That's the way it should be."

When the groups were asked to react to a concept that stressed the
idea of a cedar chest as a *hope* chest, the results were generally negative.
Here's how the trial copy went:

**A LANE CEDAR CHEST HOLDS MORE THAN JUST KEEPSAKES.
IT HOLDS HOPES AND DREAMS.**

*In her Lane cedar chest, she'll keep the things she plans to use in her own home
one day. Her secrets are here. And her start on the future. In fact, contemporary
young women across America see the things in their Lane cedar chests as
their first steps toward lives of their own.*

The results quickly showed which way the wind was blowing:

"I think it's dumb."

"I'd never buy one for that use."

"I would like to see young girls get back to this tradition, but I don't see that happening."

"My oldest daughter is 21 and when she graduated from high school, I suggested she choose her silver, crystal, and china patterns for her hope chest. She thought I was crazy."

Next, we tested the "tried and true approach" of the cedar chest as a romantic gift—with disillusioning results. The trial copy headline read:

HOW DID SUCH A PRACTICAL PIECE OF FURNITURE EVER BECOME SUCH A ROMANTIC GIFT?

Here the reactions ranged from "I would rather receive a piece of jewelry," to "My husband better not dare go and buy me one of those without me being there to pick it out!"

In today's world, we were forced to realize, furniture isn't romantic, although tradition and sentimentality continue to be appropriate, underlying appeals. We used about a dozen different benefit boards in this test. After sorting out the varied reactions from the disparate groups tested, we prepared advertising that retained romantic echoes while linking tradition with the practical needs of today. The television commercial was filmed in rich color suffused by misty values. The scene is set in an apartment. A young woman is surprised by delivery men bringing her a cedar chest, to which a note is attached. The opening frames show the mother writing this note to her daughter, and the narration is the mother's voice as the daughter reads.

From the day you were born everyone said you were just like me. It's hard to believe my headstrong little girl is now a woman. I wanted to give you something useful, since we're both so practical. So this Lane cedar chest will hold your sweaters and blankets, but it will also hold your memories. Because not many people know it, but you and I are two of the most sentimental people on earth.

Announcer: "Lane Cedar Chests. The graduation present she'll be opening the rest of her life.

This magazine ad supported television in linking the idea of tradition with practical needs. This was the first in a series to reposition the cedar chest as a gift appropriate for the young woman about to go off on her own.

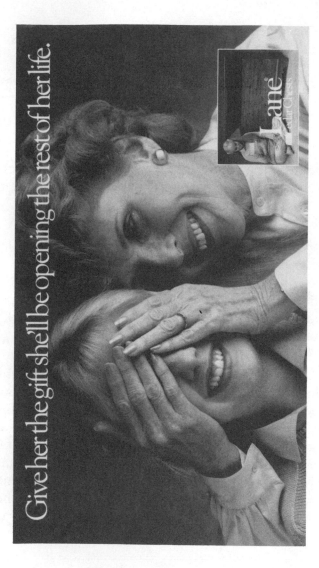

Give her the gift she'll be opening the rest of her life.

Maserati

For our client Maserati Automobiles, we recently conducted benefit testing sessions with consumers in Miami, Chicago, and Richmond. These gave us a reading on prevailing perceptions of a brand that has very little market penetration but extremely high awareness with the segment of the American public most likely to buy a luxury automobile. We learned that the Maserati is well known from its past exploits in racing competitions. Its mystique is one of high fashion and extreme opulence. Most people put it in the company of the Ferrari and Lamborghini, in the ultraluxurious, exotic class where cars are priced from $70,000 to $175,000. For the American market, however, the Maserati models marketed are in the $40,000 to $55,000 range. This is the category dominated by Mercedes, BMW, and Jaguar.

From the benefit sessions, we found that our job is to capitalize on the perception people have of Maserati's high quality, but slowly to decompress those notions down to a realization of its actual price level. People must understand Maserati's affordable reality. We know that if customers test drive a Maserati, they're likely to buy it. Our advertising therefore needs to get people in to the showrooms. The primary target is SRI International's Value And Lifestyles (VALS) "inner directed" segment: those who seek direct experience, are socially aware and, therefore, likely to be turned on by a car that is sporty, prestigious, sexy, fun—and of the highest quality.

These are the people we talked to. We showed them thirteen Benefit boards with statements ranging from "You think it's a temperamental, $150,000 race car, don't you? You're in for a surprise" to "Believe it or not, for less than $55,000 you can own one of the greatest cars in the world." We found we had to focus on price but to do it in a way that did not cheapen the marque. The advertising had to be subtle enough to dispel consumer misperceptions while at the same time preserving the product's mystique. Prospects want to feel daring, distinctive, even unique. But not ostentatious, wild, or crazy. They agree, "You only live once. Do it in a Maserati!"

The outcome of this drama has yet to be written. The advertising is just getting under way. But you can see the diagnostic value of benefit testing interviews. Instead of relying on hunches and preconceived ideas, we can address the challenge on the basis of a thorough understanding of the mind of the target consumer. We can do advertising that will precisely match up the product's dominant value point with the dominant interests and desires of potential customers.

Focused Groups

Focus groups are fine, but usually they ramble on in an unfocused way and are often nonspecific. Focus sessions in which the thoughts of subjects are directed to various concepts, as in the sessions described in this chapter, give ad creators specific input. It should be standard procedure to conduct them before starting work on any major advertising campaign. Because no matter how close you are to your market, I guarantee you, you do not know all the answers in advance.

AMMO Ammunition

To take this subject full circle, let's go back to the farm belt for another client, FMC Crop Chemicals, and see how farmers reacted to benefit testing. The product at issue was a revolutionary new insecticide called AMMO. It kills a broad spectrum of insects that feed on cotton plants. The temptation was to say something like, "Introducing AMMO, the revolutionary product that increases yields by killing 16 cotton pests you dread most."

If we had done that, however, our ad would have looked very much like the one our competitor came up with:

Introducing CYMBUSH
There's never been a cotton insecticide like this.
THE ULTIMATE HAS ARRIVED

We showed a benefit board like that to cotton farmers. They laughed. One said, "That sounds like Madison Avenue." Another said, "It sounds like you're selling pantyhose."

Extensive field tests of the product had been done before the government approved it for general use. The farmers who had used the product on test acres had been impressed with the results and they were willing to endorse it in testimonials. How would other farmers react? "Farmers will say anything if you pay them enough," one panelist said skeptically. "I'll believe my neighbor, but that's it," another volunteered. "Put my neighbor in your ad and I'll believe it." Look through the pages of agricultural magazines. You'll find page after page of ads with testimonials. I shudder at the misguided efforts of my colleagues in other agencies. A simple benefit test will save clients from wasting their dollars in this way.

We also knew that the product would increase yields. Field tests had proved this. But again the farmers laughed. "If we believed what chemical companies tell us about better yields, we wouldn't need any seed." Another pointed out: "Too much can go wrong. The weather for one thing. You *guarantee* yields and I'll buy it."

We tested about twelve possible positions with seven different groups in various parts of the country. The results were always the same. They all liked a position that showed how AMMO was superior to all other products they had used. They translated this into an economic benefit,

As in the Lane example, print was a visual mirror of the television, used to drive home the idea that AMMO renders last year's product obsolete.

because the more bugs an insecticide kills, the fewer "passes" a farmer has to take across his field with costly chemicals.

The television commercial showed competitive cans falling one at a time, in slow motion. They came crashing down like trees in a forest. AMMO was left standing. The print ad was a four-color spread showing seven competitive cans on their sides, with AMMO looming above them. The theme line: "AMMO. It takes care of 16 cotton pests and 7 of ours."

AMMO was introduced four months after the competing CYMBUSH, which was essentially the same chemical. The goal was a 40 percent market share, and media were scheduled on a share of voice basis that made it possible to produce sales at that level (see Chapter 16). Even so, our competitor outspent us, backing its "big brag" campaign, which benefit testing had told us was doubtful. The results: AMMO got a 44 percent share compared to only 36 percent for CYMBUSH.

Sum & Substance

Benefit testing presents a clear picture of what matters most to consumers. It takes the guesswork out of advertising and makes it possible to avoid false starts and failed directions. Key selling points are identified and ranked in order of importance. Some become the strategic sales position and, thus, the primary thrust of the ad. Others are recognized as secondary, but can nevertheless play an important role in the copy. It is a technique that marries the left and right sides of the brain; it makes those dominated by the left comfortable with what the right-siders come up with. It separates the triangles from the squares. It, or something like it, should be used to find the key selling approach for every major campaign before the ads are started.

Benefit testing offers one final bonus to all who work with freewheeling right-siders. It puts up a loose fence that serves to keep writer/art director teams from meandering off onto byways far from the main road leading to the product's strategic selling position.

·14·

Human Drama

It is the artist's job to accomplish at least two things—to stir the emotions of the viewer and to lay bare the soul of his subject.

—Yousuf Karsh, photographer

The ultimate objective of all advertising—and the only reason why 150,000 people are employed in the advertising agency business—is to put a convincing selling message in front of the target consumer so he or she will want to buy the product.

Ideally, you would like the consumer to see the spot, or read the ad, and drop everything, rush out to the store, pick up the phone, clip the coupon, or do whatever it takes to acquire what you have to sell. That instant! Thanks to the brilliance of your persuasive message. Sometimes that happens. More often, a sale results because your ad came along just when the consumer happened to be in the market for that particular item.

The consumer's decision to buy something moves ponderously through several stages: from the first glimmer of awareness of the need, to heightened interest, to conscious desire, and finally to action.

Your creative selling message must build awareness of the brand and of its special advantages over a period of time. It must sustain this awareness so that the brand will be remembered when the need-bug bites. Your selling argument must be there as a last-minute reminder on the page or the tube (or inside the consumer's head) to shift the consumer's need to a specific desire for *your* item.

Persuasive advertising helps move the mind from interest to desire, but first it must be provocative enough to command attention. This isn't difficult on television, the intrusive medium, providing you've intrigued the audience into watching. But print is another matter. A clever and appropriate headline will do it. Unusual graphics, of course. Sometimes the creative team wants to overpower the reader with size. It asks for spreads, color, or multiple page units to give the message intrusive power.

This is when a choice must be made by media planners and account managers. Can the budget handle big space, color, or multiple exposures? Can the advertising appear often enough to guarantee exposure at the critical moment when the sale is about to be made? Would it be better to opt for smaller units and greater frequency? Overwhelming impact may well make the difference, but sometimes a compelling creative idea must be shelved, or adapted to a smaller format, so that a media plan can deliver both impact and long-term repetition.

Creative Leverage

If your advertisement is persuasive and delivered with drama, the sale is likely to take place, but not in great amounts after a consumer's single exposure to the selling message. As you will see in the next chapter, advertising is most effective after the consumer has seen your offer, in one form or another, at least twice and usually at least three times during the period between product purchase and repurchase. But before we discuss *how many,* let's talk about *how* to make your advertising so persuasive that fewer impressions will be needed to sustain memory until it is time to buy. That's what we call *creative leverage.* Advertising agencies specializing in creative leverage are the fastest growing in the country today. Advertisers seek it to offset escalating media costs. An ad that jumps out and lodges in the mind bridges the gap between selling impressions to make fewer insertions necessary.

How can this be done? The commercials the public likes best are not as flat-out persuasive as those originating in local markets that pound away on behalf of retailers and auto dealers. They do not ask you to order, or to telephone, or to drive somewhere "before it's too late." They are "softer," and heavy on entertainment value. Any suggestion that the viewer or reader should take some kind of action is usually left to the imagination. The ten favorite television commercials of 1987,[1] selected by the viewers themselves, were heavy on entertainment and light on direct salesmanship. Perhaps you remember them:

	TV Spending ($ million)	Subject
1. California Raisins	$ 5.4	Claymation
2. Bud Light	51.9	Spuds Mackenzie
3. Pepsi/Diet Pepsi	90.1	Michael Jackson
4. Miller Lite	79.8	Jocks
5. McDonald's	344.1	Mac Tonight
6. Bartles & Jaymes	33.4	Frank & Ed
7. Coca-Cola	39.9	Max Headroom
8. Isuzu	34.1	"Liar" Joe Isuzu
9. DuPont Stainmaster Carpet	22.8	Sloppy kids
10. Domino's Pizza	41.0	The pizza "Noid"

By sending awareness up into the stratosphere, these commercials are successful without hitting the consumer over the head. The California Raisins spots are especially so considering the small budget that put them before the American public. In popularity, the dancing animated clay raisins ranked alongside previous classics like Wendy's "Where's the Beef?" and Coke's "Mean Joe Greene" spot (which, you may remember, showed the touching encounter between the football star and a young boy outside a locker room).

Beguile (as in Charm or Delight)

If the advertising is effectively prepared, there should be no doubt in viewers' minds that you want them to buy the product (or idea) being presented. This desired action can be implicitly stated; the "call to action" does not have to be articulated in an obvious way. The public is sophisticated. The clever rascals grew up with advertising. What cannot be obscure is the benefit, whether it is psychological or real. The consumer should leave the ad at hand with a clear understanding of the product's advantage over other brands in the category. The message must be *specifically relevant to the beholder*. Assuming the brand's *dominant value point* is desired, felt to be unique in some way, and remembered, the viewer or reader can be trusted to decide for himself when or where to buy and to act accordingly.

Not to ask for the order, not to urge a specific action to take place, is somewhat contrary to what I was taught. My early mentors insisted that every advertisement must have the following ingredients: (Get) Attention, Promise (something), Rationalize (the promise), Ask (for the order). Sometimes this is hard to do on television in 15 seconds; and in longer spots, a hard sell at the end often interferes with the tone and mood of what has gone before. You want positive images of the brand left lingering in the mind. The A-P-R-A formula was concocted from what was learned through trial and error in print advertising back when copy was king, and titans like Claude Hopkins and mail order writer John Caples[2] occupied the throne. It is still very much the rule in direct response, and it is appropriate in print.

New research suggests that commercials incorporating a psychological appeal along with a practical benefit statement work best. Stuart Agres of Lowe Marshalk found this out through a double-blind test using independent researchers. First, ASI Market Research analyzed 168 commercials in terms of consumer recall and persuasion. Then, without knowing how they performed, Russell Belk, a research expert at the University of Utah, separated them into two groups. One group of spots used only a rational approach. The other group combined both psychological and rational benefits. Commercials that combined rational and emotional benefits scored best. Those commercials with a subtle emotional appeal combined with a practical benefits approach did even better. Apparently, when it comes to recall and persuasion, it takes two to tango. "A commercial should address product benefits such as 'Our detergent gets clothes whiter and softer,' as well as psychological benefits such as 'Our detergent will boost your esteem in the eyes of your mother-in-law,' " Agres observed.

Another key finding of the Lowe Marschalk study is that, in today's world, an implied appeal works harder than a psychological benefit flatly stated. "What this shows," said Agres, "is that emotional ads have to be done right if they're going to be effective. A subtle approach works better because it has a chance to get past the consumers' natural barrier of skepticism."[3]

Prime Movers

Emotion works in television. What about print? A 1981 study of 142 insurance ads with the highest or lowest Starch readership scores demonstrates that basic human needs and interests—the prime movers in human behavior—are also the basic motivators in what people read. Advertisements with high "read most" scores were found to have three characteristics in common. They all contained (1) something new and fresh; (2) something of self-interest to the reader; and (3) something with human drama ("a presentation of the vital needs, problems, benefits, and solutions through the vehicle of the actions, attitudes and behavior of people. . . .").[4]

While these findings are new, knowledge of the value of using a psychological appeal in advertising is not. The case for directing advertising to human needs and desires was forcefully made in 1925 in the textbook *Psychology in Advertising* by Albert T. Poffenberger, Ph.D., a professor at Columbia University.

The other day I found this rare Poffenberger volume in the library of the American Association of Advertising Agencies (AAAA). I had been looking for a copy ever since I first learned of its value while working on a college term paper. Interestingly enough, I discovered from an inscription on the flyleaf, it was given to the AAAA by the late James Webb Young in 1954, two years after I graduated. Young himself influenced the advertising business with concepts and ideas over a fifty-year career, most of it spent with J. Walter Thompson. These are still referenced. He wrote several books of his own. In one of them he said, "[A]dvertising . . . is all about people. And about how to use words and pictures to persuade people to do things, *feel* things, and believe things. Wonderful, mad, rational and irrational people. About their wants, their hopes, their tastes, their fancies, their secret yearnings, their customs and taboos."[5]

Poffenberger's empirically documented text inventoried the relative strength of motives. Given the fixed nature of human desires, this handy checklist is well worth recapturing and presenting here. It is based on a study of seventy-four men and women conducted by Daniel Starch. Respondents were asked to rate motives on a scale of 0 to 10. The results are shown in Table 14-1.

Poffenberger also presented the findings of a study conducted by H. L. Hollingworth that measured the persuasive strength of fifty appeals presented in the form of advertising copy. Forty persons—twenty men and twenty women—served as subjects in this experiment. Each was asked to read the copy and then to arrange the cards on which the advertising appeared "in an order of merit, according to their *persuasiveness*, that is, according to the degree in which they make you *desire* the article or *convince* you of its merit."

Nine years later, H. F. Adams, making use of the exact same material and instructions, repeated the Hollingworth experiment with forty men and twenty women. The combined results of the two experiments are shown in Table 14-2, where 12 represents the weakest appeal and 1 the strongest.

Human desires are woven into our basic natures. They do not change

Table 14-1. The Relative Strength of Motives

Motive	*Value*	*Motive*	*Value*
Appetite—hunger	9.2	Respect for Deity	7.1
Love of offspring	9.1	Sympathy for others	7.0
Health	9.0	Protection of others	7.0
Sex attraction	8.9	Domesticity	7.0
Parental affection	8.9	Social distinction	6.9
Ambition	8.6	Devotion to others	6.8
Pleasure	8.6	Hospitality	6.6
Bodily comfort	8.4	Warmth	6.5
Possession	8.4	Imitation	6.5
Approval by others	8.0	Courtesy	6.5
Gregariousness	7.9	Play—sport	6.5
Taste	7.8	Managing others	6.4
Personal appearance	7.8	Coolness	6.2
Safety	7.8	Fear—caution	6.2
Cleanliness	7.7	Physical activity	6.0
Rest—sleep	7.7	Manipulation	6.0
Home comfort	7.5	Construction	6.0
Economy	7.5	Style	5.8
Curiosity	7.5	Humor	5.8
Efficiency	7.3	Amusement	5.8
Competition	7.3	Shyness	4.2
Cooperation	7.1	Teasing	2.6

Source: Albert T. Poffenberger, *Psychology in Advertising* (London: A. W. Shaw & Company, Ltd., 1925), p. 85.

Table 14-2. The Relative Strength of Appeals

Appeal	Order	Appeal	Order
Appetite	1	Recommendation	7
Family affection	2	Activity—sport	8
Protection	3	Conformity—fashion	9
Sympathy	4	Superiority—ambition	10
Health	5	Group spirit	11
Economy	6	Beauty and attractiveness	12

Source: Albert T. Poffenberger, *Psychology in Advertising* (London: A. W. Shaw & Company, Ltd., 1925), p. 88.

with lifestyles or external environmental stimuli. The late Bill Bernbach put it this way.

> There may be changes in our society. But learning about those changes is not the answer. For you are not appealing to society. You are appealing to individuals, each with his own ego, each with the dignity of his own being, each like no one else in the world, each a separate miracle. The societal appeals are merely fashionable, current, cultural appeals which make nice garments for the real motivations that stem from the unchanging instincts, and emotions of people—from nature's indomitable programming in their genes. It is unchanging man that is the proper study of the communicator.[6]

We will always have a desire for food and drink, for rest and comfort and security, for a sense of self-worth or social acclaim, for independence, power, success. Parental feelings will always run strong: the desire to nurture, protect, and provide. Human nature is a constant. It's dependable. We were born with our four instincts: fear (self-preservation), hunger (for food and drink), sex (love), rage (anger). People have five senses: sight, touch, smell, hearing, and taste. The instincts and senses are often a starting point for advertising appeals. They are easy to fall back on. Of course, they aren't always used; sometimes they play merely a small role in copy, like a dash of Accent on a steak.

Dramatic Moments

Each advertising campaign must present a series of dramatic moments that cleverly appeal to our expectations as well as clearly define the practical benefits we can expect to get from using the product. The *dramatic moment* is the end result, the essential result of all the consumer interviews, benefit testing, strategy statements, product evaluations, and position statements that have preceded it. Your ad should never go out without it.

"Give me an example of a dramatic moment," you ask.

"Remember Volkswagen's 'Lemon' ad?" I reply.

"No."

I'm dumbfounded. "Were you alive in 1964?"

"Yes," you reply, "but I was four years old then and not in the market for an automobile."

Once again I'm reminded of the swift passage of time and of the need to put everything in context.

"There's a new book out," I offer. "It's called *Bill Bernbach's Book*. It's by Bob Levenson, a writer Bernbach raised from a pup. Look it up. Buy it. Check it out of the library. You'll find a dramatic moment on every page."

But, true to your age group, you want instant gratification, not a trip to the bookstore. "You brought up 'Lemon.' Aren't you going to make your point?" you ask.

"The Volkswagen campaign is a symbol of the creative, revolutionary 60s," I explain, resigned to the fact that a campaign I regard as contemporary and relevant is now hopelessly old. " 'Lemon' was an ad in the series along with 'Think Small' and 'Nobody's Perfect.' "

The assignment at hand was to dramatize how exhaustive, how zealous, how persnickety Volkswagen inspectors are when it comes to approving a car and releasing it to the public. Here is what Bill Bernbach had to say about the ad in 1980:

> Suppose the Volkswagen ad, positioned to tell its inspection story, had said: 'The greatest inspection system in the world' instead of the single, shocking word: 'LEMON.' Do you think anyone would have got the idea that we meant it? But in one stroke, we drew attention to the fact that this was a great inspection system.[7]

A dramatic moment is often stumbled upon accidentally. Later, of course, it is presented to the world as an example of the brilliant execution one should expect from a gifted, creatively driven advertising agency. The VW event was not unlike our own experience with "Virginia is for lovers."

The creative team assigned to Volkswagen consisted of Helmut Krone, art director, and Julian Koenig, the great writer responsible for dreaming up the breakthrough campaign. Krone had the idea for the visual. The photo would show a perfect, unblemished car. The headline would offer an unexpected twist, something like "This car looks perfect, but it isn't." Koenig had jotted down some possible lines, but he knew none measured up to others he had done in the series. The idea just wouldn't come, so Julian decided to go to the race track to clear his mind. He loved the horses, and maybe there in solitude, midst the madding crowd, he would find inspiration.

A young writer by the name of Rita Selden happened by Krone's office and saw the layout on his drawing board.

"Why don't you just say 'Lemon'?" she offered. Of course. That

Imagine this ad with a headline like "Reject." It just doesn't have the bite. Writers who can lift the mundane to the sublime are worth their weight in gold to advertisers. They lift awareness for a fraction of the media dollars others pay.

Lemon.

was it! I think she's got it! The nugget. The pure distillation of the idea at hand.

The creative process is unique to the human mind. Facts can be programmed into a computer, which, when asked, will spit out new facts in combinations calculated to solve a problem. With the creative mind, facts come back in all kinds of wild and wonderful ways that you know at first sight will work. Give it input and back comes an unexpected idea, like "Lemon," reflecting brightly in the strong light of human experience. An idea with just enough twist and top spin to make it memorable.

Obviously "Lemon" has memory power for me. I remember it after twenty-five years, and so do avid Volkswagen customers, I'm told. The nostalgia they feel for the Beetle, the 1960s, and those old ads is the basis for the campaign appearing today. The type style is the same, and so is the format. Everything about the color spreads is suspiciously reminiscent of the old Beetle ads. As with their ancestors, they feature short headlines like "Roads scholar," or interesting new information like "Volkswagen presents another radical idea: rear wheels that turn." They are definitely the grandchildren of the earlier campaign, retaining (as smart advertising should) a well-established product personality. They find a dramatic moment and milk it.

A dramatic moment makes an indelible impression on the thousand or more synapses assigned by the brain to remembering a particular point, assigned to that given task from the hundred billion or so available inside every human skull. Even so, as dramatic as a moment may be, there is a good chance the consumer will forget the product with the passage of time.

The skillful advertising practitioner understands the fallibility of human memory and overcomes it with emotional and dramatic moments. Equally important is a well-orchestrated advertising schedule. With that cue, let's bring in the media people.

Sum & Substance

Advertising today serves up *dramatic moments loaded with* indirect *sales appeals*. By skillfully blending emotional and pragmatic appeals, and by camouflaging persuasion with wit and entertainment, advertisers allow consumers to draw their own conclusions about the brand and its advantages.

This indirect persuasion permits the delight of individual discovery. It is the most effective way to win over an audience of TV addicts, those jaded viewers who have seen and judged thousands of commercials since infancy. But while a blunt, hard-sell approach is seldom appropriate, it is selling suicide to be obtuse. Drama without a selling raison d'être is worthless.

·15·

How Much?
How Many?

A man who advertises at all must keep it up until the public knows who and what he is, and what his business is, or else the money invested in advertising is lost.

—P. T. Barnum, *Struggles and Triumphs*

In a presentation to a client or new business, people always respond to words, pictures, ideas. Creativity stimulates the imagination. As layouts are presented and the copy discussed, the left side of the brain is forced to sit in the back and leave the driving to the right.

Then the agency shifts gears. The discussion progresses from how the ads will be done to how many should be run and how much they will cost. When the presenter says, "Its time to look at the media plan," eyelids begin to droop. The right side doesn't want to let go of the wheel. It's true, handling the media is mainly a left-side speciality. It means coming to grip with details. But it isn't boring. An imaginative media plan is just as creative as the advertising it delivers.

The most effective campaigns are built through a collaborative effort between the creative team and the media planners. Together they decide what size print units should be developed and what length the commercials should be, whether to include radio and outdoor advertising, balancing frequency and impact—all with an eye to the budget and a profitable return on advertising investment. In time, the plan comes together like a masterful tapestry richly woven to cover the market, minds, and emotions of those falling within the demographic and geographic targets.

The battleground is the product category. The fight is for share of mind.

In the hundred years since Ebbinghaus first conducted his experiment, many advertising studies have verified the rate of forgetting identified by his exhaustive tests. Half is gone in the first 60 minutes; the rest fades gradually to a low level as time passes.[1]

In the late 1950s, Hubert A. Zielske of Foote, Cone & Belding confirmed the rate of learning and forgetting relative to product advertising.[2] He did this by conducting an awareness tracking study among two control groups of housewives, using a different schedule for each. One group was sent an ad a week for thirteen weeks. The other group received one ad every four weeks for a year. Both groups received a total of thirteen ads. The results were quite different and reconfirmed the Ebbinghaus memory decay theory—and the value of repetition. The chart on the next page shows the sawtooth pattern of rapid rise, followed by sharp decline, in ability to remember among those exposed to ads once a month. As time passed, the rate of forgetting dropped gently until memory of the advertising was gone. Those who saw ads once a week quickly became aware. However, the awareness gain was quickly lost as repetition stopped. Interviews were conducted weekly by telephone with the women receiving the ads to measure the percentage of recall among each group. In all, 3,650 telephone calls were made. No housewife was ever interviewed twice.

Because memory fades, the question most often asked is, how many repetitions are needed to switch the consumer to our client's brand precisely when he or she is in the market for the product we have to sell? Several inquisitive scholars have probed for that answer.

Get Off to a Fast Start

In the early 1960s, a young professor by the name of John Stewart was hired as a consultant by my client, A. H. Robins. He was a brilliant Harvard psychologist, a Ph.D., and much in demand in academic circles. The University of Richmond wanted him for its business school but couldn't meet his price tag at the time. Robins agreed to pay half his salary in return for part-time consulting. It was an excellent way for the school to add a valued resource to its faculty. It was also a stroke of good luck for me. John taught me a great deal about reach and frequency, the number of exposures needed to make an impact, how quickly people forget, and how much repetition is necessary to sustain recall.

When I met him, John was finishing up an incredibly complicated study and writing a book on this subject. He had started it at Harvard's Graduate School of Business when the Newsprint Information Committee approached the college and provided it with a grant to conduct basic research on the effects of repetition. With the help of the committee and the willing participation of two advertisers, Sara Lee and Lestare, Inc., Stewart implemented an experiment using an intricate series of split runs in the Fort Wayne newspapers. Two 1,000-line advertisements ran, one for each product, without change, over a period of five months. Stewart divided the city into four areas. One area received no exposure, another

Shown here are the percentages of housewives who could remember advertising when exposed weekly and at four-week intervals. Like the hare, weekly exposures burst into the lead, but the tortoise wins in the end.

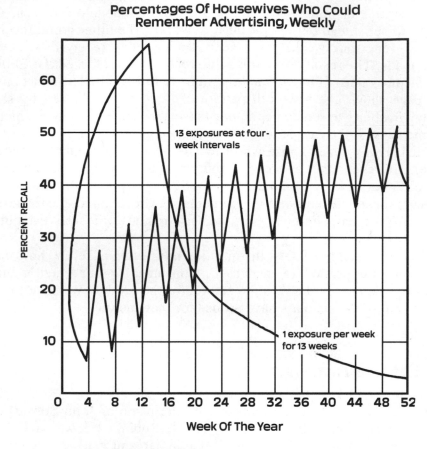

Percentages Of Housewives Who Could Remember Advertising, Weekly

was exposed once a week for four weeks, another once a week for eight weeks, and the fourth area was exposed for twenty consecutive weeks. Six thousand personal interviews were conducted to determine changes in brand awareness and preference. After all this was done, Stewart concluded:

> If we had known originally what we now know in retrospect, *we would have run the advertisements weekly for the first four weeks, every other week from week 5 through 12, and monthly from week 13 through 24.* We believe this frequency of scheduling would have been nearly optimum. The first four insertions would have obtained the sudden and widespread awareness of the products and would have started the development of firm conviction about the product. Some extra purchases would have been obtained—at least enough to help hold whatever shelf space had been obtained in retail stores. The biweekly frequency from weeks 5 through 12 would have sustained awareness at a level only slightly below a weekly frequency, and we believe that the slightly lower level of awareness would not be a serious loss in comparison to the economy gained. . . . The monthly

insertions would have been efficient per dollar spent in reminding the "previously prepared" prospects to make a trial purchase.[3]

Three for the Money

In 1968, Robert C. Grass of DuPont undertook some laboratory experiments with television commercials in an attempt to learn how many times to run them. He measured the attention, or interest, generated in respondents when exposed to the message. "This measurement was obtained by means of CONPAAD equipment," Grass explains, "which requires that the subject perform physical work in order to see or hear the commercial. When subjects were exposed to the same commercial again and again on this equipment, a generation-satiation pattern was obtained." Grass concluded: *Attention or interest was maximized at 2 to 4 exposures* of the commercial, depending upon the particular conditions being employed, and was followed by a decline up to the total number of exposures used in this study."[4]

In 1972, Dr. Hubert E. Krugman of the General Electric Company presented a paper at a television workshop sponsored by the Association of National Advertisers (ANA). It was entitled "How Potent is Television Advertising?" He concluded that three exposures to a TV commercial might be the minimum needed. Here is what he said:

> We spend a lot of money on repetition of advertising. Some explain this by noting that recall of the advertising will drop unless continually reinforced, while others note that members of the audience are not always in the market for the advertised product, but that when they are, the advertising must be there, so that there's no choice but to advertise frequently. So we can have advertising campaigns of equal magnitude, but based on quite different assumptions about the nature of the effect.

> Of course, these two views are apparently quite opposite. One says that the ad must be learned in the same way that habits are learned—by practice. The other says that at the right moment (when one is "in the market") it just takes minimal exposure to achieve appropriate effects. . . .

> I'd like to offer a view that argues against single-exposure potency, and also against any large number of repeated exposures. I think it is important to understand how communication works and how people learn, and to do that, some attention has to be given to the difference between 1, 2 and 3—i.e., the difference between the first, second, and third exposures. One to make ready, two for the show, three for the money and four to go, or just what? All more complex campaign effects based on twenty, or thirty exposures, I believe, are only multiples or combinations of what happens in the first few exposures. . . .

My own and Bob Grass's work were both primarily laboratory. However, in September of 1970, Colin McDonald of the British Market Research Bureau gave an award-winning paper at the annual conference in Barcelona of the European Society of Market Research . . . a paper ("What is the short-term effect of advertising?") which reported purchase diary data interrelated with media data, such that McDonald identified two exposures as optimal. There are others as well, but the point I am making should be clear: that *a wide variety of research procedures agree on the special significance of just a few exposures as optimal.*[5]

The McDonald diary study referred to above was carried out among housewives who were asked to record both their purchases and television viewing so that "opportunities-to-see" advertising (OTS) could be identified. The study fitted two records together. "The most significant finding of the study," McDonald concluded, "was that where a switch in brand occurred on consecutive purchasing occasions, the shopper was more likely to have been exposed to two advertisements than one for the brand switched to."[6]

In 1979, Michael J. Naples, (then) director of marketing research for Lever Brothers (now he is president of the Advertising Research Foundation), compiled a scholarly work on advertising frequency that was published by the ANA. In it he compared the McDonald study with the findings of a major advertiser "who carried out an analysis involving 38 brands over a four-week period, using change in unaided brand advertising awareness as a measurement criterion." The study involved nearly 3,000 respondents and confirmed that "unaided brand advertising awareness over a four-week period did not attain a sufficiently positive level *until three exposures were received.*"[7]

The weight of evidence from these and other studies suggests that *an individual reader or viewer must be exposed to at least two, and preferably three, advertisements within a purchase cycle for optimum results.* This, of course, does not mean three insertions. Depending on consumer viewing habits, the commercial will reach some people once, others twice, still others three times, and so on. Even in print, repetition beyond three times during the target period may be required to reach enough people with three exposures to deliver the message to a sufficiently large audience to build share of mind to the levels needed. As we know, the *awareness-interest-desire-action* funnel inevitably narrows. Unaided awareness levels must be up to twice the amount of market share targeted. Even when the market can't actually recall the advertising, however, it may still be working to change attitudes and create sales; this is sometimes referred to as the "sleeper effect."

A Case for Greater Frequency

In 1982, Time Inc. and Joseph E. Seagram's & Sons, Inc., released the results of an exhaustive three-year joint study of the effects of advertising frequency on people's buying habits.[8] The research was conducted over a forty-eight-week period in test markets where absolute control was maintained over the advertising for the products included. Except for the ads in *Time* and *Sports Illustrated,* all other advertising for the Seagram's brands tested was withheld from the markets under scrutiny. There were eight Seagram's brands in all: four with high awareness and four that were not well known. Some people received copies of the two magazines containing no ad; others were exposed to one, two, or four ads per month. The ads were changed every thirteen weeks.

The study found that even a single ad can have a major impact on people's awareness levels. Awareness curves did not flatten out, but continued to rise even after forty-eight weeks. Each week, a sample of the population was queried about its buying habits and brand attitudes.

Awareness and attitudes rose much more rapidly than did actual recall. In other words, people may forget seeing an advertisement, yet still be influenced by it. The greater the frequency, the better the results, which is bad news for skeptics who question advertising's value. The researchers found that it was hard to change attitudes about established brands, but that those brands starting out with low awareness had higher gains overall, probably because consumers had no preconceived opinions or entrenched attitudes to overcome.

For brands starting out with high awareness, the sharp increase in "willingness to buy" after the first insertion is followed by a temporary dip. This rises again as advertising continues. The line at the top tracks weekly frequency; the middle, twice every four weeks; and the bottom, one insertion per four-week period. Gains continue even after 48 weeks.

Campaign Curve

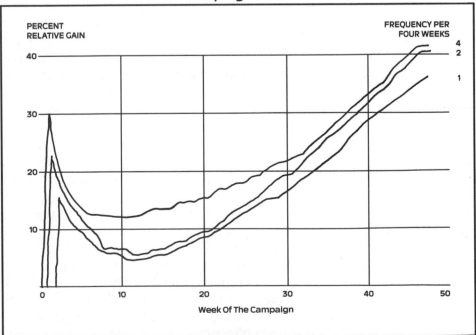

PERCENT
RELATIVE GAIN

FREQUENCY PER
FOUR WEEKS

Week Of The Campaign

Measure of Exposure

In advertising, the standard measure of total exposure is known as gross rating points (GRPs). The number of gross rating points on a given schedule is equal to *reach* (the percent of the population exposed to the message) times *frequency* (the number of times the population is exposed during that time). For example, 200 GRPs = 40% reach × 5 frequency, or 10% reach × 20 frequency. (In television, especially, agency media buyers negotiate with representatives of stations or the networks to get the lowest cost per "point" possible.)

Media planners are interested in Target GRPs, that is, reach and frequency against the ideal consumer segment for the brand advertised. In our planning, we usually reduce GRPs by a third or a half to allow for the loss of those people who leave the set or change channels during a commercial break. Homes exposed to programming do not automatically translate into individuals exposed to the advertisement.

Reach and Frequency: Optimum Dosage

The key considerations here are the amount of reach needed and the number of times the commercial should appear. The objective is twofold: (1) to expose the customer to the advertisement at least three times during a purchase cycle; and (2) to reach enough potential customers to establish an optimum level of share of mind. The length of time between purchases is another variable. As shown by Ebbinghaus, and confirmed by many advertising studies since (including those reviewed here), we know that there is a precipitous decline in memory over a four-week period. By the second week, 75 percent is lost; by the fourth week, our beholder has forgotten 95 percent of the information we provided. Frequency must be scheduled with this in mind.

The size of the media budget and the amount of repetition needed to build awareness to desired levels are matters for the individual advertiser to determine through telephone tracking studies. These findings can then be compared over time with sales results during the period. Ideally, different test markets, exposed to various levels of media weight, should be studied to determine precisely the most cost-efficient amount of advertising to use to build unaided awareness to the levels needed to produce sales. (A technique for doing this is discussed in Chapter 17.)

What can be known for sure, however, is that our advertising must register at least three direct hits on the target audience during the interval between product purchase and repurchase. Ideally, the three should be scheduled to impact on the reader or viewer as closely as possible to the time of a purchase decision. For some products, this is quite possible. Vacation decisions or insecticide applications are two good examples. For products that are not seasonal, it is better to start with a burst against the target, then throttle back to maintain awareness over time.

Sum & Substance

Nowadays, when advertising as a selling force is often called into question, it is interesting to review studies that have probed the question of "how many?" rather than "why bother?" Those with a scholarly and scientific bent should write the Association of National Advertisers in New York to order a book by Michael Naples of Lever Brothers entitled *Effective Frequency: The Relationship Between Frequency and Advertising Effectiveness*. You'll come away from it enriched by information that goes beyond charts and case studies. It is an affirmation of advertising's effectiveness tracked through the years.

What jumps out at me from my own experience with many campaigns, as well as from a review of documentation by others, is the need to burst into public consciousness with heavily weighted advertising up front, followed by less frequent exposure over time. The key is to carve out a share of mind with your advertising proposition and to keep it there. At least three reinforcements of your message are needed during a purchase cycle, that is, between purchase and repurchase of a given item.

If we are to believe the findings of the Seagram-Time study, we must also keep in mind that it is easier to establish new attitudes for new brands than it is to change attitudes that are already entrenched. This suggests that we should go with the flow on products with an established image, reinforce that image, not try to change it. With new products, we start with a blank canvas and, thus, with a tremendous opportunity to relate product attributes to customer desires. This lesson is not limited to package goods. It can be applied to product categories from farm machinery to insurance policies, from locomotives to liquor.

·16·

Share of Voice

*Brands that spend much more on advertising as a
percentage of sales than their leading competitors
tend to capture a larger share of their market.*

—Dr. Bradley T. Gale,
The Strategic Planning Institute

The skeptical CEO always wants to know: "What is advertising's impact on the bottom line?" Until recently the response was subjective, about as clear-cut as the answer to John Wanamaker's classic lament, "I know half my advertising is wasted, but I don't know which half."

As we found in the preceding chapter, one way to answer the retail pioneer's question is to schedule various media weights in test markets and then compare awareness to sales. Another way is to have the strongest share of voice in the product category.

The first piece of evidence to prove this point comes to us from a ten-year study of brand loyalty in twenty product categories conducted by the NPD Group of Port Washington, N.Y. It is a by-product of NPD's work for subscribers, for whom consumers keep diaries noting all purchases of products in the categories under study. These include typical high-profile package goods: food and beverages, household and personal products, and pet food—fifty major brands in all.

With this diary panel method, consumer purchasing behavior can be observed over six-month time periods. Loyal buyers are defined as consumers who make at least three purchases of a given brand during the six-month period, and who satisfy their desires and needs for that kind of product by selecting a particular brand more the half the time. Advertising expenditures for each of the fifty brands over ten years are also factored into the analysis, as are promotions. The information is representative of the nation as a whole.

After analyzing the data, Tod Johnson of NPD concludes that brand loyalty among major package goods hasn't declined very much during the past decade. When brand loyalty does decline, there are two causes, both induced by the marketers themselves: (1) a segmentation strategy that cannibalizes the flagship brand through brand extensions and flankers; and (2) advertising practices that are erratic or fail to keep pace with others in the category. In contrast, Johnson finds, "Brands tend to show actual improvement in loyalty when both their advertising expenditures (in absolute dollars) and their share of category expenditures increase."[1] This is shown on the chart below.

Advertising vs. Promotion

As marketers look for a quick fix to make their numbers in the short term, they earmark a larger percentage of sales for promotion. This means that either advertising or profit suffers. During the past ten years, promotions for package goods have grown at an annual rate of 12 percent, compared to a growth rate of 10 percent for advertising. As you might expect, short-term promotional tactics usually come at the expense of the long-term advertising strategy necessary to build and protect the brand. In Chapter 2, we saw that this practice was decried by David Ogilvy as long ago as 1955. But today the problem is even more acute as the cost/price squeeze intensifies and marketers scramble for sales.

Back in 1975, 23 percent of all sales for the fifty brands were on consumer-recognized deals. By 1985, the figure had increased to more than 40 percent of all retail transactions involving some kind of deal obvious to consumers. The theory behind the trend, to paraphrase Gertrude Stein, is that an ad is an ad is an ad. When it comes to building loyal customers, however, it isn't so. A coupon, for instance, may influence trial, and cause a blip on the sales chart, but it doesn't lasso and corral a repeat customer. In fact, coupons don't even please the shopper very

The 1975 level equals an index of 100. Although these findings show the value of maintaining or increasing share of category expenditures, they do not take into account the leverage potential of an outstanding advertising execution.

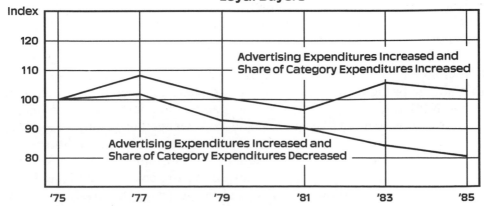

much. Another recent study concludes that "a considerable proportion" of the people who redeem coupons do so grudgingly: "They resent coupons, feel they are caught in a rising spiral of prices triggered by the coupons themselves, and the only way to maintain a balanced budget is to get involved in coupon redemption."[2] Of course, the marketer, not the retailer, gets blamed for the practice. More than 75 percent of shoppers believe that prices would go down if couponing ended.

The NPD study shows the danger of relying on promotions to build and protect the brand franchise. While conceding that "promotions can move lots of volume," and that "promotion is a tremendous stimulus for short term sales," Johnson concludes that "there is very little apparent difference in Brand Loyalty no matter how the brands are broken out by their measured levels of consumer recognized dealing." Promotions supposedly reward "loyal" buyers, but also encourage consumers to be "unfaithful" to other brands. They do not woo customers away from brands that are effectively supported. With all this in mind, Tod Johnson advises marketers to have two budgets to build both brands and sales: (1) a *strategic budget* to build the franchise over the long term, using advertising and a few selected, consumer-oriented promotions; and (2) a *tactical budget,* which would be for promotions tied into pricing, and aimed at managing the amount of sales revenue at different price levels.

How Budgets Get Set

It may be helpful at this point to review the four different methods by which advertising budgets are set: decree, task, share of voice, and the ratio of advertising to sales (A-to-S).

Budgets set by *decree* are usually handed down by top management after it has looked at the previous year's budget and cast a beady eye on the following year's profit plan. Industries relying on this method are usually half-hearted about the need for advertising, or view advertising as something that doesn't directly influence sales. Examples are heavy industry, insurance, and investment banking. The guideline is: "How much can we afford?" Usually, when things get tough, the ad budget is the first to go.

Ordinarily, budgets are set by *task.* The first step is to set objectives by defining what is to be accomplished by advertising. For example, is it to maintain brand loyalty by holding on to share of voice in the category, as the NPD study suggests? If so, the agency and client work together to "task" the budget. Marketing expectations respecting volume, revenue, income, profit, and market share are listed. Competitive expenditures are taken into account. Reach and frequency against the target market are evaluated. A preliminary plan is produced. Media costs are budgeted. All this is compared to product margins and profit goals. Obviously, the task method makes a great deal of sense, but its use depends on a CEO and budget director who have some appreciation of advertising's power and its importance to corporate health. When they do, an ideal and practical budget can be plugged in along with overhead, research and development, direct sales, and profit to move the company forward.

The *share of voice* method is based on current or desired market share. For example, Zipco has a 10 percent share of market and will spend 10 percent of all category spending on advertising. When the objective is to increase market share, ad budgets are often set at 200 percent of the desired share increase. For example, Zipco wants to increase its share from 10 percent to 11 percent. It will, therefore, increase share of voice by 20 percent (from 10 percent to 12 percent). No matter which method is used to come up with the budget, share of voice in advertising markets must be considered. There is compelling evidence that success depends on it.

The *advertising-to-sales* ratio method is based on a fixed percent of estimated sales (or fixed dollar amount per case shipped). For example, Virginia Gentleman bourbon projects annual sales of 300,000 cases. A total of $2.50 is built into the price of each case for advertising, thus producing an annual ad budget of $750,000. Although the method has merit, it ignores the fact that advertising can cause sales. It also does not take competitive share of voice into account. When sales are trending down, so does advertising support. This may happen just when it is needed most. The advertising-to-sales ratio, however, with all its faults, is a good method if sales are tracked on a current basis and the ratio makes sense.

Spend More, Make More

A recent study of 749 consumer businesses tells us that those using a higher relative A-to-S ratio earn a higher return on investment. A higher A-to-S ratio also has a positive influence on perceived product quality, market share, and relative price—the factors driving profitability. The study was conducted by the Ogilvy Center for Research & Development and the Strategic Planning Institute (SPI), a nonprofit membership organization formed to help managers apply scientific methods to marketing strategy. SPI does this through the use of the PIMS (Profit Impact of Market Strategy) data base containing detailed operating and competitive data on more than 2,700 companies, consumer as well as industrial. This information allows managers of member firms to compare their businesses with others' on a confidential basis.

This project began in 1986, when the Ogilvy Center for Research & Development approached SPI with the idea of jointly sponsoring a project to investigate the impact of advertising expenditures on consumer businesses. The consumer product companies included in SPI's data were divided into five categories according to their A-to-S ratios (higher, lower, or about the same) as compared with direct competitors'. The extremes in terms of return on investment (ROI) are dramatic. Those companies spending substantially more than their competitors relative to sales, it was found, have a signficantly higher return on investment. The big spenders averaged a 32 percent return. Those spending a smaller proportion of sales dollars than direct competitors earn less on invested capital (17 percent average ROI). The three middle categories are as follows: less (22 percent ROI), equal (22 percent ROI), more (25 percent ROI). The brands with higher advertising-to-sales ratios have a better return because they are seen by consumers as being superior products.

This perception of product quality, when widely held, leads to greater market share, as this SPI chart shows:

A-to-S Ratios vs. Direct Competitors	Average Share of Market (%)
Much less	14
Less	20
Equal	25
More	26
Much more	32

When brands have perceived superiority, they have market flexibility because marketing costs are lower and because prices can be raised without losing market share.

As the pendulum of power swings to the retailer (see Chapters 2 and 3), this analysis, along with the NPD study, underscores the need for marketers to hold the line and not give in to short-term pressures that substitute promotional tactics for long-term strategy.

Dr. Bradley Gale, who supervised the SPI study, summarized its findings in this way:

> Businesses that spend more than their leading competitors on advertising as a percentage of sales tend to have superior perceived quality in the market place. . . . A business's relative product/service quality has a strong effect on customer loyalty and on repeat sales.
>
> Superior quality also insulates your business/brand from price competition. Our data show that when a product/service offering is perceived as superior it commands a premium price (on average—nine percent higher than competitors). Together, relative perceived quality and relative price determine relative value. Businesses or brands that offer superior quality at a comparable price tend to gain market share.[3]

In other words, if you have a quality product, and customers know it and like its distinctive advantage, they're willing to pay for it. As a result, they'll be satisfied, and you'll make out like a bandit.

Sum & Substance

When it comes to brand loyalty, the situation is not unlike that found in Wonderland. "Now, here, you see," the Red Queen told Alice, "it takes all the running you can do to keep in the same place. If you want to get somewhere else, you must run at least twice as fast as that!"

When advertising is erratic, and exposure drops below that for competitors in a category, brand loyalty drops. On the other hand, loyalty rises when the advertiser's share-of-category expenditures increase. Coupons, premiums, sweepstakes, sampling, games, bonus packs, and other forms of consumer promotions stimulate short-term sales, but have little effect on long-term brand loyalty. Consumer promotions, coupled with trade promotions—deals, push funds, case allowances, shelving allowances, and the like—eat away dollars otherwise available to protect and build the brand franchise.

Those companies that bite the bullet, that somehow find the resources to (1) keep the trade appeased, (2) promote for short-term results, but (3) still come up with a higher advertising-to-sales ratio than others in their respective categories, end up earning a higher return on investment. They do so because customers regard their products more highly, associate them with quality, and are willing to pay more for them. This leaves a greater margin to play with, which, of course, makes biting the bullet less painful.

·17·

How to Increase Market Share

*For effective awareness-to-market-share conversion,
genuine effort should be made to establish an
awareness character that clearly differentiates a
business's capabilities and products from competitors'.*

—William L. Burke and Sidney Schoeffler,
The Strategic Planning Institute

As we learned from Keith Jones, a healthy category market share is the
first line of defense against brand hostaging. And, as the SPI/Ogilvy study
demonstrates, it also means greater profit and market flexibility. The
question is, how best to use advertising to directly influence market share?
While many factors (such as distribution, price, deals, and promotions)
influence market share, in the final analysis, the trump card is high
awareness on the part of consumers of a distinctive product difference.
Dominant category share of mind leads to dominant category market
share.

With all that has been said in the previous chapters, we now know
exactly how to go about introducing or revitalizing a brand so that it can
compete with formidable competitors. If we're operating on a shoestring,
we need to limit the markets on our hit list. We'll start by solidifying
distribution. This means making the deals, buying the shelf space, lining
up distributors, dealers, or whatever. To do that we'll also outline our
advertising plan to our trade customers. This won't be just a transparent
merchandising sop, but an *innovative campaign based on product difference and quality,* scheduled with sufficient weight to capture share of
mind. Part of our effort will go into publicity. We'll do some crazy things
to get people talking.

In the markets we've selected, we'll want to know everything about
the category. We'll start by studying competitive activity: How much
advertising is run, by whom, and what does it say? Let's be sure ours is
different. What is the relative share, relative awareness, relative spending?
What do our customers want? What appeals do they find meaningful?
What do they think about the products they're already using? Is there

154

something we can say that hasn't been said before to give our product a perceived advantage? We must "own" a dominant value point no other product has, and this benefit or property must be something the customer desires profoundly. If we don't have a point of leverage, we shouldn't waste money trying to overtake the leaders through advertising. We must have a unique benefit, attribute, or feature. Our success depends on it.

Awareness Leads to Share

Given two conditions—that distribution is equal to that for other brands in the category, and that consumers like our point of difference—there is a direct correlation between unaided brand awareness (UBA) and market share. Table 17-1 shows some examples of this correlation in two paper categories. Try to recall the value attributes owned by the two leaders in their respective categories.

Bounty absorbs spills and mess more quickly and thoroughly than competitive brands, according to Rosy, its spokeswoman. Charmin is the tissue you love to squeeze, but don't do it!—the value point owned is "softness." Whether you liked Mr. Whipple or not in those commercials that ran a few years ago, they established the softness feature clearly. Do you remember what each of the others claim as a dominant value point? If you do, do the claims strike you as meaningful?

The share percentages shown below are, of course, snapshots at a given point in time, and these are about as stable as rankings week to week in the NFL. Obviously, advertising isn't the only dynamic at work. Trial and use pushes back through the selling funnel to influence UBA. In other words, the more satisfied customers there are, the more awareness for the brand there will be. That's why it takes repetition and extraordinary creative execution based on a competitive benefit to gain on the category leader.

Table 17-1. Relationship of Unaided Awareness to Market Share

Brand	UBA	Share
Paper Towels		
Bounty	60%	18.4%
Scottowels	40	12.6
Viva	30	7.0
Brawny	28	9.9
Bathroom Tissue		
Charmin	74%	19.2%
Northern	51	14.5
Scottissue	34	7.9
White Cloud	31	8.2

In 1980, Leo Burnett announced the results of a ten-year review of advertising support, awareness, and trial data on clients' new product introductions of some 124 package goods products. This is what David W. Oson, associate research director for the agency, observed after studying the data: "The more ad support the greater the awareness, and the higher the awareness achieved by the brand the higher its trial will be. However, once the brand has attained a high level of awareness, a small increase in awareness from that point on tends to lead to a large increase in the amount of trial for the brand."[1]

About the same time, Cahners and SPI released the results of a study of brand awareness and preference data among readers of four Cahners publications matched against SPI's Profit Impact of Marketing Strategy (PIMS) data base. As Burke and Schoeffler report, "The study focused on the six-year business experiences of participating member companies of the PIMS Program whose industrial and construction products were reported in brand awareness market research studies conducted by the Cahners Publishing Company. Seventy-three lines of business of 25 different large multi-market member organizations of PIMS were evaluated."[2] As with the Burnett study, these findings also show that increased brand awareness improves the potential for increasing market share.

Not surprisingly, when more is spent on advertising as a percentage of sales, brand awareness levels increase more sharply. In announcing the results, Cahners president J. A. Sheehan said, "Although the impact of market share on profitability has long been identified, the connection between brand awareness and market share had not been demonstrated until now."[3]

Two factors were found to be vital in converting awareness to increased market share: (1) adequate production capacity, and (2) unique product characteristics (that is, a value point of leverage). The study also warned category leaders not to feel complacent. When leaders rest on their corporate laurels, the competition can gain in awareness and, therefore, market share.

AdPlan: How to Predict Sales

So now we know, if we want to be the leader, our brand must have high awareness and also offer unique value in the category. To get this awareness, with the greatest media efficiency, we have during the past ten years conducted more than 100,000 telephone interviews to probe both unaided advertising awareness and consumer understanding of the brand's unique advantage. From these studies, we see a direct link between unaided recall and product sales. This linkage for transaction-oriented products exists when a competitive benefit point of difference can be identified.

In our continuing analysis, awareness is compared week by week with actual sales. The products range from food to whiskey to agricultural chemicals to tickets to theme parks. The first task is to determine precisely how much advertising weight is needed to bring awareness to desired levels. Usually, advertising begins on a base of awareness. Past efforts are the springboard, which is why a consistent brand "personality" is important. This residue of awareness will change weekly as the campaign unfolds.

Since we've been tracking many products over a long period of time, we find we can predict sales based on the number of target GRPs needed to push awareness to optimum levels. All media—broadcast, print, whatever—are reduced to GRPs for this exercise.

To put the question simply, we want to know how much advertising we must use to get the awareness we need to get the sales we want. That's logical, you say. You buy media exposure to make people aware of what you have to sell and of the benefits offered. *Voilà!* Some will buy. Why do we need a media model?

The reason is that people forget. They remember with repeated exposures and forget with the passing of time. Also, the rates at which people remember and forget vary, depending on such factors as competitive advertising activity, availability of the product, and inherent interest in what is being sold. The AdPlan model developed by my partner (and brother), Steve, takes all this into account. It allows both learning and forgetting to occur during the same week. The formula is:

$$A = bX + cY$$

A equals the amount of unaided advertising awareness at the end of the week, *X* equals the number of GRPs run during the week, and *Y* equals the percentage of unaided awareness at the beginning of the week; *b* is the learning coefficient, *c* is the retention coefficient. These variable factors are identified through an awareness tracking study for the particular brand. Once the learning and retention coefficients are known, together with the relationship of unaided advertising to sales, a media schedule can be developed to generate the awareness necessary to produce the sales forecast.

The Case of Virginia Gentleman

We used this technique successfully on behalf of our client Virginia Gentleman. This bourbon was the No. 3-selling brand in the state of Virginia, a quality product that is popularly priced along with Jim Beam and Early Times. Old Grand Dad, Jack Daniels, and Wild Turkey were the premium-priced market leaders. There had been no advertising to speak of for the brand for five or six years.

The fitted line is our prediction of sales expected from various levels of awareness at each point in time. The black squares show what actually happened. As you can see, market share and unaided awareness came close to what we expected.

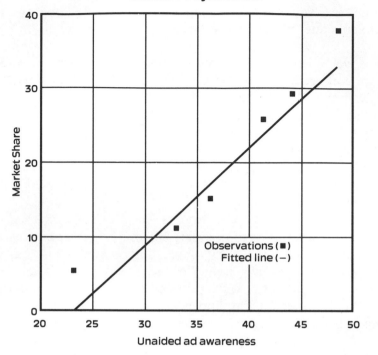

Sales Projections

From consumer interviews, we knew that the most appealing and believable strategy would be to position the brand as equal to or better than its premium-priced competitors. The benefit was, in effect: "This is a gourmet, quality whiskey, as good as the three well-known quality brands, but, as you'll see, it is priced below them." To find this out we used the benefit testing techniques previously discussed.

Our comparison advertising featured a tongue-in-cheek fillip. Intuitively, we knew we should have fun with this. Bourbon is a product associated with good times, getting together with friends and sharing a drink. We created ads showing our bottle next to a more expensive competitor, using headlines like these:

Why settle for a Turkey when you can have a Virginia Gentleman?

If Jack Daniels were a Virginia Gentleman, he'd make a better drink.

Sorry, but your Old Grand Dad is not a Virginia Gentleman.

The copy was short and sweet:

Virginia Gentleman still comes from cypress tubs and copper stills. And, like any gourmet item, it's still made in small batches. By hand. You see, we do more than we have to. But, then, that's how you get to be a Virginia Gentleman in the first place.

The strategy paid off. Tracking study readings showed monthly awareness gains at various media weights, which we related to sales in selected markets. With these data in hand, we then used AdPlan to determine the awareness we needed—and could afford—to get the market share we wanted *throughout* our distribution area during the next twelve months.

The results were significant. Market share increased 12 percent, while sales volume for Virginia Gentleman went up 5.3 percent despite a 7.8 percent decline in the brown liquor category.

Promotions and deals were nonexistent because Virginia is a control state, that is, one where the state runs the liquor stores. This makes it a pure test, in which advertising is the only variable. There is an important footnote that should be considered with this success story. Competitive advertising expenditures were taken into account. Our share of voice was greater than the competition's against our targets in the geographic markets selected.

A New Vodka From Virginia

At the time the campaign was run, A. Smith Bowman Distillery, the maker of Virginia Gentleman, was run by three Virginia gentlemen: Delong Bowman, who has since retired, his brother-in-law, Robert E. Lee IV, and Delong's nephew, John Adams. The operation is nestled on seven acres between Reston, in Fairfax, Virginia, and Interstate 66. The Bowman family once owned most of the Reston land, and when I first called on Bob Lee, years ago, before the building boom in northern Virginia, the tiny Williamsburg-style office building, with the distillery out back, was out in the country and hard to find. Now it is dwarfed by giant developments and highways around it.

Delong had reservations about referring to competitors in his ads. It didn't seem the gentlemanly thing to do. I pointed out that we weren't being mean about it. The ads were in good fun. Besides, consumers had told us in advance that they would like this kind of approach.

Later, with the trend continuing away from brown liquors to vodka, gin, and wine, the company asked us to name a new vodka, design the label, and develop an introductory strategy. Distribution would be limited to Virginia.

Yankelovich Monitor told us that there was a strong undercurrent of local and regional pride running across America, something the Commonwealth of Virginia exploited with great success by promoting Virginia products to Virginians. "We've got it made in Virginia" banners and shelf talkers were displayed in stores throughout the state.

These comparison ads were all in good fun. By associating Virginia Gentleman with best selling brands of premium whiskeys, the product was positioned for quality and value.

Straight Bourbon Whiskey. 80 proof. A. Smith Bowman Distillery. Sunset Hills, Virginia.

WHY SETTLE FOR A TURKEY WHEN YOU CAN GET A VIRGINIA GENTLEMAN?

Virginia Gentleman still comes from cypress tubs and copper stills. And, like any gourmet item, it's still made in small batches. By hand. You see, we do more than we have to. But, then, that's how you get to be a Virginia Gentleman in the first place.

After testing a dozen fancy labels and different names, we decided to call the product Bowman's Virginia Vodka. We settled on a simple red label with block letters in white to give the brand high visibility in self-service liquor stores. We wanted to convey an inexpensive, almost private-label look. The key to success was the price point. It was priced as low as or lower than any other vodka. Vodka consumers are well aware that all vodkas taste pretty much the same. This, combined with regional pride, made Bowman's Virginia brand the best-selling vodka in its distribution area within six months.

Advertising was minimal, but in this case it wasn't needed to get high unaided awareness. Product publicity was well orchestrated. Word of mouth did the job. Bob Lee, a direct descendant of General Robert E.

Straight Bourbon Whiskey. 80 proof. A. Smith Bowman Distillery. Sunset Hills, Virginia.

SORRY, BUT YOUR OLD GRAND-DAD IS NO VIRGINIA GENTLEMAN.

Virginia Gentleman still comes from cypress tubs and copper stills. And, like any gourmet item, it's still made in small batches. By hand. You see, we do more than we have to. But, then, that's how you get to be a Virginia Gentleman in the first place.

Lee, was interviewed all over the state. In-store product displays were extensive. The combination of these four—hard work at every level of DeVoe's iceberg—combined to give us the share of voice necessary to gain market share. Top of mind against the target soon reached 90 percent, where it continues to hold.

If your voice is loud enough, it doesn't matter whether you paid for a microphone. The object is to be heard and remembered. When share of voice leads to top share of mind, market share climbs.

Ask your agency to get you a high level of share of mind in your category, and never mind how they do it. Tell them to think out of the box.

Sum & Substance

In the reach for dominant category market share, keep the following points in mind:

1. Identify a product difference and drive it home. Talk with customers to learn which psychological and practical attributes make a difference. If the brand lacks a unique advantage, find something to say that hasn't been said before. For advertising to work, there must be a point of leverage.

2. If the brand lacks a dominant value point, and has weak category share, consider alternatives other than advertising unless unique emotional values can be established and driven home over time. To gain category ground, the brand must stand out with a unique and desirable personality. If you are unwilling to commit to a long-term effort, it is best to rely on promotion or to revert to value positioning (discussed in Chapter 3).

3. If advertising is indicated, be the A-to-S leader. Advertise consistently. Start big and sustain the effort over time. To do it right, and be able to afford it, you might initially have to limit advertising markets. Roll out as your share climbs.

4. You may have to limit the number of products selected for advertising support. If there are several products in the line, go with the few that offer unique advantages. Promote the rest. A strong "umbrella" brand identity will help pull the others through.

5. Track awareness in each market and relate it to sales to determine the optimum number of GRPs needed to meet share goals.

6. Find a way to generate word of mouth.

7. Take a risk. Take a deep breath and go with that crazy, offbeat, innovative idea that might, just might, capture popular fancy.

To own category share, the brand must be top of mind. Do what it takes to get it.

·18·

Corporate Advertising

Many consumers gladly pay a little more, if necessary, for an article that bears a name they respect.

—George Burton Hotchkiss, author,
Advertising Copy

There are times when corporate objectives call for advertising to make the company better known and more highly regarded by certain segments of the population. By investors and security analysts, for example. By acquisition targets. By potential employees. The approach to corporate advertising is essentially the same as it is to selling any other product. Only here the corporation itself is the product. All the principles we've discussed so far apply.

Someone once characterized corporate advertising as a man in a conservative suit, standing in a dark corner peeing quietly in his pants. He's happy, and no one notices. I'd say that's fairly true of puffed-up, image advertising that offers no benefit, or is not of inherent interest, to the reader or viewer. However, a 1978 Yankelovich Clancy Shulman study for *Time* magazine proved that corporate advertising can lead to broad support of a company by enhancing a company's image and function in the business world.[1] It showed that corporate advertising can influence *behavior* with regard to the purchase of stock; it can attract bright employees and gather support for controversial issues; and it can sell products.

I've been involved with dozens of corporate advertising campaigns. Too often the objectives are unclear. They should be precise. Unless someone can pin down the goal to be achieved, the money should be saved for a more fundamental purpose. Given vague objectives, I would rather romance the brand to generate sales. Sometimes, however, corporate advertising can be the most powerful method available to create sales. Two examples come to mind.

The first involved the A. H. Robins Company—the pharmaceutical company—in the early 1960s. I was with the Cargill & Wilson agency at the time. One day, Bob Wilson ran into Claiborne Robins at a chamber of commerce meeting. "I'm thinking about doing some corporate advertising," Claiborne said. Bob came back to the agency all excited by this news. He called in Al Cascino, John del Cardayre, and me to talk about it. "Claiborne wants A. H. Robins to be better known by the investment community," Bob said. "He would also like for doctors to read the ads and think favorably about the company." This is an example of an unclear objective. Robins himself knew exactly what he wanted to accomplish, but we didn't. As luck would have it, however, we stumbled upon an approach that fit the company's needs and helped it to grow into a major factor in the pharmaceutical field.

"Doctor of Tomorrow"

In the days before it moved some of its over-the-counter products into consumer marketing, most of Robins's sales came from doctors' prescriptions and recommendations. Doctors knew the company primarily through such basic products as Robitussin, the cough medicine, and Donnatal, a skeletal muscular relaxant often regarded by physicians as "a poor man's tranquilizer." Now the company was investing heavily in research to develop sophisticated products. The company had come a long way since Claiborne Robins's early days when he traveled around detailing prescription medicines compounded by his grandfather in a small corner drug store. Claiborne wanted the ads to sell products.

Al and John worked out two ads, each representing a different campaign approach. One made use of a color photo of a small boy, a tiny figure on a beach, as he walked along the water's edge, stopping to pick up a shell. Over his shoulders, the vast ocean stretched into the distance as the first light of morning cast a shimmering glow on white caps far out on the horizon. It was a beautiful ad that captured the essence of man's quest for knowledge. It provided the setting for a theme emphasizing Robins's research. It would be a lofty and high-minded campaign to make the public think warmly of the A. H. Robins Company. The copy was simple, a quote from Sir Isaac Newton:

> *I do not know what I may appear to the world; but to myself I seem to have been only like a boy playing on the seashore, and diverting myself in now and then finding a smoother pebble or a prettier shell than ordinary, whilst the great ocean of truth lay all undiscovered before me.*

The other ad was like a minidocumentary. It showed a young man in a white coat, with a stethoscope around his neck and a startled look on his face. He had stopped dead in his tracks while making his hospital rounds. The headline revealed the reason: "The man said Doctor, and the man meant me." The copy tells the story and emotions of a young third-year medical student the first time he ventures out in the ward and a patient calls him "Doctor." The closing paragraph describes the many years of sacrifice it takes to train a physician, and draws a parallel with the years of steadfast laboratory work required to develop a new medicine. The theme was "Doctor of Tomorrow."

Bob and I showed the two layouts to Claiborne Robins. He looked at each just for a moment or two, then held up the layout showing the young doctor and said excitedly, "This is it! This is exactly what I want. By providing a public service for the medical profession, we'll be making our company better appreciated by the people who prescribe our products." The campaign ran for the next eleven years in *Time, Newsweek,* and *U.S. News & World Report*.

To develop material for "Doctor of Tomorrow," we invited physicians to dinner, usually at the Rotunda Club. We encouraged them to reminisce about their days in medical school. "What incidents stand out?" we asked. "It doesn't matter how trivial—if you remember it, it was important." The doctors warmed to the subject. As one told a story, the others nodded in agreement; soon medical school tales rolled out across the table one after the other until we had enough anecdotes to write a novel. John del Cardayre, a prolific old pro who had joined the agency from Foote, Cone & Belding, wove each story into a tightly written, 145-word narrative of pathos, hardship, joy, or discovery.

Doctors saw themselves in the ads. It didn't matter where they had gone to school—Harvard, Johns Hopkins, the Medical College of Virginia, wherever. The minidramas we presented were shared experiences: the endless, boring "scut" work an intern is obliged to do; the 48-hour shifts in trauma service that heap fatigue on top of fatigue; the apprehension and sleepless nights before an exam. The public shared the physicians' interest in the subjects. Starch readership reported "noted" and "read most" scores consistently high. The ads usually ranked first, second, or third among the best read of all the advertisements in the issues studied.

The series spoke directly to the interests of the target audience through the technique of drawing the subjects from the targets themselves. It prompted hundreds of letters of appreciation from doctors, while at the same time improving public understanding of the years of expense and sacrifice made by young people to become physicians. The campaign both enhanced the doctor-patient relationship and cemented the bond between practitioners and Robins. It helped several Robins products to become leaders in their respective categories. It set the stage for A. H. Robins to emerge from a small company to a major player in pharmaceuticals.

Corporate advertising can sell products as well as company goodwill.

"Whose Famous Hands Are These?"

The second example has to do with a Fortune 500 company called Robertshaw Controls whose main competitor in some lines is Honeywell.

Two examples of ads written directly from information supplied by the target audience: in this case, practicing physicians. The campaign won doctor friends for Robins by influencing regular people favorably about the medical profession.

DOCTOR OF TOMORROW

You get no pity in "the pit"

This is the school of decision. This is "The Pit" where each young doctor-in-the-making must stand alone—and "present" a patient" to faculty and fellow students.

As he gives his diagnosis and recommended treatment, he faces a bombardment of questions from the shadowy figures that rise above him. If there is oversight, fuzzy thinking or indecisiveness, those probing questions will find it out. There's no pity for him in "The Pit." The ordeal is a pretaste of lonely decisions a physician must make all his

life . . . a vital part of his long, tough, costly years of study and training.

The same pitiless probing marks every step in A. H. Robins pharmaceutical research. For only on the most conclusive evidence can we base the better medicines to aid your doctors of today and your doctors of tomorrow.

A. H. ROBINS COMPANY, RICHMOND, VIRGINIA
Making today's medicines with integrity . . . seeking tomorrow's with persistence

Although Robertshaw makes thermostats and appliance controls that are ubiquitous and vital in American life, the company is seldom credited as the manufacturer making them. Who knows who makes the oven controls on the kitchen stove? Robertshaw wanted investors to know. The company also wanted customers and prospects to know that it was a leading supplier in the category.

Bob Wilson had a brainstorm. "To use Robertshaw controls, you

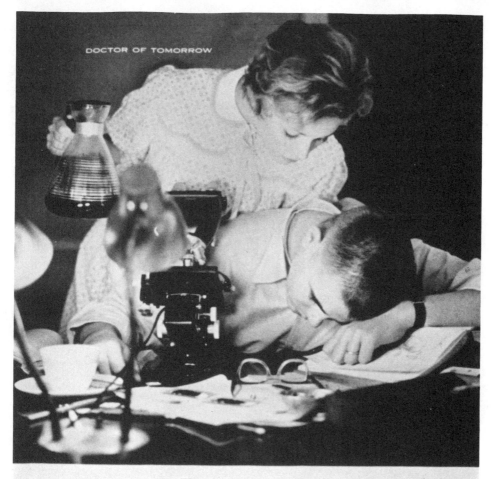

have to turn a dial, or punch a button. This means you use your hands. Suppose our ads show the hands of famous people, doing what made them famous. In a smaller photo we'll show the same hands adjusting a Robert-shaw control. The headline will always be the same: 'Whose famous hands are these?' We'll make readers guess by giving some clues in the copy, then in a smaller ad on another page we'll identify the famous person.''

Harry Jacobs comped up some layouts and Bob and I went to Robertshaw's headquarters to show them to Tom Arden, the president. It was late in the afternoon, and Tom had had a hearty lunch. The ads featured the famous hands of Artur Rubinstein, Norman Rockwell, Art

Wall, the golfer with a baseball grip, and Warren Spahn, a southpaw pitcher.

Midway through the presentation, I noticed Tom Arden nodding at the far end of the conference table. Then his chin fell to his chest. He was sound asleep. I coughed loudly, reached for a water glass and knocked it over. Everyone jumped up to avoid the flood. Arden blinked and shook his head to see what the fuss was all about. When the presentation continued, we had his full attention. The campaign ran for several years, until Arden got tired of it. In the meantime, according to our tracking studies, it did the job of building the desired awareness for Robertshaw. Starch told us we had a winner. The ads were seldom outscored for "noted," "seen associated," and "read most."

This campaign inaugurated Harry's specialty, the three-dimensional direct mail piece. Each ad was merchandised to security analysts with a unique item relevant to the ad packaged inside an attractive box. We sent out a baseball autographed by Warren Spahn, and a box that opened to become a golf hole for use in putting practice. The ball inside was imprinted with the Robertshaw logo and Art Wall's signature. We re-printed Rockwell's Tom Sawyer series, suitable for framing. And we mailed out a Rubinstein stereo record. Each mailer was autographed by the famous personality featured. The merchandising pieces were also sent, or given, to Robertshaw customers and prospects. With our target audiences, Robertshaw became as famous as the hands the ads featured. We went to a great deal of trouble to photograph the actual hands of the famous people. But it was worth it. The campaign was one of those that gets talked about. The famous "hands" opened doors that had been locked previously.

Romance and Enhance

A way can always be found to sell products while selling the company's image. And, except in those cases where the company name is subjugated to the brand advertised, every product ad an advertiser runs should be calculated to advance the personality of the corporation. The style of the ad, the graphics, the tone of voice should all be consistent. Remember those General Electric commercials from the 1950s with Ronald Reagan as the spokesman? I can hear the music now and the closing line, "G.E.— the initials of a friend." This phrase first began to appear in G.E.'s institutional advertising in the early 1920s. Every ad you do should add up to the personality of a friend. Your ad may be selling product benefits, but it carries your company image along with it. The personality and tone must be consistent with what the company is and what the company leaders want it to be. Conservative, forward thinking, witty, stylish, thoughtful, responsible? When you call your agency in to talk about advertising, give the creative team some adjectives you would use to describe your company in the context of human personality. It is one way to be sure you'll be comfortable with the personality (image) they project for either product or corporate advertising.

All of the above is especially true for business-to-business advertising, but it also applies to advertising for banks, insurance companies, and investment firms, where individual product names sit in the back while the company name does all the driving.

Sum & Substance

Like product advertising, corporate advertising should be founded on specific, measurable objectives. What is expected? Enhanced customer loyalty? Interest in the company's securities? Are we fluffing up the baby to sell it? What is it we want to happen?

The agency should be let in on the secret. Once a clear set of objectives has been established, all the techniques we've been talking about apply. Offer benefits from the point of view of the target audience. Package those benefits in a series of dramatic moments. Get people talking. Stick with it. The A. H. Robins series went on for a dozen years. Robertshaw's campaign was cut down in its prime. If it's worth doing, it's worth continuing. When corporate advertising is done well, it enhances a company's image and function and helps it become the perceived leader in its corporate category.

·19·

Something to Bank On

*The best way to get new business is to do a bril-
liant job for the clients you already have.*

—Bill Bernbach, in *Bill Bernbach said . . .*

If you are in the agency business and want to win a reputation for
innovative creative work, start by impressing the home-town folks with
the work you do for a bank. Banks are consistent advertisers. They use
all the media. The advertising you do for them is highly visible. Besides,
for a young agency, it's good to have a bank connection: You never know
when you'll need an operating line of credit and it is always helpful to
have a friendly banker on your side.

From the day we opened in 1965, we wanted a bank client. Unfortunately, all the big ones were already signed up with established agencies.
Then one day, just three months after we started in business, I got a call
from Ed White, The Bank of Virginia's advertising manager. "We're going
to review agencies," he said. "We've picked you and two others, plus our
present agency. When can we come and see you?"

The Bank of Virginia had been a fixture at an agency called Lindsey
& Company for twelve years. Lindsey was the oldest agency in Richmond,
and for many years, prior to the surge of my old outfit, Cargill, Wilson &
Acree, it was the largest. I wanted to work at Lindsey when I graduated
from college, but without any skills to offer, I didn't get a job. A few years
before our competitive jousting for the bank account, Dan Lindsey had
merged with his friends Liller, Neal and Battle, in Atlanta, to form
LNB&L. The combined operation was one of the largest in the South.
But despite the agency's size and tenure, the advertising it was doing for
the bank looked shopworn, and Ed White was a new advertising broom.
He wanted a fresh look, and powerful persuasion, for his $250,000 budget.

When a client starts shopping around, most agency incumbents are
dead in the water, so I figured we had a good chance to win the account.

This was our first new business opportunity and we went all out for it: Figuring in our own time, we probably spent $1,000 on the pitch. Today we ante up $100,000 or more.

Many years before, Rosser Reeves had been advertising manager for The Bank of Virginia. When Tom Boushall, the bank's founder, realized Rosser had gotten too big for the job, he let him take the account, which then billed $30,000, with him on a job hunt in Manhattan. With the hip-pocket account, Reeves was launched on an advertising agency career that led to his preeminent position at Ted Bates, where his unique selling proposition (USP) and hard sell influenced advertising in general.

As you might suppose of an enterprise that Reeves found interesting, the bank had roots in retail, which meant advertising results came through the door into the bank's lobby the following day. Boushall had started it in the early 1920s to bring banking and credit to the little guy, while other banks concentrated on lucrative commercial customers. With this kind of heritage, the bank was aggressive and receptive to anything, within reason, that would bring in business. It was, and is, a dream account.

Pitching *The* Bank

To prepare ourselves, we did an awareness survey and found the bank had been running an invisible campaign. Invisible, not subliminal (whatever that is). But, as we also learned, the name of the bank was a great asset. It was easy to remember. It sounded important. After all, it was *The* Bank of Virginia. Virginians like things preceded by the article "the": *The* River, *The* Club, *The* High School, *The* University, *The* Store, *The* Bank. We built a campaign around the phrase: *The* Bank.

It was, in a way, a status mnemonic. But it had its humorous aspects too. Best of all, it set The Bank apart. Imagine the chagrin of competitors when their wives or husbands said they had to "stop by the bank." We stole the phrase from their vocabularies.

The committee came to see us in our penthouse apartment, where we had set up shop. Our office was as stylish as the advertising we produced. It was on top of the newest building in town, with floor-to-ceiling windows overlooking Virginia Commonwealth University. For the presentation I ordered some showcards made by a local artist, Mike Kimmel, who had been doing them for thirty years. His cards heralded movies as far back as silent films. He lettered Thursday specials for grocery stores and presentation cards for every agency in town. George thought the $75 expense was an extravagance we could do without, and threw a fit about it. That was the first time I realized that our otherwise smooth partnership might be in for some bumps along the way.

Every new business presentation must be carefully orchestrated. From what Ebbinghaus had taught us, we knew much of what we said would soon be forgotten. This is especially true when six or seven agencies have their day in court over a two-day period. New business presentations often seem like revolving doors. You go in while someone else is coming out. This means the nugget you want to have remembered must be showcased and dramatized. The two most important segments are the opening and the close. Impressions are formed during the first few minutes, as you set the stage; and prospects are likely to remember what you say at the end. The long middle section often blends into a haze. When the selection committee meets later to compare notes, it can't remember which agency said what. "We liked that campaign that showed the product in the middle of a baseball diamond," a prospect told us recently. The campaign wasn't ours.

New Business Gimmicks

I wondered if we needed a gimmick to make our bank presentation memorable. They can work. I once made a presentation for the Virginia industrial development account. It was a standard pitch, with speculative ads and a well-thought-out media rationale. A competitor, Dick Athey, chartered a jet and took the entire committee on a tour of Virginia by air to point out industrial sites and Virginia's unique advantages. As they flew along, he related his ads to the views below. And they got the account. Never underestimate the value of showmanship, as long as it is relevant to the problem at hand.

Sometimes gimmicks get out of hand and succeed only in diverting prospects away from what are the most important considerations in selecting the agency partner. "In efforts to demonstrate their creativity many agencies skid over the line that separates bright creative ideas from absolute zaniness," Ed Buxton wrote in 1988 in *AdDay*. "The recent pitches for the loose Microsoft business demonstrate some of this wild-eyed foolishness. Competing agencies used outdoor highway signs, a skytop restaurant banquet complete with a window washer floor show, a live boxed tarantula, plus a bizarre assortment of communications. None of these creative mindblowers won the account."[1]

I agree with this assessment. The key is relevancy, just as it is in advertising itself. Recently, when we were one of several agencies invited to pitch the Maserati automobile account, we knew we had only one disadvantage. All the others were within a half-hour drive of the company's headquarters. We were three hours away by even the fastest Maserati. Distance was a potential problem. To mitigate this situation, we dreamed up a way to show how accessible we really are.

As Maserati's management walked into their conference room for the start of our presentation, my colleague, John Adams, dialed my number long distance and handed the phone to Don Morrissey, Maserati's president. I told him he was in good hands; he would hear first from the people who would work on his business, and I hoped to meet him soon. Then, accompanied by an artist with a Polaroid camera, I set out for the airport where our King Air was waiting. He snapped photos of various stages of the brief journey and mounted them in a folder. Forty-five minutes later, midway through the pitch, I walked into the client's meeting room just as the last in the series of photographs was coming into focus. I shook hands all around and handed Don the folder with the photos inside. Copy on the cover in bold letters said, "We went door to door to convince you The Martin Agency is even closer than you think."

We did get the account.

Of course that wasn't the only reason. That was just one positive mark on the scoresheet. We get our accounts by doing our homework. This includes scouting for obstacles that the agency must overcome to win the account, as in the example just cited. Having done that, however, the key to success is to identify the client's "marketing problem" and then to show how your communications approach will solve it.

"The Demon"

Start by describing "the Demon" your thinking must exorcise. To find out what it is, you must send a team into the field to gather as much information as possible. Every industry has experts. Find the best and talk with them. Record their comments. Talk to consumers. Talk with the trade. Pour over market data and syndicated research. Where there are gaps, conduct some research of your own. You might need research you can project to the customer universe. Or qualitative research to give you insights. Today we often conduct value point (benefit) testing sessions, then videotape and edit them for a dramatic effect. By the time you're finished with all this homework, you should know as much as the advertiser does about the obstacles separating the brand from success. Then, show how to eliminate failure, how to chip away at the obstacles, until the solution you offer seems the only sensible way to proceed. Always direct the presentation to solving the problem at hand: Put "the Demon" out up front, then hack away at it until only the agency's unique "answer" remains.

That is what we did for The Bank of Virginia, our first new business presentation. Finally, the big day came. The visitors arrived in our glass penthouse suite, the first aliens to see us in our natural habitat. Ed White introduced Bill Gordon, president of the bank, and Dick Chumney, its planning director. They sat down impassively, arms folded, and waited "to be sold" by this upstart of an agency. I looked at them around the circular walnut table, sitting there in the white Knoll mushroom chairs with bright red cushions, took a deep breath, and proceeded to set up "the Demon." The bank was being outspent by competitors, I argued. Advertising awareness was low. They were fourth in the market, in share, top of mind, spending, everything. I pointed out that they had to get unaided recall up to the top spot, on less money, in order to have any hope of climbing in category share. The answer was creative leverage: The phrase "*The* Bank" would make them top of mind with every bank customer. And it did.

The only gimmick we used was a book we gave them when they left. It described the agency and the procedures we used. The last page said, "And the media is paid with a check from *The* Bank of Virginia." An actual check from our account at *The* Bank was pasted onto the page. The president told me later that when he turned to that page there was no question in his mind but that we were the right choice.

Advertising for The Bank of Virginia captured share of mind in the market during the first four weeks without a budget increase. As described in the previous chapter, it created an image while it sold bank products. The advertising bounced back and forth between savings and loan promotions, depending on when loan ratios needed to be brought into line. But the connecting thread was always *The* Bank: "There's a loan to match your personality at *The* Bank." "Bring your nest egg to *The* Bank." "Now, *The* Bank pays more: 4½%." "Take your dream to *The* Bank." Word of mouth about *The* Bank crackled around town like a brush fire in August. Goals were met weeks ahead of time. Advertising awareness shot to the top of the category, despite our being outspent 4 and 5 to 1.

Today, twenty-three years later, The Bank of Virginia is called Signet. It operates in Virginia, Maryland, and the District of Columbia. It is the second-largest bank in the region, and for us, with billings in high seven figures, it continues to be a major piece of business, just as it was when it became our second account.

Involve the Client's Employees

We learned a lesson with our first campaign that applies to most successful advertising programs: Get company personnel involved with your advertising and promotion plans. We prepared special material to tell bank employees what the campaign was all about and when it would appear. We printed up buttons and bumper stickers. Tellers wore "nest egg" stickers on their lapels or dresses. Meetings were held around the system. When the client's staff gets caught up in the effort, it works. You must have the support and follow-through of the people who actually meet with customers. When you do, anything can succeed. Without them, anything will probably fail.

Years later, we won another major bank—Barnett, Florida's largest bank. The chairman commented after our pitch that he wanted the advertising to reach and excite his own 12,000 employees, just as much as he wanted it to sell the market. "If it does that," he said, "it's worth the $10 million we have to spend." That was a wise observation. Every successful advertising campaign should be first directed inside to make the external effort pay off.

Ferret Out "the Demon"

Our two bank clients had much to do with the agency's success. The Bank of Virginia started a roll that made us the largest agency in Richmond and the second largest in the state, all within five years. Barnett picked The Martin Agency out of a total of twenty agencies it approached, when billings were lodged at $40 million. Three years later, billings topped $100 million.

The quest for Barnett didn't start out so well. Roseann Duran, Barnett's advertising manager, sent out questionnaires to forty agencies, then whittled them down to nineteen prime candidates. The Martin Agency was not one of them. "We like your work for Bank of Virginia," she said, "but you are too far away." It's true, Richmond and Jacksonville are separated by 1,000 miles and a change of planes in Atlanta. Roseann and her boss, Bill Fackler, went to see all nineteen agencies, and when they were through, they still hadn't found what they were looking for. Roseann called us, and we became number twenty on their shopping list.

My partners, Don Just and John Adams, know the banking business as well as they know advertising. Don had been president of Bank of Virginia International at the age of 29; John had worked on the account at our agency for eleven years. We wanted the Barnett business and spared nothing to get it. Two teams went to Florida for two weeks to ferret out "the Demon."

Don and John alone called at 45 of Barnett's 220 branches. They opened accounts at 12 of them. They learned how Barnett did, or did not, cross-sell services. We studied signage, literature, competitive advertising, and the bank's personality, and we talked to Florida's banking commissioner, to national banking experts, to New York security analysts, and to customers, both individual and commercial. We comped up several possible approaches on benefit boards, and conducted and videotaped benefit testing sessions in several Florida cities. We did a PRIZM[2] study to pinpoint selective customers for specific services by Zip Code analysis. We learned about the Florida market and about Florida attitudes. It is sophisticated and rich. Retirees bring their nest eggs with them. They want a bank with clout, but they want local service. With state barriers disappearing for regional and national banks, the market is attractive to big banks everywhere. Florida banks are being bought up. Local bank autonomy is eroding as executives and credit committees from out of state call the shots. However, despite $20 billion in assets today and offices within ten minutes of every household in Florida, Barnett is still a local bank. It stands apart. Because it is decentralized into twenty-nine regions, each with a local bank president and credit committee, major decisions can be made locally. This, buttressed by Barnett's leadership position, is a distinct advantage. Responsiveness, size, leadership, a full menu of services, and convenient locations were all good reasons to bank at Barnett. We needed a way to state these advantages simply.

Our agency was selected as one of the four finalists. We made our presentation in Jacksonville, in Barnett's impressive board room. Around the walnut table half the length of a football field sat the marketing directors of the twenty-nine regions. When we finished, they gave us a standing ovation. That was a first for me. Then, following an abbreviated presentation to members of the executive committee, Barnett gave us the account.

To deal with the distance problem, we leased office space across the street prior to the presentation. And we identified a service team to be our local arm. Our King Air gets to Jacksonville in 2 hours and 45 minutes.

"Florida's Bank"

The theme that started running in the year we won the account continues today: "Barnett is Florida's Bank." It sums up all Barnett's advantages in just four words. It plays directly to regional pride (which Yankelovich tells us is an important factor). It sets the stage for showing how this big bank, with local roots, delivers quick and responsive service. It is a leadership statement.

The first commercial was filmed in Silvercup Studios, a former bread factory with 200,000 square feet of studio space in Long Island City, just across the Queensboro Bridge from Manhattan. Inside, the producer constructed a papier-mâché mountain 20 feet high. At the base, a jungle was created. There were birds, an eagle, and a 15-foot python.

The commercial opens with a disheveled little man in a blue suit, tie askew, clawing his way through the underbrush. Behind him are several luggage bearers carrying filing cabinets. An announcer says,
"At most banks in Florida, bankers have to go to great lengths to get an answer for you."
The man comes upon a wise man wearing a turban, as jungle sounds are heard in the background.
"I'm from a bank in the west and I need to get a decision on a matter of great importance to our customer."
He brushes away a python.
The wise man replies wearily,
"You'll have to go higher than me, my son."

This isn't the Himalayas, nor is it a scene from *Raiders of the Lost Ark*. It is a bank commercial filmed in an old bread factory.

The announcer says,
"Major decisions usually have to go all the way to the top."
Our man comes upon a Yul Brynner type who leers at him.
"You have only just begun, blue suit. HaHaHaHa!"
The man jumps back, startled. He continues to climb the mountain.
Announcer:
"At Barnett we don't work that way."
Another wise man in a cave, with an eagle perched behind him, waves our hero on despite his plea,
"A customer is waiting for a decision!"
No luck, the answer is the same,
"Higher, my son."
He is exhausted now, but on he climbs, ever higher, clawing his way up the mountain as thunder claps in the background and lightning flashes. Announcer:
"Barnett is structured so that local decisions are made locally. That means decisions that affect you are made by people close to you."
He reaches the top. A white-haired guru is sitting cross-legged on a rock in the snow near a chasm that is spanned by a swinging rope bridge. He points to the bridge.
"Higher, higher."
The frustrated banker trudges on across the bridge.
"I know, I know."
Announcer:
"When you need an answer, Barnett doesn't make a mountain out of a molehill."
Mood music now builds to a crescendo. The man and his bearers come back across the bridge. He looks up at the guru and says,
"He said come back next Tuesday."
Guru nods knowingly,
"It has always been thus."
The man mumbles to himself,
"It has always been thus?"
Slide and music come on the screen as the announcer says,
"Florida's bank stays close to Florida's people. And Barnett is Florida's Bank."
These last four words are shown on the screen.

Two years later, another spot came down hard on the loss of local autonomy by bank competitors.

The sound starts with a drum roll and marching music, then the roar of a truck convoy. Trucks begin to roll by loaded with bankers in black pinstripe suits. The announcer says,
"A lot of bankers are being shipped out of state these days. That's because many Florida banks are being bought out."
Trucks continue to whiz by.
"And now have to answer to offices in Georgia, New York, even California."
A truck goes by with this sign on the side: "CALIFORNIA OR BUST."

A yuppie banker type walks into the frame. He stands in front of a Barnett office and looks at the passing parade.

"Not Barnett. We've stayed home and now have more offices offering more services than ever before."

Music up.

"You see, Barnett has to answer to somebody, too—the people right here in Florida."

The banker looks up at his colleagues in the trucks, grins, takes off his glasses and waves. The announcer closes by saying,

"After all, Barnett is Florida's Bank."

Theme music over super of the four words.

Not exactly what you would expect from bank advertising. But the point is clearly made. It is squarely on position. And awareness of Barnett advertising shot up to the 90 percent level. During the past three years, Barnett deposits, a measure of a bank's size and success, shot up as well, from $12 billion to more than $20 billion.

When a bank wants great advertising, and gives the agency the latitude to do it, it hands over an opportunity that rarely comes along: highly visible advertising that pays off in growth and increased market share for both the client and the agency.

Sum & Substance

This chapter is especially for agency people. The formula for a successful agency is exactly the same as for a successful brand. The agency must first have top-of-mind awareness with its target customers. A good way to get it in its own backyard is to do outstanding, successful, provocative advertising for a bank. Bank advertising is highly visible. When it works, the agency attracts more work.

If the agency wants to move out beyond its own market, it must find other ways of extending its reputation for outstanding work. The object is to make the short list of agencies being considered by a prospective client. A creative reputation often gets the agency in the door, but it takes hard work to leave with the business. It also takes inventive problem solving, showmanship, and clarity. Agencies should talk about the client's business, not their own. They must set up "the Demon" that prevents the client and its brands from gaining category success. Then it must hack away at "the Demon" until the agency's solution is seen as the only way to proceed.

Personal chemistry has a great deal to do with agency success. The client asks, "Are these people I want to work with? Are they honest? Are they smart? Do they understand my business? Can they come up with answers? Are they innovative? Can they produce great advertising? Do they listen?" And this gets back to the original question, "Can I work with them?" Other clients will provide that answer.

An agency is a brand too. It must be romanced like any other.

· 20 ·

Truth or Consequences

*Advertisements are like people. If a man is sincere,
you can forgive him almost anything.*

—Roy S. Durstine, founder of BBDO

People often ask: "Who decides on matters of truth and taste? Is this left to the agency? The advertiser's legal department? Uncle Sam? The media? What are the checks and balances? Who keeps you guys in line? Is advertising really honest, or do you shade the truth?"

It's a matter worth exploring here, because every day we see ads, or have to approve them, that teeter on the edge of truth and over the brink of taste.

Truth is a matter of fact. It's cut and dried. You lie or you don't. In advertising, as in all things, you must tell the truth or accept the consequences.

Taste, on the other hand, is in the eye and mind of the beholder. What offends one person is ho-hum to another. I wouldn't want to wear a ring in my nose. The women of Chad think nose rings are lovely. Tastes change over time. Hemlines rise, then zoom back to the floor; men wear pleated trousers or buttons on the backs of their collars, then wake up one morning to find they are passé. Wide ties are out, somebody reminded me the other day. Those bright shirts everyone wore a few years back are now ghastly (I still have a drawerful).

Clever advertising people observe contemporary culture, take advantage of it, and sometimes push right to the edge of prevailing taste to shock people into noticing their output. "Virginia is for lovers" did that in 1970. It wouldn't raise an eyebrow today.

Consider this recent assault on prevailing folkways. The photo shows a female athlete with a suspicious bulge in her running shorts. The headline reads, "Steroids will make a man of her yet." This got attention, and it got the point across. It dramatizes a significant problem in athletics and makes athletes think twice about abusing their bodies. It was a masterstroke for a worthy cause. It also backfired in the fast lane of public acceptance. A small segment violently objected.

A powerful idea, one that goes straight to the heart of the problem at hand—and often to the edge of public tolerance—commands attention in the midst of today's media clutter. The best creative minds often come up with something crazy to get attention. Sometimes crazy ideas are ahead of their time.

Taste Isn't Static

A couple of decades or so ago, we had the bright idea of putting Massengill Douche Powder on television. In those days, the National Association of Broadcasters (NAB) had a code that spelled out in detail what could or could not be said on radio and television. To get Massengill on television, we had to pass muster with the NAB, so we mocked up a storyboard and copy that presented the brand in the most oblique way possible. The spot featured "beauty" shots of the package against a Jamaican waterfall, as I recall. I took it to Washington to show to the code's director. He flatly refused to let us proceed. "You are ten years before your time," he said. I pointed out that Preparation H commercials were on the air. But he showed me a specific exclusion in the code permitting that particular product to be advertised. Hemorrhoids were O.K., it seems. Douching was not. "Come back in ten years," he suggested.

Somebody did. The company was sold and a new agency, at a new time in history, put Massengill on the air. Now almost every night I see a commercial for Massengill—something with a mother and daughter delicately discussing the subject of feminine hygiene. Mores change.

So do regulatory constraints.

Ironically, the NAB went out of the code business in 1983 when the Justice Department challenged it on questions pertaining to restraint of trade. The key question was the NAB's limitation on the number of commercial minutes allowable each broadcast hour. When challenged on this, the NAB opted to drop both that rule and the advertising code as well. Now each station decides what advertising content it will or will not accept as well as how many commercial minutes it can sell. That's a loose arrangement considering that there are 999 commercial television and 8,807 commercial ratio stations in the United States.

Local Watchdogs

At the local level, for all practical purposes, the burden is now on the advertiser to deal with sticky questions *before* its advertising appears.

Not everyone found this motley gang to their liking, but it stopped people and drew attention. I noticed my dentist posted it on his wall. It also drew winning votes of Clio judges for Doug Mallott of Hawley Martin Partners.

WE CAN FIX THEIR CHOPPERS IN LESS THAN 24 HOURS.

When denture wearers get bugs in their teeth, it's no laughing matter. That's why we offer same day quality service for all repairs and relines in by 11 a.m. The next day, your customers hit the road smiling with the kind of polished choppers you just don't see on the street every day.

DRS DENTAL LAB
All our customers walk out smiling.

Return To A Time When You Had Basketball In The Gym, Football On The Field

And Gymnastics Here.

My classmates gulped at this idea for our high school reunion invitation. Later they showered praise as it got the credit for the large crowd.

This shocker from Fallon McElligott for the University of Minnesota was controversial—but it talks directly to young steroid users who are afraid of freakish side effects.

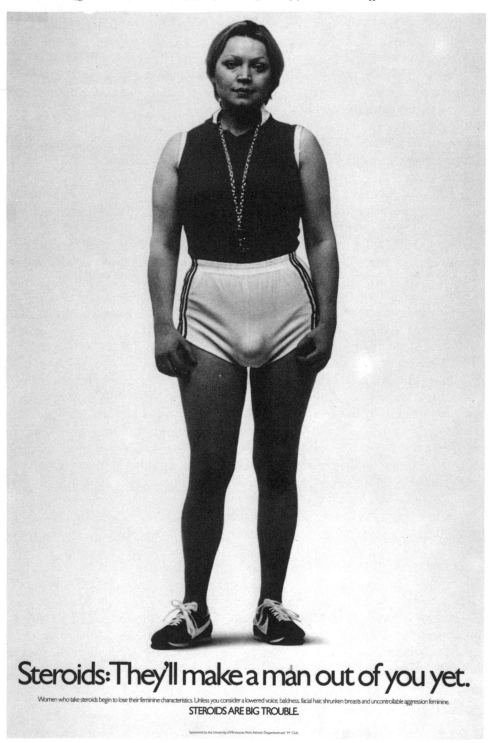

Steroids: They'll make a man out of you yet.

Women who take steroids begin to lose their feminine characteristics. Unless you consider a lowered voice, baldness, facial hair, shrunken breasts and uncontrollable aggression feminine.
STEROIDS ARE BIG TROUBLE.

Sponsored by the University of Minnesota Men's Athletic Department and "M" Club.

Once it does run, however, a local Better Business Bureau is there to lower the boom, usually in concert with a local Advertising Club. As a former president of both a BBB and an Advertising Club, I can tell you this works. The BBBs and the Ad Clubs are zealous about safeguarding the public interest so as to protect the good name of business and advertising.

When I was president of the Ad Club in Richmond, I went to an ad conference in Washington in the fall of 1960 and heard the chairman of the Federal Trade Commission blast the Ad Clubs for not supporting the BBBs and local self-regulation. This was during the last days of the Eisenhower administration when Earl W. Kintner headed the FTC. He warned that nature abhors a vacuum, and that given one, the government will usually rush in to fill it. "There should be a minimum of government restriction in order that we preserve our system here in America," he said. "This, then, means that the citizen must assume certain responsibility." He was talking about self-regulation at the local level.

I found that our local BBB was floundering. Our club monitored advertising to see if we had a problem. We did. There were fire sales without fires, false price comparatives, phony peddlers, and franchise rackets. The list of tricks and swindles was endless, and the BBB was understaffed. Horace Gans, the director, and two part-time assistants had their hands full doing comparison shopping, investigating 2,000 complaints each year, and trying to answer 1,000 telephone inquiries a month, all with two lines and an annual budget of $21,000.

The Ad Club and the business community got together to turn things around. A code was drafted. I invited Kintner to speak at a rally of business leaders at the John Marshall Hotel. "I am sad," he told the 250 assembled, "that here in this important commercial center you have a Better Business Bureau which consists of one hard-worked man and two ladies. This, if I may say so, is a disgrace to Richmond. How can you expect to regulate yourselves if you do not support the instrumentality through which self-regulation works?"

We did turn it around. The next year, the BBB's budget was $50,000. Today it is $550,000. Each year a staff of sixteen investigates some 7,000 complaints and handles about 70,000 inquiries while manning twelve telephone lines. Richmond has an aggressive watchdog.

Better Business Bureaus grew out of the "vigilance committees" formed by businessmen early in the twentieth century to combat false and misleading advertising. Today they are a strong local force in 156 commercial centers throughout America. They remove the few bad apples that can contaminate the rest of the barrel. So, despite the demise of the NAB code, after-the-fact self-regulation is alive and well locally.

National Safeguards

At the national level, the networks clear advertising in advance. Agencies send off storyboards and scripts for approval like expectant authors hoping to be accepted by a publisher. Each major network has a Broadcast Standards and Practices (BS&P) department with the power to accept or reject. To give ad creators some inkling of what they might or might not approve, the networks offer BS&P guidelines in a book that covers everything from alcohol to weight reduction.

Here you can find "do's and don'ts" for comparative advertising, children's advertising, contraceptives, firearms, massage parlors, nutrition, and subliminal perception (whatever that is), just to name a few of the categories. Responsible agencies use the guidelines for network commercial development, and also to check out what should or should not be done in local or regional spot advertising.

Sometimes network approval is subjective, and "go, no-go" decisions are made outside the rule book. Not long ago we proposed a spot for Coty cosmetics that depicted a novice nun (a free spirit in the Julie Andrews, *Sound of Music* mode) walking down a hall behind her mother superior. As the older nun marches sternly ahead, the novice takes a sharp left. The scene then dissolves to our novice in the privacy of her barren room. She lifts the mattress on her metal bed to reveal a bottle of the fragrance hidden there. Two networks accepted it, another did not. The writer and artist went back to square one.

Another restraint on national advertising safeguards the public interest.

Back in the early 1970s, the American Association of Advertising Agencies, the Association of National Advertisers, and the American Advertising Federation (the parent of local ad clubs) joined forces with the Council of Better Business Bureaus to form an advertising self-regulatory organization. It is called the National Advertising Review Board (NARB). At the same time this took place, a National Advertising Division (NAD) of the Council of BBBs was formed to monitor advertising, initiate investigations, determine the issues, and respond to complaints. It also has a special division that deals with children's advertising.[1] With a staff of review specialists, it is, in effect, the investigative arm of the NARB.

Court of Appeals

The NARB is a court of appeals. There are fifty members representing national advertisers, advertising agencies, and the public. When a case is appealed to the NARB, the chairman draws together a representative, impartial panel of five from this reservoir of resources. Since 1971, the NAD has investigated, resolved, and reported the results of 2,580 cases. Of these, only 44 were appealed to a panel of the NARB.

Through the years, cases have originated from five primary sources: individuals, consumer organizations, local BBBs, NAD monitoring, and last, but not least, category competitors. Competitors are ever vigilant when it comes to protecting category share.

Often a challenge will surface in response to one competitor's seeking a point of leverage on others in the category. A recent example involved Bryan Foods, a division of Sara Lee. Its advertising was challenged by a long list of competitors spearheaded by Oscar Mayer.

Bryan operates in ten southern states selling a line of meat products ranging from beef stew to bacon and hot dogs to hams. Despite a deep southern heritage dating back to 1909, Bryan products are outsold by Oscar Mayer in many key southern markets and across the South as a whole. This shortcoming notwithstanding, Bryan decided in 1984 to use the theme, "Number one from the South," in advertising its bologna, bacon, and hot dogs. The basis for the statement is that Bryan is the largest brand of processed meats *based* in the South. The campaign provoked considerable outrage among competitors, who fired off complaints to the NAD. The controversy boiled for three years and eventually wound up for review and judgment by Panel No. 43 of the National Advertising Review Board. I was one of the five panel members.

Why did such a seemingly harmless phrase cause so much controversy? The story demonstrates the power of a strong value point and also provides insight into how the industry's self-regulation mechanism works.

Television copy out of Ally & Gargano went like this:

Up in Chicago, the number one hot dog is Oscar Mayer. But down in New Orleans, Bryan is number one. [That was true. Nielsen shows Bryan beat Oscar Mayer 2 to 1 in New Orleans, although the brand trailed elsewhere in the Southeast and Southwest.] *In Buffalo and Minneapolis, Oscar Mayer is number one. But in Birmingham and Memphis, Bryan beats them.* [This claim was also accurate.] *Say, maybe you're wondering why Bryan hot dogs aren't number one up North, too. We think it might be because we don't sell them up there. Bryan. The number one hot dog from the South.* [The key word in the last line is "from."]

The Power of Being Number One

I know from studies undertaken for our own clients, including benefit testing we've done on this point, that the "number one" claim is a compelling argument to make with consumers. A large segment of the population is traditional, conservative, conventional, nostalgic, sentimental, and unexperimental, and thus especially receptive to a leadership claim. They don't research every purchase and pour over consumer reports. They rely on the tried and true.

VALS psychological segmentation would classify people in this segment as "belongers"—a traditional mass market group comprising about 40 percent of the population. It's a big market, and spends about $200 billion a year on food and beverages alone.

These people would rather fit in than switch to an unproven brand.

They tend to go with category leaders, as do many in other VALS categories as well. This fact is confirmed by the *Yankelovich Monitor* for 1987, which tells us that "consumers demonstrate an interest in symbols of success . . . reliable anchors . . . interest and trust in well-known brands"—all as a guide to competent consumption. Many shoppers prefer brand leaders because they want quality at a fair price. When so many of their peers cast affirmative votes for a brand at the cash register, this raises the consumer's confidence level. It's easy to go with the flow. It simplifies decision making.

So here was Bryan claiming top status in the South for its hot dogs and bologna—and also reaping the benefit of this claim rubbing off onto Bryan products in other categories as well.

Of course you can't claim to be the leader if you're not. That's when somebody blows the whistle, and the NAD steps in.

Competitors Will Blow the Whistle

Oscar Mayer brought Bryan's advertising to the attention of the NAD by saying that the claim could be interpreted to mean that Bryan was *the leading seller* of hot dogs and bologna throughout the South. Bryan responded by providing the NAD with brand share data that, in the NAD's opinion, substantiated the fact that Bryan produced a greater *tonnage* of hot dogs and bologna than any other southern-based company, and indeed led in sales in some markets, but not in the South as a whole. The question, then, boiled down to tonnage versus category share to justify the number one claim.

After reviewing the data, the NAD asked Bryan to modify the number one claim to avoid giving the impression that it was based on distribution and sales throughout the South. Bryan agreed. The NAD issued a case report stating that the matter was resolved. But two months later another competitor complained.

A letter from a lawyer representing Bozell & Jacobs, the agency for Decker Food, said: "Enclosed is a storyboard of a Bryan Hot Dog commercial that is currently airing. It contains the claim: 'Bryan's, the number one hot dog from the South.' According to the most recent SAMI[2] data," the letter continued, "Oscar Mayer is the number one hot dog, and Decker is the number 2 hot dog . . . Bryan does not even appear among the top 10 . . . in the region."

By now, however, Bryan had shifted its approach slightly to enable it to hold onto its dominant value point while relating "the number one" claim to taste rather than to sales. A typical ad said:

People who know their hot dogs really love our hot dogs. In fact, in recent taste tests, Bryan beat the leading brand by nearly 2-1. Bryan. #1 from the South.

Competitors were not mollified by the shift of body copy from sales to taste. Letters poured into the NAD complaining that Bryan was continuing to make the misleading leadership claim despite the successful challenge and apparent resolution of the matter. The situation was complicated by the fact that Bryan had conducted extensive taste tests in various cities in the South that supported its claim that its brands were preferred on the basis of flavor.

In all, more than 2,900 completed interviews over a three-year period showed that Bryan products were preferred, sometimes by a margin of 2 to 1. This then became the solid footing for the claim, from Bryan's point of view. Bryan was careful to use the phrase "preferred 2 to 1" or "nearly 2 to 1," as the findings indicated.

The NAD continued to negotiate with Bryan to get it to drop the claim. Finally, by the autumn of 1986, Bryan agreed to drop the number one claim unless it carried a tonnage disclaimer. Bryan said future advertising would shift entirely to an approach based on taste preference.

This would have ended the matter except that by now the NAD staff had reconsidered its earlier view that the taste tests were a valid indication of preference. Although it had accepted the test methodology the previous year, the NAD now questioned the testing procedure on several points. Questions of testing reliability led to an impasse. The matter was referred to a panel of the NARB for resolution. Bryan's official reaction to this step was published in a NAD case report:

> Bryan believes that these tests were accurately designed, conducted and reported and are accurate in their assessment of the consumer preference for Bryan hot dogs and bologna over leading competitive brands. We believe that the NAD owes a responsibility to advertisers to be consistent in its findings, particularly when those findings are the basis for future advertising claims and we look forward to presenting our case to the Panel.

Day in Court

The hearing room was packed. The panel meeting convened at 9 A.M. in the conference room on the thirty-third floor at 155 East 44th Street, the New York headquarters of the ANA, in late July 1987. Bryan had present its marketing executives, lawyers, marketing research experts, and representatives of its research firm and advertising agency. Oscar Mayer sent its chief legal counsel and market research director. There were research experts advising the NAD, staff representatives of the NAD and of the NARB, and, finally, the five NARB panel members.

Dr. Ronald Smithies, a NAD vice-president, made the opening comments. He strongly questioned the methods used in Bryan's taste test research, implying that there was a large margin for error, and opportunities for the interviewers to bias the respondents. Down at the end of the table, Jim Nelems, president of The Marketing Workshop, the company conducting the research, flushed and held himself in check. He felt his professional reputation was being impugned. But he said nothing. He would have his chance to speak.

The lengthy controversy had gone on for three years, consuming time, energy, and patience. In the meantime, Bryan's market share in the hot dog category throughout the South had climbed impressively, doubling in several markets, even tripling in some, and moving a minimum of three share points for the market as a whole. This was not at the expense of Oscar Mayer, however, whose products maintained share position throughout the region.

Because Bryan had opted to drop the phrase "Number one from the South" from its advertising, the original challenge (and primary source of the controversy) was now moot. By this time copy appeared over the theme line: "Bryan. The flavor of the South."

The original question, then, had been settled before the NARB panel could rule on it. Now the issue was whether or not the taste tests were valid and could support the 2-to-1 preference claim. The findings of the panel on this question would go beyond this particular case. What was allowed or disallowed as a result of this hearing would send signals to the industry as to what procedures were to be followed in future taste testing when the findings were to be used as the basis for an advertising campaign.

After hearing all the arguments and studying the thick dossiers submitted by the NAD and Bryan, the panel met privately to reach a decision. Some members were troubled by the research. Others felt it was valid for the purpose. There is no question that the number one claim would have been disallowed or a disclaimer required whenever it appeared. Discussion was polite, but brisk, and opinions varied on the various issues. A tentative decision was reached, but refinement of the opinion continued beyond the meeting. Correspondence and telephone calls honed it, finally, to reflect the unanimous consent of all five.

Bryan's research was found to be "marginally acceptable" as the basis for development of the taste claim.

Don't Miss the Point

For readers interested in increasing market share, rather than in lessons on the fine points of taste tests and NAD/NARB procedure, there is a moral to this story rooted in advertising effectiveness. This marketer went to great lengths to ferret out and defend a dominant value point to use in its advertising. Whether you applaud or disapprove of the tactics employed, the fact is that the use of a distinctive claim paid off in market share gains.

The obvious question to any advertising observer is: Given this extensive effort to find and keep a leverage point, and the obvious success it produced, why do some marketers spend millions without bothering to use one? Advertising should never get produced unless it identifies a point that gives the brand added value and makes it crystal clear to readers and viewers exactly what it is.

Sum & Substance

Successful advertising campaigns break with precedent, but they cannot break the rules. Every means must be found to push concepts as far as you can take them, to find a dominant point of difference, and to stick with it. When advertising passes over the line of truth or taste, however, the industry has mechanisms in place to deal with it. This is as it should be in a free country fueled by free enterprise. The best place for Uncle Sam is in the umpire's chair, to make a call when needed, but not down on the court with the players.

·21·

Where Are You Going, Little One?

Some men have a peculiar genius for writing a striking advertisement, one that will arrest the attention of the reader at first sight.

—P. T. Barnum, *Struggles and Triumphs*

Barnum is right. But there aren't very many of them available to do it. And therein lies the greatest threat to agencies and to the clients who entrust them with their brands.

Where do people with a "peculiar genius" come from? One of ours was a waitress who wrote short stories. Another was a helicopter pilot. A partner in a hot creative shop told me his best writer was a housewife who was out looking for a second career. But such cases are rare. Creative directors would rather bring in people who don't have to be trained. So who trains them? Journalism schools? They train journalists. Even if the schools knew how to do it, some look down their noses at advertising. A few good schools do prepare future writers and art directors. The Portfolio Center in Atlanta is one. The University of North Carolina in Chapel Hill turns out good writers. Syracuse University, New York School of Visual Arts, and several others give kids practical exposure to the advertising business. But where does a young, untrained person with a good liberal arts education and a flair for writing go to get a job in advertising? Tell me. I don't know. Every writer you meet has a unique story to tell about how he or she got started.

Somehow a few break in—but only those with a fierce, abiding passion to do so. Many of the most promising talents go elsewhere and are lost to the advertising business. As a result, there is a shortage of great creative advertising minds entering the nation's agency farm system. A great young talent can soon write his or her own ticket. Agency CEOs all over the country are scrambling to find the best. These are the same CEOs who say to an untrained individual, "What can you do for me? Come back when you've had some experience." But they don't come back. The seasoned best will only go with the agencies that "feel right," those with the environment and proven reputation for producing great advertising.

Genius Is Rare

The United States Census tells us that there are only 8,190 people in this country who classify themselves as copywriters. And 8,925 more who are artists and art directors. Think how small that number is! It's frightening to realize that the entire output of the $60-billion advertising agency industry rests with them. All the brands in the land depend on them. Apply the 80 to 20 rule and you have about 3,400 creative people you might say are those with "peculiar genius." Subtract those who are partners in their agencies, and 7,000 agencies are left to fight it out for a few thousand (at most) with creative magic in their genes. These are the precious few who can truly romance a client's brand.

In recent years, most of the advertising news has focused on mega-mergers as agency goliaths joined together to form big worldwide communications companies. The manipulators who make these deals seem to forget that leverage and stockholder investment depend on the dubious devotion of a few talented creative minds. Without those minds, the devotion of clients is likely to evaporate.

This megatrend has caused a lot of problems for creative people. These people were more comfortable when the business of advertising was making ads.

If you read the trade press, like *Advertising Age* and *Adweek,* you get the idea that billings are everything. They place much emphasis on agency size and ranking. The headlines have to do with shifting accounts and who is "hot" based on billings growth. Creative people couldn't care less about such matters. What they want is a place to work where they are free to think and free from fear. They don't want to worry about job security and company politics. They prefer to be left alone to work in peace.

The Megatrend

Today, sixteen agency groups have worldwide billings exceeding $1 billion, and three exceed $4 billion in billings. If size means interesting accounts, and freedom to do exciting work for those accounts, all is well and good. But more often than not, size means restrictions on creative freedom, layers of approval, competitions between creative teams, testing and retesting, advertising produced to formula, fear of risk, and hours of effort that never see fruition in print or on the television screen. Like a salmon driven upstream by an inward urge to spawn, a creative person survives by spawning creative offspring and is driven to find a place to do it. I once had one of the most talented copywriters I've ever known call me to plead for a job. She was stuck in a place where creative teams were pitted against each other on every campaign. "I've been here two years and haven't had an ad produced," she said. "You've got to get me out of here." She took a job at half her former salary.

The advertising agency business has changed profoundly in the past ten years. Back then, the largest agency in the world billed less than $500 million. Even adjusting for the value of the dollar, goliath matchmaking and escalating media costs have driven the largest agencies into a different category of operation and size. The "little ones" have grown up. Twenty years ago, during the golden age of creativity, agencies like Ogilvy and Doyle Dane Bernbach billed less than $150 million. Yet they were in the top ten. Their size fostered a sense of family. Their leaders were passionate advertising men, not financial manipulators. A psychological environment existed that made New York the mecca for creative people everywhere.

Advertising Decentralization

People wonder why some of the best advertising today is being done in such unlikely places as San Francisco, Portland, Minneapolis, Providence, Boston, Raleigh, and Richmond. The answer is simple. New York is no longer the mecca. Bernbach is dead. Ogilvy is in France. Hal Riney is in San Francisco. Tom McElligott is in Minneapolis. Harry Jacobs is in Richmond.

The best advertising is created where the best creative people work. The best creative people work where they

- Are encouraged to take risks
- Have their work produced
- Can be proud of what they do because it is seen, admired, and judged by the people they respect most—their peers in the business

There are still smaller agencies in New York that meet these needs, and because client orientation continues to be focused on the Big Apple, they are growing more quickly than their brethren in the outback. Some "creative pockets" in the monolithic, amalgamated shops do great work— the best in the business. But the output from the huge shops as a whole is spotty and uneven. Except for a few of the megaboys, focus and tradition were lost when moneychangers entered the business. It remains to be seen whether or not they can regain them.

I got a letter the other day from a writer who has been creative director at three of the largest and best-known agencies in the world. He managed a 280-person creative department in New York. Here is what he said:

> As you may have heard, New York is not exactly the promised land of the ad world these days. So I'm looking to get out. My resume says I've had some fancy titles, but I never got far from writing ads. I love making good ads. The best ads are being made outside of New York nowadays. That's why I'm writing you. Maybe we could make some great ads together.

If this were the nineteenth century, writers and art directors would be poets and artists, starving, perhaps, but happily pursuing their muse in secluded ateliers. In the twentieth century, "artists" collaborate with the "merchants" in society in order to survive and feed their families. Thus art and money joined together in an alliance called advertising agencies. But it is an uneasy alliance. "Artists" shun bigness. They are uncomfortable with agency managers who put money first and advertising second. They agree with Leo Burnett, who once said, "When an agency starts counting money instead of making ads, it is in trouble."

The Magic of Advertising

Money alone is not the motivator for the creative personality. It helps. But it is less important than the chance to realize creative expression and get peer recognition. These two factors, rather than money, provide the drive to project a brand above its own peers in a category. For an example, let's turn the clock back a hundred years to the time when a new restaurant opened in Paris. It was one of many in the restaurant category and, to succeed, management knew it needed top-of-mind awareness with target customers. A twenty-seven-year-old artist-aristocrat, starving for recognition more than for money, accepted a few francs to design a poster. Media planners had it plastered on kiosks all over Paris. The results were electrifying. The Moulin Rouge was an instant success, and the artist, Toulouse-Lautrec, was an overnight sensation.

The needs of both were served: the client jumped to a huge category share and the artist got the respect he craved.

That's the magic of the advertising business.

Sum & Substance

The advertising agency business is getting bigger at the top and stronger in the middle. The rarest resource is not money or clients, it is creative talent.

There is a subculture in the agency business. It is a subculture of creative people—those who turn out the work. They know everything about the creative side, which campaigns are popular, which are bombs (from a creative perspective), who's hot, who's not. It's not a very large group, put them all together and they would make a dismal crowd showing at Yankee Stadium. There are, after all, only 148,000 people altogether in the advertising agency business in the country. About 17,000 people can be classified as doing creative work in advertising. This tiny talent pool is responsible for turning out the $60 billion of advertising developed and placed by advertising agencies.

All agencies scramble to attract the best talent. To do this the agency must have a strong reputation for believing in the creative product. Before these rare birds flock to an agency, they want to be sure that management is serious about great work. The size of an agency is of no consequence, nor is its location. What is essential to them is that the agency's underlying position is for creativity, that management is dedicated to it, and that the agency's clients appreciate it. The most talented people avoid places where creativity plays second fiddle.

Clients want the best talent assigned to their accounts as much as the agencies want to have it on staff. A big idea can build a business. Brilliant advertising can lift even parity products out of a category and make them highly successful. Companies who recognize this follow the talent to unlikely places like Minneapolis, Portland, and Richmond. If this trend continues, America will, for the first time, have a decentralized advertising agency industry.

· EPILOGUE ·

The Name Game

*Better be called ever so far out of your name [by a
nickname] if it's done in real liking, than have
it made ever so much of, and not cared about!
What's a name for? To know a person by.*

—Mr. Williams, in "The Haunted Man"
by Charles Dickens

When you work in an advertising agency, you're often asked to come up
with a name for a new product or enterprise. I relish doing it because
names have always fascinated me.

This is the way it happens. The account executive returns with the
assignment: an amusement park needs a name for a new rollercoaster,
R&D has produced a new insecticide, developers plan a new community,
a bank wants to rid itself of single-state identification, or maybe a client
has a new line of apple sauce.

The account executive writes a memo describing the product characteristics, competitive names, and a description of the market to be
served. This is distributed to everyone on the staff along with a call for
entries. "Give us three suggestions, and we'll give a hundred bucks to the
winner," the account executive proclaims. And so the name game begins.

After the entries are culled by a committee, the leading candidates
are turned over to a lawyer to be sure the trademark can be cleared.
Finally someone in authority makes a subjective decision and our baby
has a new name.

Names and words are sounds the mind uses as shorthand for things
that have full and broader meanings. Look at simple, everyday words like
"chair," "bike," "dish," and "pencil." Since we've all had experiences
with them, these words call up highly personalized, visual images: your
favorite chair with the frayed arms, the time Dad brought home your first
bicycle, that priceless china dish of Mom's you broke, the teeth marks
you made in the yellow wood during a math test.

The same is true for brand names: They are a verbal shorthand that
stands for specific products and services. And, if we in marketing do our

196

jobs well, they stand for something good, valued, and distinctive. It is our mission as marketers to be sure a brand name conjures up an association instantly with the specific product and its desirable attributes. We do this with advertising, packaging, logotype design, signage, public relations, and most of all, with the quality of the product itself. Every opportunity is taken to drive home a lasting impression that is relevant, consistent, and positive.

Public figures and celebrities do this for themselves very well. They take great care to hone their images so we know what to expect from them. For example, what comes to mind when you see or hear the following names?

> Churchill
> Reagan
> Cher
> Iacocca

The custodians of these names did their jobs right. They polished their image at every opportunity and, as a result, your mental association with them is clear.

Image polishing is a job that is never done. One major deviation from what the public has been led to expect can, like Humpty Dumpty, destroy what took years of experience and millions of dollars worth of media exposure to establish. That's why we, as custodians and builders of brands, have a serious responsibility entrusted to us. The manufacturer must everlastingly offer both quality and service. The agency must keep public perception in mind as it comes up with ideas for fresh new ways to romance the brand.

Words Grow on You

When it comes to naming a new product, it is hard to look at a list of suggested brand names and feel comfortable with any of them. Each one seems so strange. What does the word mean? The fact is, a new name means nothing in advance. Only with time and usage does the name that seems so awkward in the beginning become associated with the object and what it stands for. *Exxon. Kodak.* These strange assortment of letters mean nothing by themselves. With care and promotion, however, Exxon has come to mean quality automotive products and services, while Kodak has been associated instantly with reliable film and popular cameras for over fifty years.

Sometimes we name a product that sounds or looks like a word that stands for something else. This can be an accident, or done deliberately to borrow established values. When that happens, it is harder to accomplish the task of creating our own meaning. To register our own distinctive brand identification, we have to overcome or diffuse the baggage—good or bad—that the word brought with it. Cadillac Rug Cleaning is an example. A name like Cadillac sets up a wall that's hard to scale. It has been preempted by the automobile. Crestar, a perfectly good name for a bank, has needed time and effective advertising to separate it from the brand of popular toothpaste. That was an unforeseen complication.

Early Origins

I was once asked to come up with a name for a new mountain resort. It would be built on a magnificent site embracing 4,000 acres high in the Blue Ridge Mountains, forty miles southwest of Charlottesville, Virginia. We wanted an appropriate, appealing name to suggest a resort for all seasons: where you could golf, play tennis, and go hiking in the spring, summer, and fall; and go skiing in the winter.

My first inclination in naming a place is to find a natural link with the past. What significant events or landmarks can be identified? One of them could be the ideal name. In this case, Meriwether Lewis was born nearby. For me the name conjures up romantic fantasies of rugged exploration from Lewis' exploits with Captain William Clark in tracing a new land route to the Pacific. We advanced the word "Meriwether" as a possibility. But when some suggested altering it to "Merriweather," it was obvious it didn't work. Our list of candidate names continued. There are several mountain peaks that make up the site and they had some fascinating names: "Potato Patch," "Devil's Knob," and "Black Rock." These went into the hopper along with the name of a nearby village called "Wintergreen." Wintergreen was an ideal name. It said what we wanted to convey. The problem for me was, that word also meant the flavor of chewing gum. We went with it anyhow and overcame that association with our advertising. Wintergreen is now simply what it is—one of the most successful vacation home resorts in the country.

Sometimes you can find clues to early origins in the assortment of letters used to form a name. This is especially true for those you find in England. An example I like is the name, "Lincoln." Until recently I thought it was uniquely American. Most of us associate it with our sixteenth president and so we should. But where did the name originate? Actually, "Lincoln" is an acronym. The first three letters go back two thousand years to the celtic word "Lindon," meaning a "hill near water." Later, when the Romans swept into central Britain they established a colony on the Lindon site, but their name for it, "Lindum Colonius," proved too unwieldly. Over the centuries the natives shortened it to a word more easily said: "Lin-coln."

Of course, the name "Lincoln" also conjures up instantly an image of a sleek automobile as well as the tall man in a dark suit, top hat, and chin whiskers. Or if you are from Nebraska, you may think of Lincoln as the name of your capital city. If you are British, it is probably none of these. It's that town on the hill in Lincolnshire, the one with the most beautiful cathedral in England, located 132 miles north of London.

We seldom stop to think about where words come from, they're just there—handy references for distinctive objects, places, beings, and actions.

The Agency Name Game

With all the mergers going on in the advertising agency business, it's hard to keep up with the names, and even harder to guess where they originated. It is as if someone swirled letters around in alphabet soup, reached in with a spoon, and used what came up. Venerable Ted Bates is now Becker, Spielvogel, Bates (BSB). Batten, Barton, Durstine & Osborn is now known simply as BBDO, those letters that sound like they are falling down the stairs.

Doyle Dane Bernbach and Needham Harper joined to become DDB Needham. Sullivan, Stauffer, Colwell & Bayles became SSC&B, then SSC&B:LINTAS, and now just Lintas. Lintas? Where did that come from? In 1979 SSC&B bought an in-house agency from its client, Lever Brothers (Unilever). It was called Lever International Advertising Services (LINTAS). So it seems, the agency business reflects real life. Time and usage brings about a shorthand that makes a name easier to say and remember, as it was with "Lincoln."

In my own small way, I have contributed to the agency name game. When I conceived the idea of starting an advertising agency twenty-three years ago, it was a simple matter to call it Martin & Woltz. George Woltz, my partner, was amenable to putting my name first, and so we did. Somehow it sounded more natural than Woltz & Martin. When George left to start his own firm in 1975, I simply changed the name to The Martin Agency after discarding other possibilities such as Martin Associates, Martin Partners, and David Martin Advertising.

New Agency, New Name

Two years ago, I sold my interest in The Martin Agency to Scali, McCabe, Sloves (SMS). By then, my associates and I had made the agency stand for creative excellence within the ad fraternity. This is the fact that attracted SMS and the interest of clients all over the country. Having sold my stock (and like all good managers, having put my successors firmly in place), in August 1988, I left the agency George and I founded to strike

out again. This was done with the blessing and good wishes of my
partners, as well as Marvin Sloves and Sam Scali. I wanted a new setting
where I could put the lessons learned, and have told in this book, directly
into play.

My brother Steve and I bought a smaller agency and then wrestled
with what to call it. We wanted to relate the new name somehow to
"Martin" without creating confusion with "The Martin Agency." All my
gifts of coinage came into play. Here's a partial list of the names we
considered—keep in mind there was no editing here, we just gave the right
side of the brain free rein:

Marmar, Marmark, Maramark, Admar, Admart, Starmar, Markstar,
Marstar, Adstar, Marplan, AdPlan, AdMartin, Marta, Martas, Martac,
MarketSource, Marimar, Marbros, Advanta, Marsource, Adsource,
Target Marketing, The Martac Group, Stephen & David Martin &
Associates, Martin & Martin, Martin Brothers, Creative House,
Martin Partners.

None of them worked. They were all cold and strange and awkward.
We toyed with the idea of Martin & Martin, but this seemed to us to be an

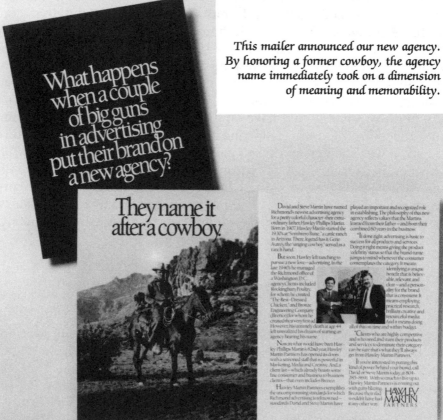

*This mailer announced our new agency.
By honoring a former cowboy, the agency
name immediately took on a dimension
of meaning and memorability.*

imitation of Saatchi & Saatchi, the agency that has gobbled up a large part of the agency world. Martin Brothers was a possibility, but it sounded too much like an automobile dealership or an appliance store.

Finally, we went back into our own history. Our father, Hawley Phillips Martin, the first ad man in the family, had been named for his mother's parents. He was a colorful character who started his career as a cowboy on a ranch near Tucson, where I was born. He is the one who gave me Aesop Glim's book (see Chapter 4) and stressed the importance of "The Hat Trick." He managed an advertising agency the last few years of his life. With his copies of *Printers' Ink* and *Advertising Age* and our talks at the dinner table, he kindled my interest in advertising. Unfortunately he died in 1952, at the age of forty-four, so he never got to start his own agency. At the time, I was still in college, and Steve was only seven. To honor him, we named the agency *Hawley Martin Partners*. Mother, who is now eighty-two, said he disliked the name "Hawley." It was too sissy for a cowboy. He always insisted on being called "Phil." Even so, she says, he would be pleased.

Coming up with a name is the easy part. What's harder is to make any new "brand" not only recognized but stand apart. Our job is to advance—and romance—a meaningful, desirable difference in our respective, crowded and competitive categories. We know, as you do, that the perception of a quality difference is essential for survival and success in the marketplace.

▪ CHAPTER NOTES ▪

Chapter 1 "The Angry Lion"

1. *The Unpublished David Ogilvy,* edited by Joel Raphaelson, The Ogilvy Group, 1986, p. 75.
2. *The Mirror Makers* (New York: William Morrow & Co., 1984), p. 226.
3. Ibid., p. 232.
4. *The Art of Writing Advertising* (Denis Higgins), 1965, reprinted by NTC Business Books, p. 79.
5. *Newsweek,* September 18, 1986, p. 64.
6. *The Art of Writing Advertising,* p. 82.
7. *Bill Bernbach said . . .* published by Doyle Dane Bernbach, compiled by Bob Levenson.

Chapter 2 "Something of Value"

1. Leading brands, 1925 and now, listed by Peter Georgescu in *The New Definition of Advertising,* presented to AAAA, Oct. 9, 1987.
2. *Yankelovich Monitor,* 1987, Chapter III, p. 36. By permission Yankelovich Clancy Shulman.
3. "Every inch counts": Martha T. Moore, *USA Today,* 9/26/87, copyright 1987, *USA Today.* Excerpted with permission.
4. Ibid.
5. Graham Phillips, Ogilvy & Mather, *The Role of Advertising,* Conference Board, New York, Oct. 29, 1986.
6. *The Unpublished David Ogilvy,* edited by Joel Raphaelson, The Ogilvy Group, 1986, p. 109.
7. See *Business Week,* January 26, 1987, p. 65.

Chapter 3 "Hostage Brands"

1. Much of the material in this chapter is drawn from conversations with and speeches and articles by Keith M. Jones, V.P., Summa Group, Stamford, Conn.
2. *Business Week,* January 26, 1987, p. 64. Reprinted by special permission © 1987 McGraw-Hill, Inc.
3. "Advertising as a Productivity Force," speech given before the Chicago Advertising Club, February 17, 1988, p. 15. Also reported in *Advertising Age,* March 14, 1988, p. 18.

Chapter 4 "The Hat Trick"

1. Albert Lasker, Lord & Thomas, *The Lasker Story* (New York: Advertising Publications, 1963), p. 13.
2. Claude Hopkins, *My Life in Advertising,* reprinted by NTC Business Books in 1986.
3. As reported in *Advertising Age,* April 24, 1967.
4. *The Lasker Story,* Chapter IV.
5. Aesop Glim, *How Advertising is Written—and Why* (New York: McGraw-Hill, 1945), p. 21. Reprinted with permission.

Chapter 5 "How to Deal With Creatives"

1. Henriette Anne Klauser, *Writing on Both Sides of the Brain,* (San Francisco: Perennial Library, 1986), p. 27.
2. Ibid.

Chapter 6 "Ideas Start Where the Buck Stops"

1. John O'Toole, "Some Thoughts on Polynesian Navigation," AAAA annual meeting, April 1985.

Chapter 8 "Did You See the One? . . ."

1. "Advertising that gets talked about," *Advertising Age,* November 16, 1987, p. 18.

Chapter 9 "Personality Is Permanent"

1. "Image and the Brand," speech before the AAAA, Chicago, October 1955, reproduced in *The Unpublished David Ogilvy* (The Ogilvy Group), p. 77.
2. *Adweek,* December 14, 1987, p. 19.
3. The discussion of Ebbinghaus and Bartlett is based on material appearing in Alan D. Baddeley, *The Psychology of Memory* (New York: Basic Books, Inc., 1976), Chapter 1. Copyright © 1976.
4. See the article "Putting the Advertising on the Package," *Viewpoint,* July/August 1988, pp. 25–26. Published by the Ogilvy Group Inc.

Chapter 11 "Television Is Entertainment"

1. *Yankelovich Monitor,* 1987, Chapter IV, p. 65.
2. *Advertising Age,* December 28, 1987, p. 12.
3. David A. Aaker, Donald E. Bruzzone, and Donald Norris, *Viewer's Perceptions of Prime Time Television* (1981), and *Irritation in Advertising: Causes and Remedies.* (1983). Copyright by Marketing Science Institute, Cambridge, Mass.

Chapter 12 "No Risk, No Gain"

1. Douglas Durden, "Changing the Cheers Chemistry," *Richmond Times Dispatch,* August 2, 1987, Section F, p. 2.
2. Remarks at the Effie Awards ceremonies, New York, June 12, 1985.
3. *Some Thoughts On Polynesian Navigation,* report of the chairman, AAAA annual meeting, May 1985.
4. John Philip Jones, *What's in a Name,* (Boston: D. C. Heath, 1986), p. 139. Reprinted by permission of the publisher, Lexington Books, Lexington, Mass., D. C. Heath & Co. Copyright 1986.
5. Ibid., pp. 139–140.
6. Levi's 501 jeans' cost per 1,000 retained impressions for 1987 was $8.17, compared to $8.44 for Lee and $13.93 for Wrangler, according to Video Storyboard Tests' "fifth annual measure of efficiency," as reported in *Adweek,* March 7, 1988.
7. Mike Hughes, *Pencil Pointers* (newsletter of The One Club for Art & Copy, Inc., New York), Jan./Feb. 1988, pp. 1 & 7.
8. House ad for J. Walter Thompson USA, Inc., *Death of an Idea.*

Chapter 14 "Human Drama"

1. As determined by Video Storyboard Tests Inc., New York, through its tenth annual study of America's most popular television commercials.
2. It was Hall of Famer John Caples who wrote, *"They laughed when I sat down at*

the piano, but when I started to play. . . .'' His name is the most famous in tested advertising.

3. From report on the Lowe Marschalk study in *Adweek,* August 31, 1987, p. 38.

4. A study in 1981: Starch Tested Copy. Vol. 2, No. 18.

5. James Webb Young, *How to Become an Advertising Man* (NTC Business Books, 1975), p. 7.

6. From a speech, "Facts are not enough," to the AAAA on May 17, 1980.

7. Ibid.

Chapter 15 "How Much? How Many?"

1. Alan D. Baddeley, *The Psychology of Memory* (New York: Basic Books, Inc., 1976), p. 8.

2. John B. Stewart, *Repetitive Advertising in Newspapers,* Harvard University, 1964.

3. Zielske study, p. 20 (from an article in the *Journal of Marketing,* Vol. 23, No. 3, January 1959, pp. 239–243); Stewart conclusion on frequency, pp. 298–299.

4. Robert C. Glass study: *Satiation Effects of Advertising,* ARF, New York, October 15, 1968, pp. 20–21.

5. See Hubert E. Krugman: *How Potent Is Television Advertising? Some Guidelines from Theory,* ANA Television Workshop, New York, October 11, 1972; Also Michael J. Naples, *Effective Frequency: The Relationship Between Frequency and Advertising Effectiveness,* ANA, New York, 1979, pp. 24–25.

6. Naples, *Effective Frequency,* pp. 64 and 69.

7. Ibid., p. 68.

8. *A Study of the Effectiveness of Advertising Frequency in Magazines* (New York: Time, Inc., 1982).

Chapter 16 "Share of Voice"

1. *Update 1985: Reconciling Loyalty Trends and Promotion Growth* (Port Washington, N.Y.: The NPD Group, September 1986).

2. Summary of study by Clayton/Curtis/Cottrell, Boulder, Col., reprinted from *Presstime* by SCAN, The Advertising Checking Bureau, Inc., Vol. 35, No. 11, November 1987, p. 13.

3. *How Advertising Affects Profitability and Growth for Consumer Businesses,* results of a joint research project by The Strategic Planning Institute/The Ogilvy Center for Research & Development.

Chapter 17 "How to Increase Market Share"

1. *Marketing News,* May 16, 1980.

2. William L. Burke and Sidney Schoeffler, *Brand Awareness As A Tool for Profitability* (Cambridge, Mass.: Cahners Publishing Co., 1980). Copyright © Strategic Planning Institute.

3. As reported in *Industrial Marketing,* February 1981, p. 13. Reprinted with permission from *Business Marketing,* formerly *Industrial Marketing.* Copyright © Crain Communications, Inc.

Chapter 18 "Corporate Advertising"

1. The study was based on 1,533 in-home interviews in twenty-five markets. *Corporate Advertising Study* for Time Magazine by Yankelovich Clancy Shulman, 1978.

Chapter 19 "Something to Bank On"

1. Ed Buxton, "Losing Creative Cool, *Ad Day View,* February 23, 1988. Reprinted with permission from *Ad Day.*

2. PRIZM is an acronym for Potential Rating Index by Zip Market. The service categorizes the population into groups according to lifestyle and demographic characteristics.

Chapter 20 "Truth or Consequences"

1. The NAD is an aggressive watchdog. It monitors national television, radio, and print. Sometimes an informal query to the advertiser will quickly put the matter to rest. The issue raised must be of public interest and must involve national advertising as opposed to local issues, which are handled by local BBBs. A special unit, the Children's Advertising Review Unit (CARU), handles children's advertising. It considers questions raised by consumers and conducts an ongoing review of advertising directed to children under the age of twelve.

2. SAMI (Sales Area Marketing Inc., New York) measures sales by periodically checking warehouse inventories to track movement into retail outlets.

▪ INDEX ▪